THE SPOOK
WHO FLEW OVER
THE CUCKOOS NEST

GARY TULLEY

Gibson Publishing

First published in the UK by Gibson Publishing

Printed and bound by CMP (uk) Limited

The Spook Who Flew Over The Cuckoos Nest
Text copyright 2013 by Gary Tulley
Image copyright 2013 Gary Tulley

ISBN 9780 9927-1183 2

This is a work of fiction. All the characters and events depicted in this book are
fictional and any resemblance to real people or occurrences is entirely co-incidental.
Some locations that appear in the story are real enough, and others have been used
rather fictitiously.

Gary Tulley asserts the moral right to be identified as the author of this work.

I would like to dedicate this book to my brother Brian.

Gary Tulley

CHAPTER 1
BRIGHTON REVISITED

"Mike!....can you get that please darling? I'm in the kitchen it could be important, my hands are tied at the moment." Either he was out of earshot, or maybe Mike Eastern, wasn't in the room at all. Whichever way, it didn't stop the phone from continuously bleating away. Patience on tap can be a virtue providing of course, that the circumstances aren't debatable. In this case, leaving his malcontent partner, Joan Travers, into playing the Devil's advocate, as she appeared in the doorway leading to the apartment lounge. "I hope, for your sake, that damned newspaper that your head is buried in is of more interest than......." She stopped short of castigating as the phone decided to cease ringing. Probably in sympathy to her cause. Slowly and trance like, Eastern, lowered the paper and glanced intently towards her.

"Oh....sorry, Joan, you were saying?" Then without more ado he returned to the paper and duly lost himself again.

"It really doesn't matter much now, does it!? She replied brusquely. "It's fairly obvious to me that the sports page is in control....right?" Having ventured this far, her kitchen task had somehow lost it's appeal, leaving her to edge toward him. In the past, Joan had never been one for verbal dress rehearsals, rather she had written the script. "On the other hand, Mike, if the content is that captivating then maybe we need to share it." It wasn't so much what she had implied in her approach, but moreover in the way that she had said it, that finally persuaded Eastern, to engage her line of thought.

"I suggest, that if you get round to reading this particular article here on page two, then you'll appreciate why I appear to be somewhat distant. To be honest, the bureaucratic bullshit it contains, makes me feel like I want to throw up!"

His apparent terminal view on the subject, totally transformed her delicate attitude. Without further prompting, she became instantly aware that possible grief written or otherwise, seemed to lodge an infinity with him. And that he also thrived on it. But then he was a specialist 24/7 PI, and what was food and drink to him inadvertently became another man's poison. "In that case, I'll take your word for it, Mike." She responded. "And allow you to explain the lurid details. It all sounds very intriguing to me I have to say."

"I certainly wouldn't argue the point with you on that one, Joan. Unfortunately your'e going to have to wait awhile for an answer, I suggest that we discuss the matter fully over dinner later. In the meantime, I intend going missing for a short while....grab some fresh air, and reflect on a spot of business at the same time." A perfectly engineered smile then washed over Joan's face as she replied in a knowing manner.

"As I recall, Mike, the last time I heard you say that, you decided to go missing for twenty four hours."

"Did I?" he questioned loosely. "Well, if I did, it figures that Rogon, had a say in it." The reference to the latter, came by way of a former undercover Government security agent affiliated to Spooks, whom Eastern, by indelible circumstances had found himself embroiled with. In a political and torrid association when cracking a Police conspiracy case, some 6 months previous.

"Strange, when I think back." she mused. "especially the love hate relationship that you both shared."

"Meaning?"

"The way you harp on about him at times, it's almost as if the man never really went away."

""Uhm, I hadn't really noticed, Joan, although familiarity can become a two way thing if you let it. Having said that, I don't suppose for a minute the guy has ever reflected on my input in that particular case." Determined to get the last word in, Joan astutely concluded.

"I'm bound to say that you got that part right, Mike. You've always maintained that a log has got more feeling than a spook!"

Minutes after exiting their apartment, Eastern succumbed to an involuntary shiver, as the chill wind bit through to his body. Just to add to his plight, he cursed the fact that his car was parked at the seaward end of Brunswick square in Hove, where he resided. Burying his chin deep into the lapels of his overcoat, he strode away briskly, head down into the night. Engrossed as he was in a satellite of his own making, the outside world quickly became a vision of the past.

Meanwhile, and close to where his car could be found parked, a short heavily built figure emerged from behind the shadow of a large blackened out limousine.

The exclusive cut and colour of the garb, including the trilby that he was wearing, seemed to compliment the vehicle by generating a sinister air to their joint existence. Shrouded by the darkness, the figure chose to remain lurking in a position consistent with an element of surprise if called upon. Completely oblivious at that point, to his presence, Eastern literally walked directly into an unavoidable confrontation, as the alien figure stepped out from beyond the shadows intent on waylaying him. Totally unaware as he was, Eastern found himself hard pressed not to retaliate. And in the process, humbled into becoming a highly disgruntled spectator. From the offset, it quickly became aware that the aggressor had pre-knowledge of his existence. "Mr Eastern I believe? I apologise for invading your space and my selfish timing. The situation arising." he strongly emphasized, "is one of necessity aligned with state security...."

At this point, Eastern's intuition had now revolved 360% by unlocking the key to what was rapidly becoming an altercation too far. Cutting his inquisitor short, he readily referred him to the only language he knew that they both shared. "Hold it right there! I'm not interested in your bureaucratic crap, so get to the fucking point. On second thoughts I'll say it for you, Rogon sent you didn't he? Why the hell couldn't he have phoned, and, more to the point you moron, how the hell did you know I was going to be here anyway!?"

Almost immediately, realization gripped him as his senses returned full circle. "I should have known better." he rebuked himself. The motionless mask on the agent's face, indicated to Eastern that he was wasting his breath, should he decide to pursue that specific line of enquiry. "You fucking sad brainwashed idiot." ran through his mind, "You should have read the small print in the advert and stopped when you arrived at Spooks!"

A further, and what would have been a feeble attempt to appease the agent , came to an abrupt ending. Leaving the latter deciding to vent his own stamp on their addled conversation. "I need to make you aware Mr Eastern, that I carry no official jurisdiction in forcing you to...."

"Yeah...yeah, I get the picture, just spare me the bollocks that goes with it. I can only surmise that if Rogon wants a 'meet', then this situation has to be a priority."

Damned if I do and damned if I don't, a cajoled decision that Eastern could well have done without. And with as less time to debate the consequences. As a result, a whirlpool of mixed emotion, mingled with contrived scenarios, swirled around in his head, in opposition to his reluctance to say no. Fumbling around in his coat pocket, he produced his mobile and proceeded to make an enforced call. "Give me a couple of minutes", he proffered, "this happens to be a private call". Some 5 minutes later, the obtrusive limousine exited Brunswick square and headed along Western road. It's destination privy to only the driver. Sitting in the back while completely blindfolded, a disorientated Eastern sat wedged between two further agency personal. The ludicrous experience in itself was nothing new to him. In the not too past he'd succumbed to the 'calling' a dozen times or more. Although Eastern could well attune himself to the necessity for overall security, he did have this problem when coming to terms with Spooks translation of protocol. In his tried and tested experience, it paid to sit back and relax whilst reflecting on the thought that Rogon was about to infiltrate his private life once again.

Deep down, having monopolised the role of a free spirit while acting as a PI. Eastern, nevertheless, had this love hate relationship that had developed over the past between himself and Rogon, had now moved on to establish a successful combination based on mutual respect. As was the norm, the journey, he reminded himself, seemed to take for ever. Finally the limousine ground to a permanent halt, and Eastern was unceremoniously bundled out.

Still blindfolded while remaining in a state of complete secrecy, he completed the last steps of his ordeal on foot, some minutes later. His blindfold was then removed thus allowing his vision to adjust to the alien light. And also to familiarise himself with his immediate surroundings. "Welcome to the world of 'plastic' beings" became his initial thoughts. "Where night and day have no meaning" swiftly followed. The inevitable third option soon transpired into one of stark reality, brought about by the unmistakeable and enigmatic tones conspicuous only to Rogon. Cutting through a blanket of silence from behind him, his opening gambit was brief and to the point.

"Mike! it's so good to see you again. I trust that you are keeping well?"

Full of expectancy, Eastern swung round hesitantly to acknowledge his presence. "Under the circumstances I wish I could I say it was a pleasure too,' Rogon!" He fired back with inbuilt attitude. And continued his verbal assault in the same vein. "The next time that you decide to come calling when it suits you, then give me the benefit of 24 hour's notice. Or had you conveniently forgotten that I happen to live in the real world?" Briefly, the merest hint of a smile struggled to live with itself, on Rogon's face, as he proffered an outstretched hand for Eastern to shake. Inwardly, the glimpse of a disc slotting into 'play' engaged Eastern's sub-conscious prior to Rogon replying.

"You should be well aware by now, considering our past history, Mike, that your request is virtually meaningless. Unless of course there comes a time and a reason to justify it."

"That's total bollocks!" retorted Eastern, "You know damn well where to find me when it suits you."

"Same old, Mike, nothing really changes does it? Except to say of course that I've always been a staunch admirer of your maverick genre. And not forgetting your acute independence of course."

"Don't patronise me Rogon, I don't do reunions full stop! Just cut the crap and make your point." Momentarily he broke off, before pursuing another line of thought. "By the way, you never said. What is it this time, a 'bent' MP maybe? or better still, how about a political defection? Now there's a good enough reason to fuck with wouldn't you say?" As was to be expected, Eastern's choice of sarcasm fell way short.

Leaving Rogon to make it clear that he was eager to progress.

"Your wit as usual becomes you, Mike. Needless to say I'll come straight to the point. The fact that I've sent for you anyway must tell you that your presence here at HQ. Is not I stress a social call of convenience. On the contrary, your business here is confined to a State-related 'brief', which entails an undercover third party arrangement. Additional to a vested interest into organized crime."

"Oh, I get it, so straightaway you thought", I know, let's get good old Mike Eastern involved. He likes a bit of excitement! Yeah, well fuck you, Rogon. If I happen to have a problem then I deal with it...end of story. So you and your Spooks can do likewise. You seem to forget that I have got a life too."

"This is the second time I've laid my life on the line before in the name of the State. And for what? Besides, my pension is looking good from where I'm sitting, and I mean to keep it that way." Now reclining in his favourite chair while looking completely relaxed, Rogon appeared to be oblivious to Eastern's accustomed rant aimed at the Establishment. Not once did he allow a flicker of emotion to jeopardise his frame. A following pregnant pause seemingly allowed response to sail over his head, and then to disintegrate out of mind. Finally, he replied in a robotic manner.

"I take it, that means that you could be possibly interested in the 'brief' on offer then, Mike?" In response, Eastern reluctantly held his arms aloft akin to a token of submissiveness.

"Why the bleedin hell do I get the feeling that I've been suckered again? Okay Rogon, I'm in, so what's the SP (information) behind the story?" Shaking hands on their enforced deal, Rogon spilled the contents of a large file onto his desk before continuing.

"Tell me, Mike, what does the name Victor Brezznov mean to you?" Without any prompting, Eastern raised his eyebrows in instant recognition as to his enquiry. And not before delivering his own personal assassination attached to the name in question.

"Fucking bad news comes to mind, Rogon. As far as I know, he's been enjoying a 12 stretch (years) in Bellmarsh Prison as we speak. Although according to a Press report that I read earlier on this evening, that might not be the case. So, why do you ask?" Rogon hesitated before replying.

"I'll come to that later. Is there anything else that you'd care to add?" In a moment of madness, Eastern couldn't resist a sudden urge to wind Rogon up, by quipping.

"I'm seriously considering leaving him off my Xmas list this year." As was to be expected the craic (joke) fell way short on delivery, leaving an unimpressed Rogon to carry on where he had left off.

"For your information, including the rest of the world apart, Brezznov has spent the last 18 months of his sentence languishing in Foredown open prison in Sussex, while awaiting a release date. Which I hasten to add, could be possible at any time this coming month. Apparently, the power's to be are saying he's eligible to return to society." Stopping short, he sat bolt upright before continuing in a meaningful manner. "And therein, Mike", he emphasised, 'Lies the crux of the matter!'" Eastern's immediate response to Rogon's explicit dilemma, came by way of burying his head in his hands in a show of defeatism.

"I can't believe that your telling me this crap. In my book the guy is a professional career criminal, who in the past has literally got away with bloody murder. And now your telling me that he's going to walk at any moment. On that basis, I would suggest to you that somebody has got a paid-up holiday with money over, for making a decision that's beyond crucial. I'm sorry, I just don't buy it, he asserted, and continued, "From where I'm sitting, the very idea that Brezznov, could shortly become a free man...stinks! From beginning to end."

Without any formal doubt, Rogon had anticipated Eastern's summing up, and concurred in his own assessment. "In the end Mike, it all comes down to money, meaning that everybody has got a price. The higher that you are up the ladder the easier it becomes to name it." Nodding aggressively, Eastern was forced to confirm that at worst, they were both in the same ballpark. And allowed his further interest to grow.

"I have a mental picture of where all this is leading up to now. So, please continue." Glancing up from the file, Rogon commenced by easing him into a factual insight relevant to his own covert abduction. He then continued their in-depth prognosis concerning Spooks latest 'brief'.

"This could take some time, Mike, because I need to dwell on the past so that you can see where I'm coming from. Brezznov". he indicated, 'is the only son of a post war mixed marriage, between a white Russian and an English girl. Both of whom were heavily involved in running a small corporation, linked to wheeling and dealing in mainstream finance circles."

"Uhm, sounds familiar."

"Under normal circumstances I would be forced to agree with you." Rogon exclaimed. And then proceeded to ambush any misgivings on the subject, by verifying certain facts. "Any dealings that the company were party to, I hasten to add, were legitimate in every respect. Unlike Brezznov himself, who decided at an early age that money and the power that it could yield would, in later years, become a symbol to crown his egotistic desire to succeed."

"Typical 'silver spoon' case", Eastern remarked dryly.

"Exactly!" exerted Rogon and continued, 'Having decided that a one-man assault on the open market would be the way forward, he embarked on a pre-planned crusade. His intention being, to take on the Stock market per se.'

"Christ! Monetory suicide comes to mind." Eastern interjected.

"On the contrary, Brezznov got lucky, it seems. His business acumen prospered very quickly, allowing him to become a predominant status figure, as speculators go. Not only at home, but also within the foreign market as well."

"It's got the beginnings of a bloody malignant fairytale if you ask me" mused Eastern. "And I wouldn't mind betting he's upset a number of people in the process, to achieve his ranking."

"Touche, Mike, I couldn't agree more so. But to continue. By the time that Brezznov had reached thirty or so, he'd managed to accrue a substantial fortune while trading specifically within the diamond market. The majority of his holdings at the height of his prowess, centred in and around Holland......."

"The latter being the heart of the industry" Eastern interrupted.

"Quite! With doorstep knowledge plus the finance to back it, enabled his holdings in turn to create a superlative power over the market as a whole. Hence the expression 'money makes money'."

" Although, let's not forget the grief that embodies it" echoed Eastern.

"I certainly wouldn't argue with you on that point, Mike, knowing that the flipside to that has handed the agency a more contentious story......."

".......And I guess that's the reason why I'm here?" he cut in. "Your agency colleague happened to mention earlier on something to that effect.....right?" For once, Rogon appeared to come across as relieved, and was quick to acknowledge it's origin.

"It's comforting to know that we both agree on one aspect, Mike, especially when the situation, as you put it, entails a crock of shit!" Averting his gaze back to the file in question, Rogon continued in a more serious vein. "As I stated before, monopoly creates resentment and then in turn, enemies begin to appear. A spate of incidents, including death threats on Brezznov's life, finally convinced him to take the law into his own hands."

"So now we're looking at a severely pissed off, but wealthy financier, looking to play God! Yeah?"

"I couldn't have put it better myself, Mike. In the short space of two weeks, four 'hits' (assassinations)-three in Holland and one in London, were systematically carried out on his behalf, as a show of reprisal would you believe?" The enormity alluding to Rogon's latest revelation, finally came home to roost on Eastern's doorstep.

"No Shit!" he retorted. "To me, it sounds like the guy has got shares in 'Murder Inc'!" His intended version then became lost in transit, as Rogon continued where he had left off.

"On investigation, the Dutch police were primarily at a loss when detailing charges against him. It seems that any effort, on their part, to collect vital evidence and witnesses, remained thwarted. It became clear that the diamond industry as a whole, was set on maintaining an enforced code of silence." An expression of distaste clouded Eastern's face, leaving him to voice a dormant point of view.

"As I stated before" he reminded Rogon, "to my mind the arsole has got away with murder!" A rare mark of expression, resulting in a smug smile, quickly evaporated.

Which allowed Rogon a brief moment of satisfaction before responding.

"Not quite, Mike, you'll be pleased to know. The 'hit' that occurred in London, took place at a certain merchant's jewellers based in Hatton Garden. And! In broad daylight!" he emphasized strongly. "And that, as it turned out, resulted in becoming Brezznov's first mistake......"

"And the crucial one?" Eastern interjected, "There has to be a follow-up surely?"

"Absolutely, and without doubt, it all centred on the hiring of the 'face' (villain)- that Brezznov employed to carry out the 'hit'."

"Now your getting warm, in what regard?" Pausing for breath, Rogon spelt out the remaining facts in a contrived manner.

"Would you believe, that Brezznov, stupidly allowed himself to fall into the economy trap?"

"From where I'm standing, nothing would surprise me. I can only surmise that you mean a cheap job in exchange for a big deal?"

Nodding in agreement, Rogon remained unflinching in reply. "Precisely that! The 'hit' itself was doomed to failure from the word go. The 'face' employed to carry out the job, was a small time career criminal, known by the police as one Freddie Earnshaw." Eastern's face then registered a look that didn't warrant an explanation, as he exploited his own character assassination.

"Yeah, the name's familiar alright. From what I can recall he's been on the 'Bill's' (police) shopping list from way back. To my reckoning the guy's done more time (internment) than a poxy carriage clock. I can only assume that Brezznov must have been on 'crack' (cocaine) when he got him involved." Once again Rogon concurred with a nod, whilst electing to retain an unrepentant attitude.

"The fact still remains though, Mike, that, like it or not, Earnshaw still managed to carry out the 'hit' and seriously wound a security guard in the process."

"Please, go on."

"Fortunately, the injured victim was in a position to oblige the Flying squad with a one-on-one ID. So, with that and the CCTV coverage at close proximity, finally enabled the police to apprehend Earnshaw within 24 hours of the crime being committed." For the first time since their conversation had opened up, Eastern now felt relaxed within himself. And decided to pursue an alternative line of enquiry.

"So, tell me, did the police manage to make a connection between Earnshaw and Brezznov after interrogation?" In contrast, Rogon appeared to be somewhat at ease with the question when replying.

"Not at that particular time, Mike, although suffice to say, the police would have broken him down eventually. Besides which, Earnshaw had nothing to lose by implicating Brezznov as being the paymaster."

"Uhm, you stated eventually?" Clearly, Eastern was shadowing some doubt, "can you elaborate on that, Rogon? I think I'm missing something here."

"I won't bore you with the details as such, so I'll make it brief. While he was on remand awaiting trial, Earnshaw's lifeless body was discovered on the floor of a shower room."

"Presumably murdered?" Eastern conjectured. In return, Rogon was adamant concerning the latter's calculated demise.

"There was never any doubt whatsoever in that direction. His mouth, we were told, had been forcibly stuffed with bars of soap, causing him to ultimately choke to death." Forced to wince, merely out of habit rather that sympathy, Eastern then decided to come clean himself, by informing Rogon of Brezznov's alleged repatriation scenario, prior to his own secondment earlier on.

"The amount of coverage put out by the 'CLARION' itself, it seemed to me, that it was small enough to be missed.." and went on to suggest, "That the Press to my mind had been artificially leaned-on to keep the reported facts reasonably low key. Unless you know different of course?" he hinted. Rogon retaliated with a smile, in a manner that remained exclusive to the agency, before replying.

"Your subservient observations become you, Mike. There's no fooling you, is there? Although you're right of course. The decision to sanction certain injunctions, stemmed from Whitehall, as you've probably guessed already." Acknowledging his patronising explanation, Eastern issued a token nod of gratification, but not before exerting his own brand of sarcasm.

"In that case, then maybe bloody Whitehall can give me a good enough reason as to why they obviously wish to contaminate my life once again!?" From then on, any form of contact appeared to be put on hold, leaving Rogon to ease himself back into his chair. Having made himself comfortable, he ordered some fresh coffee over the intercom. His hidden emotions at this stage, gave no indication as to his secreted thoughts. Eastern meanwhile, was left to contemplate what might have been.

"He's building up to something, I just know it" he mused and continued his reasoning in the same vein. "I can read him like a bleedin' book. Poxy mind-games to soften me up and then bam! He's in your face and body with an offer that stinks of rhetoric." Meanwhile, the coffee had been made available , leaving Rogon to pick up where he had suitably left off.

"Black or white, Mike?" he enquired casually. "The coffee that is." The moment became glaringly obvious, that he intended to keep Eastern negotiating a slippery tightrope of expectancy.

"Oh,...eh...white will be fine thanks. Sorry I was miles away." At least the coffee appeared to be genuine, and he took full advantage of it.

The moment he lowered his cup, Eastern's perception kicked in, and he steeled himself for what Rogon had allegedly got in mind. Slowly and methodically, the latter placed his cup to one side and glanced upward. His unflinching gaze honed in on Eastern's own eyes like a magnet drawn to metal. Finally, he uttered a single strategic word, "Prison!" and continued to penetrate, Eastern's, mind while awaiting a reaction.

Seemingly unmoved by Rogon's premeditated verbal offering, knowing there could well be a hidden motive lurking behind it, forced him into shifting the onus into retreat. "And!?" he demanded guardedly. It wasn't the feedback that he had been anticipating. For once Rogon had been caught flatfooted.

"Touche, Mike, I get the impression that you know me better than I know myself these days, so I will get straight to the crux of the matter. Basically, the agency, and not forgetting myself of course, felt that we would like to send you to prison for a while! How do you feel about that?"

"And you can go to hell!" would normally have sufficed as a suggestion to any such proposal foisted onto him. As it was, their past relationship of late had now matured to a higher level entwined with mutual respect. Given their circumstances when confronting him, Eastern elected to absorb what was on offer before passing judgement. Meanwhile, sensing a reprieve surmounting from a verbal backlash, Rogon continued to exploit his guardian role.

"As I mentioned previously, Mike, as alternatives go, prison isn't going to be the best solution on offer. But from the agency's standpoint it becomes one of sheer necessity. Thus far and with Brezznov in mind, any history that we have touched on is only the tip of the iceberg."

"I realize that only too well." Eastern readily confirmed, "so you have my full attention. Please, carry on." He invited.

"I've no desire to cover any old ground at this juncture, Mike. Unfortunately, the fact remains that the power induced by obscene amounts of money in the past, has given Brezznov carte blanche over the years, to classify his claim as undoubtedly being public enemy number one. Moreover, the fact that he is currently being held in a controlled environment, quite frankly means nothing! His prolonged influence remains as threatening on the inside as it does on the outside."

Their in-depth conversation at that point appeared to have materialized into one of game, set and match. Derived from a fleeting image of a mocking Brezznov, gate- crashed Eastern's thoughts. And in doing so, instantly alerting him to what ever grief might lay ahead. Although even with that in mind he wasn't about to cave-in that easily, having digested the facts. "I certainly go along with your comments on that score Rogon, but consider this. The bigger they are...the harder they fall, and that son- of- a- bitch is no exception to the rule, trust me!"

Now fully convinced that he held Eastern's full attention, assured Rogon, that he could now divulge certain prime facts alluding to the heart of the matter, and Indeed, his own personal views on the agency 'brief'. "Precisely!" he echoed, "and we," he continued, "need to supply the trip-wire by bringing him down to his knees."

"I get the distinct impression, that you're going to hit me with a designer format at any moment." declared Eastern.

"And hopefully you can successfully carry it out, Mike your position, thus far, will entail you working on the inside. The idea being, will be for you to investigate the theory that Brezznov has indeed planned a multi-million pound global fraud. Unfortunately, I hasten to add, the subject matter stems from an unknown source,. Hence our desire to get you fully briefed and out of circulation full stop." The acute suddenness of Rogon's decision to move the 'brief' to another level, had now taken Eastern completely unawares.

"Christ Rogon!" he exploded, "don't you think that you've left it a trifle late to get some sort of system organized? After all." he questioned, "I seem to recall you as stating that, quote, "Brezznov could be released at any time." Rogon then assured him that intervention from a higher power could justify, as he put it........

"A bureaucratic decision to sanction an extension, at any given time, is now in place." Heaving a sigh of relief, Eastern vetoed Rogon's flexibility and enquired as to the source of the alleged planned fraud. From then on, Rogon was at a loss to clarify any solid evidence to substantiate the claim, other than collective SP (information), gleaned from a series of informative phone calls made to Sussex HQ over the last couple of months. "The caller," he went on, "as you've probably guessed, chose to remain anonymous. What I can say, with due justification, is that following a trace, the calls themselves were found to have originated in and around the Brighton area."

Disappointment, linked to frustration, was integral to Eastern's make-up. And he asserted his own personal views when summing up. "It sounds to me like it could be a classic fall-out amongst thieves, you upset me and I'll return the favour. Right?" Incidentally, did the informant at any time state the method, or indeed put any particular person in the frame, used for incorporating the alleged 'scam'?"

Once again, Rogon was forced into a climb-down. "Like I stated before, not even a hint of a motive has emerged. Putting it mildly, we have been left hung out to dry." Negativism was one thing, and Eastern wasn't about to be rubber-stamped by association.

There is of course another angle that you might wish to consider." Acting bland as ever, Rogon committed himself to acting as an observer.

"I'm listening, what's on your mind?"

"I've been thinking, those 'bent' phone calls the police received?"

"Calls? I thought that I had passed on that issue and stipulated why?"

"Maybe from where you're sitting; only it's occurred to me that they might not be coming across as being totally 'kosher' (genuine)."

"And how the hell would you go about justifying that score?"

"Just bear with me for a moment Rogon. I'm simply sticking with the word 'misrepresentation' for the present. Who's to say that the calls are only just one part of a double-edged 'scam'?" The point had been made leaving Rogon to seize the moment. "In other words, a ploy, planted specifically to draw our attention away from a hidden agenda. Given the amount of intrigue thus far, I have to say that your implication certainly holds water, Mike."

"Exactly!" Eastern retorted, "Now your beginning to think on your feet at last Rogon, by fully admitting that the 'scam' theory suddenly becomes a feasible one. Personally, I can imagine the consequence of such a scheme ultimately occurring. And in turn, resulting into a flaming nightmare in terms of policing, should the situation ever arise. The possibility being, that you could wind up throwing all your potential resources at the wrong target. Consequently, leaving Brezznov with a passport to carry out his intended game plan without any grief involved. Assuming, of course, that he's at the heart of the matter."

At that juncture, Rogon's body language could well have spoken for him, and he lost no time in concurring. "You're 100% right, of course, Mike, or should I say as usual? And as you so rightly put it, until we know otherwise we will endeavour to play our percentage card." On that note and having achieved an overall level of mutual understanding, Eastern elected to remain within the confines of the agency to further discuss various options relevant to his covert self portrayal. Also taking on board, the possible pitfalls arising from any unforeseen consequences. Prominent being, the close attention given to the body and soul makeover, consistent with a whole new identity. When physically adapting to his proposed new under-cover role.

Meanwhile, back at his Flat in Brunswick Square, much aided by the benefit of time on her hands, his worried partner, namely Joan Travers, had likewise been engaged in contemplating a few personal views of her own. That apart, the majority of women would knowingly have been divided in their respective thoughts. Once again she stopped off to check the time. "God! he's been absent for almost four hours," she remarked in a contrite manner.

Knowing him as she did, plus the erratic work pattern that encompassed his maverick way of life as a PI, had became a trait that she readily accepted on a day to day basis. Having decided to retire to bed, she left a brief note of intimacy alongside a cold chicken supper in the kitchen. Some minutes later, the last dying thoughts that entered her head, as it gratefully hit the pillow, tended to sum up her current feelings. "There's no point in staying up I'm sure to get all the legitimate excuses in the morning anyway."

CHAPTER 2
INDUCTION BY PROXY

If challenged, anybody who knew her well enough, would never question the fact that she 'knew it all'. So Joan could be excused into thinking that her predictability associated with timing, should it ever come under scrutiny, would leave her feeling a trifle jarred. It was just after 12o/c midday the following day, when Eastern finally decided to surface, preceding his unexpected and covert abduction arising from the previous evening. With that in mind, Joan didn't waste any time when getting on his case.

"Good morning, Mike, I trust your business trip went well? At the very least, you have to say that your clients are getting their money's worth out of you." With that in mind , there comes a point in every seasoned P.I's life when the reality world tends to collide with Mars. And Mike Eastern was fast becoming no exception to the rule. The time to confront his demons had arrived , and this particular nemesis, hugging the limelight, just happened to be called Rogon.

"The 'business' as you so put it, Joan, turned out to be a premeditated time bomb waiting to explode. And the guy in charge of the countdown happened to be called...."

"......Rogon!", she exclaimed quietly confident. Her verbal injection was timed to perfection as she continued to pursue her line of reasoning. "I am right, aren't I?" Looking a trifle woeful, Eastern nodded glibly in agreement as Joan continued, "When you left here last night, I happened to chance on that article in the 'CLARION' the same one that caught your attention. After that, it just became a question of putting two-and-two together. Especially after your sudden departure. Incidentally," she threw in, "how far would you have gone, before Rogon managed to convert you into state property once again?"

If there had been a ready answer on tap, then Eastern had missed the boat, and was now found wanting. To agree not to agree, became his one saving grace as an option. "There's no kidding you, Joan, is there? As it happens, you're right in every department so far. And leaving me to readily admit, that it's beginning to feel like Rogon, never really went away." Smiling coyly, she shrugged her shoulders in a carefree attitude, and centred her opinion by taking in his situation as a whole.

"I'm not about to dwell on your business, Mike. I fully understood the ground rules when we decided to get together. So, if it becomes a case of what Rogon wants...then Rogon gets. Then I don't have a problem with that. I only insist that you take the time out to consider the danger element involved."

Given that the Rogon had long entrusted his mind, body and soul to the state, many years previous, belied the fact that somewhere amongst an influx of plastic implants, and brain-washed, non-negotiable thoughts, there existed the dormant remains of a once impassioned heart. Alas, years of constant doctrine had ensured that even the use of a body scan wouldn't be capable of producing such an image. That is, until Eastern's previous unclassified assault on the agency came into opposition.

Any apology that may have been put forward by Rogon, whether it derived via a verbal directive, or a written mandate in triplicate, indicated to Eastern that their prearranged meeting, held at Spooks HQ some 24 hours later, now held the key to a session of intrigue. And one that rose above the norm. Struggling to stifle the birth of a sarcastic laugh, Eastern listened guardedly as a vintage Rogon lorded the proceedings. His opening gambit came by way of a well-rehearsed guilt trip.

"You have to understand, Mike, this isn't easy for me," he stressed. "As your aware by now, my orders come from above. I'm only in opposition while acting as the messenger boy. So I can only apologise on behalf ....."

".....Utter bullshit!" Eastern's well timed intervention, hastily put Rogon out of his misery. "For once in your life, credit me with some internal knowledge. Just forget the bureaucratic crap , and say what you've been told to say. That way we can all go home." If there had been an outside chance existing, that Rogon had been forced into submission alluding to his latest outburst, then it had swiftly evaporated. All thanks to his state institutionalized brain.

Momentarily, his face remained passive before delivering a final coup de grace.

"With all due respect, Mike, certain circumstances now dictate that as from now you won't be.........." He paused, allowing himself to emphasise his ongoing exclusive terms. "Going home, that is, at least not for the foreseeable future!" he added sheepishly. A deflated Eastern now found himself backed on the eternal ropes, akin to a ring of frustration. Fortunately, the intervention of a bell or, in his case, the cold explicit tone of Rogon's voice releasing a valve of reality, as he continued to issue more demands. "As from now, Mike, you will be interned and classified as being State property. And your new persona will be integral to Spooks jurisdiction. I will also remind you that your former allegiance to the Official Secrets Act, is still operational. Meaning that any other business in terms of diplomacy remain in situ."

Breaking off momentarily, he retained his matter of fact air but this time with added impetus, as he concluded. "Any questions thus far, Mike,?" Having dealt the cards of officialdom, he then steeled himself for a designer outburst from Eastern who could be seen suffering from a composure complex.

"How much prime listening time have I got?" would have been utterly wasted on Rogon, whose body language began expressing a non-debatable outlook. Acting on a sudden whim, Eastern finally gave up the ghost. And decided to heed the offer, rather than be forced to come in from the cold. "I've got to hand it to you Rogon. I'd always maintained that manipulation, without

being patronising, had become a dying art." A sustained silence
ensued as the onus on discretion reverted back into Rogon's lap.
Choosing his words carefully, he graciously replied at length.

"I can't tell how relieved I am that you see it that way, Mike. It
would appear that in the past I've had a problem with the phrase
' to be explicit'. Now that we understand each other, a sense of
urgency is reminding me that we need to clarify your new persona
while resident at HMP Foredown Open." Fully resigned to the
fact that a minimum of 48 hours, consisting of intense briefing,
lay in front of him, with an impromptu 'holiday', courtesy of the
State thrown in, gave Eastern a parallel twang of conscience as he
compared his lot with Rogon's.

"Poor bastard," he reflected, "You've got the rest of your plastic
life on the inside. At least I have the advantage of knowing that I'll
be back on the outside soon enough."

Rogon's take on his own observations, had he been aware,
would have been one of sheer satisfaction in knowing that his
solemn way of life, at worse come under outside scrutiny. A sad
reflection to live with you might say, but for a leading Spook
agent, an admirable one.

A dozen or so State coffees plus as many intense hours later. A
bleary-eyed and semi brain-washed Eastern emerged from within
a cocoon of convenience, bearing a designer pseudonym. As from
now, he would be constantly referred to as being one Alex Ruark.
A British Nationalist, whom some nine years earlier had been
extradited from South Africa and consequently convicted of gun
running. He was also listed as being a freelance mercenary. A half-
hearted look of disapproval shaded Eastern's face as he entered a
lightweight observation. "I should imagine you took great delight
in tagging me to a reference like that?" Rogon made it quite clear
that he wouldn't be drawn into a personality parade and elected to
stick with protocol.

"Words in this case come cheap, Mike. It's left to the man
behind them to return an investment into an asset. And myself,
and the agency, happen to think that you're more than qualified for
the role. I'm not suggesting either, that it's going to be a vicar's
tea party once you're inside. On the contrary, if you mess up, then

Brezznov has the gift of contaminating the right people to deal with any likely threat to his illicit regime. Inside, or out that is."

"I'll know when the time is right." Eastern added ruefully.

"I'm sure. In the meantime, how you deal with the mission once you're isolated is entirely up too you. Unless of course the agency are forced to intervene depending on the circumstances. Let's all hope that it won't come to that. And I don't have to remind you, that there's a hell of a lot riding on the success of your involvement, Mike......in fact." Stopping short to attune a fresh attitude, Rogon then enlarged on Eastern's covert incarceration. "The other problem, should it arise, is a question of time."

"I was wondering when you were going to get round to that one," reciprocated Eastern. "Although rest assured, I don't do pressure. So from where I'm sitting I figure it's as long as it takes.....right?" Nodding confidently in agreement, Rogon stymied an obvious sense of relief and attempted to explain further.

"Which means of course," he stipulated, "that......"

"........I could possibly be looking at a lengthy stretch, depending on the outcome?" Eastern timed his interruption to signify that he was fully aware as to what Rogon was leading up to. He then resumed their conversation. "You can relax on that score. I don't have a problem with that, only......" It was now Rogon's turn to intervene, but this time with a hint of reservation attached.

"If what!?" and prompted Eastern to continue.

"....Only that those pin-striped bureaucratic little shits up in Whitehall don't fuck with my pension when I'm banged up!" His vain attempt to inject a light ray of humour on the proceedings fell way short. And clearly washed over Rogon's plastic personality. Briefly, the moment became lost in translation , and in doing so, gave Eastern the stage to dwell on another outstanding issue. "Which reminds me, when do I get the pleasure of enrolling at HMP?"

"I can assure you that, as from now, you can rest easy on that count, Mike. You're not about to go anywhere just yet. In fact, the next forty eight hours will be crucial to you, by allowing you the time to adjust to your covert persona. ."

"I see. I presume that we are talking background data here

times...dates and so forth?"

"Precisely that! In the event you manage to get close to Brezznov, then you're going to require a reliable and fictitious memory as a means to impress the man. Hopefully, the nom de plume we have supplied you with will mean nothing to him." Breaking off suddenly, a sinister mask clouded his face, before continuing. "That is to say, that prior to your incarceration, certain factual information, relating to yourself, will be suitably leaked into the prison system via our own network. Purely for his benefit you understand?" Eastern nodded his approval, and reminded him....

"That the inclusion of a third party associate acting as a contact while on the inside, would prove essential."

Having pre-written the script prior to their discussion, Rogon was immediately on his case when replying. "I'm impressed that you recognize the importance of such a role, Mike. In fact I have a man standing by as we speak. It goes without saying that he's been fully briefed on the entire dual mission that you're both undertaking."

"Excellent, when do I get to meet the guy?" he enquired. Even for a mortal as plastic as Rogon could be, they couldn't have failed to engage with the smug look that now enveloped his face.

"You....don't!" he replied in a jocular fashion, "You see, you already have... met that is." Moments later, a small diminutive and unassuming character entered the room, fully intent on making himself known. Eastern's jaw dropped in utter disbelief as instant recognition set in. And he lost no time in making his own presence felt.

"I should have known from the start that you would be involved somewhere along the line." Smiling generously, Eastern proffered his hand and resumed their conversation in a semi relaxed mood. "It's good to see you once again 'B', especially knowing that your on side." Acknowledging his warm response, the two men then shook hands. (the reference to 'B' as a pseudonym, belonged to the Spooks operator whom Eastern had inadvertently met up with some months earlier, whilst cracking a police conspiracy case).

"At least we will be in a position to know that there's no hidden agenda to overcome this time." 'B' quipped. "And I feel sure we will make a good team this time around." Completely satisfied that the two men were seemingly compatible, caused Rogon to call for a recess, enabling the pair to formulate a future contact system when on the inside. He ended by stating that he wouldn't be available for the next 48 hours, due to a promising lead alien to the case which required prompt attention.

"The specific lead itself" he explained, "Came by way of a further anonymous phone call, made from a box in the heart of the City. Luckily we managed to trace the origin of the call to a location in North street."

"And the significance of the lead itself, is what?" demanded Eastern.

"A vital connection to Brezznov of course, but more importantly the length of the call itself. The highly volatile content that it contained , proved to be more than we could ever have envisaged."

"It sounds to me like the caller was trying to out sing a canary. It must have sounded like the mother of all conversations." Asserted Eastern.

"Most certainly, and that was almost the caller's downfall. The desk Sgt at Division, who took the call, immediately issued the trace coinciding with an APB (all patrols bulletin). Fortunately, a nearby RTC (road traffic car), which was in the vicinity, swung into action. Needless to say, they arrived too late to apprehend the suspect, who by now had long gone. Clearly he had left in a hurry. This was backed up by certain evidence that the police came across at the scene."

"Damn!", vented Eastern, "an arrest at this juncture would have been the icing on the cake."

"Thankfully, It's not all bad news, Mike." Rogon sympathised. "There's still a good chance that we can get something out of it. Whoever made that call must have been smoking at the time. This became evident from the discovered remains of a cigarette butt, found smouldering on the floor of the kiosk. Further to that, a few feet away on the pavement, a pocket lighter was also recovered. Hopefully dropped by the perpetrator in his haste to get away. As we speak, both items are now lodged with forensic and I'll get back to you on that, as soon as their report becomes available."

As a sign of surety goes, Eastern could well be excused for demonstrating his loyalty toward the agency, when replying with honesty. "That's what I like about this job. One minute you feel like your handcuffed to a bloody tank, and the next, it's raining possibilities. Mind you, if I was that anonymous caller, I'd be compelled to walk into the nearest police station and asked to be 'banged up'." Once he realizes that it's game over and Brezznov gets to know what's going down then, God help him, I can only surmise that the poor bastard is a dead man walking."

In summing up, a philosophical Rogon then rubber stamped Eastern's overall logic and pre-empted his own opinion should other facts emerge. "On a more positive note; if, as I suspect, the caller himself has got 'previous (a record), any feedback from forensic could lead us into obtaining a kosher ID of the guy. Having said that, what's your take on the situation 'B'?. I'd more than value your opinion."

"My gut tells me that we need to err on the side of caution at this stage" he chimed in. "Without more evidence to back up your assumptions, we can't be totally sure if the guy is on Brezznov's payroll. Or, indeed, it is a one-off act with a personal grudge to settle. That's the best I can offer I'm afraid." A sustained silence ensued, allowing his thoughts to sink in. Finally Eastern broke the mould.

"Uhm, I hear what you say 'B', only......"

"It's only supposition on my part" he quickly reminded him.

"I appreciate that, but knowing Brezznov he won't give a shit either way, no matter what the outcome. As it stands, forensic hold the key to his future and if he has got 'previous', then it becomes imperative that we get to him first.....right?"

Begging not to differ, Rogon nodded his overall support and finished by stating, "I suggest we keep an open mind on the subject. In the meantime, you two have a lot of catching up to do and so have I." A further dormant thought then triggered his memory as he exited the room. "It's just occurred to me feel free to use the phone at any time Mike, and if you haven't already guessed, I've placed a 24/7 security 'shadow' at your Brunswick Square apartment." With that, he turned on his heel and departed, leaving them to their own devices.

Some thirty six hours later, and with the added bonus of a civilized breakfast under their respective belts, Eastern and his adopted colleague Benny Simmons (nee former agent 'B') relinquished their freedom by becoming a selective State statistic apiece, having been inaugurated into the prison system on a pretext. The two entered into a formal induction, chaired by the Governor of Foredown Open in Sussex, on the morning of the eighteenth of March 0/5. Also present to balance protocol, included his assistant and two warders.

Acting while under a directive from Whitehall 2 weeks previously the Governor, Derek C Whiting, had been subsequently briefed on Spooks covert operation. Consequently, he was issued with the necessary documents and 'stats' surrounding their alleged records. As a principal player in the charade, it was then decided that Whiting, on a level of security, would become the sole designated official on the inside to be entrusted with specific information, alien to the operation.

Strangely enough, for reasons dictated to by agency policy (and not availlable for scrutiny). Cemented around their decision to ensure that Eastern and Simmons alike, were in ignorance as to Whiting's role as a leading player. Some 30 minutes later, having had the riot act firmly embedded in their brain, the pair found themselves kitted out and allocated a joint cell.

From that particular moment in time, life for Eastern would now change dramatically for the foreseeable future. He was now left facing the stark reality surrounding the clinical environment, stemming from a State institution. His initial brush deriving from internal discipline (although he wouldn't have been aware of it at the time) was fast becoming a grim reminder that hell on earth facing a reluctant internee, was shortly in the process of becoming a reality.

It was only going to be a matter of time before he made his presence felt. Forewarning by a bias but well meaning inmate that quote: ' I've had the word that the 'fucking nuisance' is on the wing and doing the rounds' enabled the pair the luxury of gaining an element of expectation.

Every establishment holds the rights to one, and Foredown was no exception to the rule. Chief Warden Billy Donavon was old school, and as such addicted to old fashioned values, most of which he could claim the rights to. Amongst the majority of people who were unfortunate enough to get close to him over the years was a vast collection of 'cons' (prisoners). His exclusive take on the system amounted to regimented discipline 24/7. Leaving one old 'lag' to put it in perspective by stamping his own definition: 'A bleeden dinosaur if ever I saw one, and a right nasty bastard at that!'

As ever, the internal 'hot line' had proved to be fertile. Minutes later and flanked by two surly looking henchman, Donavon entered their cell and confronted the two at close range. Drawing himself up, he exerted an immediate threatening attitude, by eyeballing the pair with intent to provoke a reaction of some kind. For his part, Simmons appeared to be impervious to any form of mind games on show, and remained completely switched off. On a par, it would take more than the verbal assault that followed to unnerve Eastern, as he now took the full brunt of a well oiled backlash from Donavon, who, by his own admission was fast losing credibility.

"Don't think for a minute I don't know what's 'going down' here, Ruark! Playing dumb in my company is one fucking bad habit. And I just happen to have the right cure for that. It means that I get to dictate what you do and what you say in here when I'm around......d'ye understand that?" Briefly, Eastern then became lost in translation as Donavon unwittingly underlined his covert persona.

"Yeah...I'll bear that in mind, Mr Donavon. I don't really need the grief right now" he gabbled innocently.

"Is that fucking so?" The throwaway remark stank of sarcasm as he continued to press home his superiority, "remember this, I alone tell you what you'll get and don't get, Ruark. So all the time you're under my roof, you belong to me. This nick is my 'manor' (home ground) and you're a bloody intruder. Step out of line once and I'll make bloody sure that the only privilege left to you, will be the one allowing you to breathe. Do I make myself clear!?" Shifting his attention away from Eastern, he levelled a menacing gaze toward an obviously disinterested-looking Simmons, who appeared to be suitably impervious to what was being played around him. By definition alone, his inner body could now be found on a covert mission somewhere in central Europe. It was then left to Donavon to inject his own personal brand of reality.

"And that includes scum like you, Simmons. I shit people like you every day. Two days from now and you'll wish you were back in Wandsworth nick." Gritting his teeth, Donavon reverted his attention back toward Eastern who, through mounting frustration, was doing a master job of sub consciously throttling Rogon and the world at large.

"Which brings me back to you, and what have we got? I ask myself. Alex Ruark. A self confessed firearms ponce, no less, and now in the throes of an 8-year stretch." What ,transpired next could have been misconstrued as a smile, but quickly overlapped into a grimace as Donavon entered into yet another non-negotiable deal. "If you ever piss on my parade in future, Ruark...." Stopping short, he indicated toward Simmons, "and that include that piece of shit! I will personally see to it, that your poxy release-dates get an overhaul with fucking interest thrown in."

Methodically, he then motioned a designer-look toward the two adjacent warders. Acting on cue, they systematically proceeded to trash the cell, Leaving him to milk the moment and not before having the final word. "I'm glad that we've got that little misunderstanding sorted out at last, I feel sure that we're going to get along just fine from now on." Wearing a perpetual sneer, he turned on his heel and headed out of their cell closely followed by his two henchman.

Seconds later, a much relieved Eastern was the first to break the silence. "Is that demented bastard implying that we qualify for a ticket for the end of season Warders Ball?" Simmons smiled sparingly at his remark. As a seasoned 'hit man' (assassin), humour and death on demand, when mixed, often became a cocktail too hard to swallow.

"Personally, I would readily have settled for a funeral. I had the wanker in my sights from beginning to end.....bloody shame really."

"Yeah, why do you say that?"

"Oh, just something that Donavon, will never know about."

"Know?....you've lost me. Know about what?"

"That I could so easily have killed him. I'm talking a hundred times possibly more on a good day and yet he still managed to walk out of here alive."

Eastern, then made up for both of them, as he laughed uncontrollably at Simmons, spontaneous black humour. Between them, they then set about reinstating their cell before heading down to the recreational facility, in an attempt to suss out life in the 'village'. (prison).

CHAPTER 3
A CHANGE OF SCENERY

After some lengthy forty eight hours of mixed emotions, concerning their arranged confinement, Eastern and Simmons, could well be seduced into thinking that there just might be a real world beyond their cell, and that they were only experiencing the mother of all nightmares. That particular morning, having 'slopped out' and breakfasted, the two found themselves summoned back to the Governor's office for work assessment purposes. Although he couldn't have been aware of it at the time, Brezznov's previous ongoing assignment of cookhouse duty, had inadvertently created a prime solution in allowing Eastern an outlet in which to capitalize on, as a means to get close to him.

Without hesitation, Whiting immediately sanctioned Eastern's posting by placing him on kitchen detail. Simmons drew the short straw by being down-graded to general duties. And then, just as quickly, Eastern found himself thrust into an ordeal deriving from a system initiation. Five minutes later, he leant his full weight onto the two-way door, closely shadowed by a 'screw', (warder). And entered the food preparation area. This, in turn, he quickly noted, lay adjacent to a large open-plan kitchen. As if manipulated by strings, a dozen or so preoccupied 'cons' immediately looked towards him in unison, blatantly intent on catching a glimpse of the new 'face' on the block.

In spite of his inbuilt granite exterior, Eastern swallowed hard as he experienced a cold wave of controlled hostility buffet his body, reminding him that it was crucial that he should now exercise his latest persona to the full. He needn't have worried, as instinctively his covert personality kicked in. Acting in a threatening manner, he glared back at their zombie-like faces. The 'screw' meanwhile, merely through experience alone, had already sensed the birth of a cold silence and acted swiftly to rectify the situation. "Okay...okay you lot, get back to work, he's not wearing flaming stockings!" On glancing round, he continued to take centre stage, "where's that cretin, Fuller?", he demanded, "the lazy bastard seems to have more time off than I do lately."

As if on cue, a dishevelled figure emerged from behind the door of a nearby stockroom. "Ah....so there you are, Fuller. Have a nice kip did we? You'd better get your bloody arse back into gear. Lucky for you, I've got another pair of hands to help bale you out, he stormed, and indicated directly at Eastern, "oh, and before I forget, his name is, Ruark, or whatever he lets you get away with, and, just for the record, I'm told that he's spent more time in solitary than you have on the outside. Rumour has it , that his last supervisor narrowly missed being on the menu!" Chuckling under his breath, he walked away and left Eastern to his own designs, who, by now, was left seething with anger at the 'screw's' misguided intervention to break the ice, by using an overcooked reference as a means to an introduction. To his way of thinking, the 'screw's' paltry remarks had inadvertently rebounded by compromising his new persona, while at the same time, branding him as a threat. The vital importance of gainfully forming an association with Brezznov, built on trust, had now disintegrated by default.

He was now left into making a snap decision as to whether he should continue in the same vein, or as the 'screw' had adversely portrayed him. To renege, now, on his imposed persona, could leave him out in the cold and wearing a cloak of vulnerability besides. Fortunately for him, Brezznov happened to be employed elsewhere, overseeing, a bulk food delivery. Without hesitation,

Eastern arrived at a decision, or, rather the unrehearsed figure of his nemesis entering the kitchen cajoled him into it.

Having previously carried out an-depth makeover, he was left in no doubt as to the latter's identity. For such an insignificant-looking figure, he found it hard to believe that the man was capable of yielding the huge amount of power and influence, available to him on demand, at any one time. His loss of attributes, Eastern observed Were more than compensated by a magnetic aura that held the key to his exclusive personality. In truth, he was capable of asking for nothing, and ending up with everything, purely as a token of respect.

When bearing in mind the adage, 'if you throw mud at something for long enough, some of it is bound to stick!', then Brezznov figures in the credits. The mud in this case being organized crime, and the alter ego pseudonym of 'little Caesar', Which rapidly becomes a designer label which he wore, denoting a symbol of fear. As yet, Eastern had gone unnoticed, allowing him the advantage of requiring a personal and reserved opinion that didn't warrant any forethought. "So, this is 'Mr 'grief', he told himself. "If the little jerk is as dangerous as he is ugly, then I've got my work cut out", he convinced himself. Any other observations then went begging as Brezznov captured Eastern in his sights, and promptly made a move towards him. Short in stature and short on words, led Brezznov expressing the thought for the day, as he elbowed his way through to confront him. "Who the fuck are you?", he demanded, with the charisma of a cobra on heat.

A fair question for an unrehearsed meeting given the circumstances. Electing to bite the bullet, Eastern chose to remain unaffected by Brezznov's stance , and contented himself by eye-balling his aggressor. Just then, the 'screw' reappeared to intervene, before the hostile silence erupted onto another level. "Okay you two, you've both made your point. Now let's draw a line under it. I don't need the bloody grief on my shift. As for you Fuller, get that lazy crew of yours back to work....no...not you two, I haven't finished with you yet." Stepping between the two he made a formal introduction, "In case you were wondering, Brezznov, this happens to be, Alex Ruark, and you'll be seeing a lot more of him. I'll leave you to take it from here."

Meanwhile, ignoring the 'screws' plea, Fuller, glanced toward Brezznov as if anticipating a second opinion. It wasn't short in coming. A curt nod of the head, followed by a firm directive, finally put a seal on the delicate situation by erasing the tension. "Do as the man says, Fuller. In the meantime I've got a few house rules I need to spell out for Mr Ruark's benefit." Satisfied that he'd dealt with his part of it, the 'screw' slunk away, leaving Eastern to contest, or not, a Steward's inquiry relevant to his future within Brezznov's self-imposed rule.

For his part, showing face had to out do no face at all. Unwittingly, he'd been handed a 'get of goal card' for free. And he intended keeping it that way. Appeasing Brezznov at this stage was the only way forward, should he hope to out do him. Eastern's bottom lip was showing raw, as he succumbed to 'little Caesar' lording up his role within the system, "It's nice to know that we have an understanding, Alex....I can call you, Alex. Can't I?" Eastern nodded glibly, as a vision of his hands encircling Brezznov's throat featured in his sub-conscious. Meanwhile, his aggressor continued to rant on, "let me remind you, power isn't a gift that you can fuck with my friend. Used the right way you can get it back with added interest.

And by that I mean respect. That alone", he went on, "more than gives me the right to do and say what I think." Eastern was now left to flounder in a sea of verbal diarrhoea. Having been stripped of self opinion, he found himself nodding mechanically in agreement with what ever Brezznov expounded. Unfortunately for him the latter was still capable of lording it up, "so you see, Alex, the sheer power of being in control is a bespoke medium that works for me, equally on the inside as it does on the outside. This", he gesticulated in every direction, is my 'Manor', and with your given track record you could become part of it. It's obvious that your nobody's mug and so I respect that. The other thing, of course, is your experience with firearms. From what I've been informed, it appears that your contacts in the business do you justice. That in itself makes you a viable asset."

For the first time, Eastern slowly began to relax, enabling him to breathe and think more easily. Brezznov's latest revelation, had favourably evolved into a springboard of mutual trust. Thus opening up a window of opportunity for prime development. The added inclusion of being able to retain his no-nonsense persona, had now reverted into an additional bonus. This in turn meant that he now felt reconciled into handling any given situation, should one come into play. Brezznov then brought him back down to earth, by capping their altercation per se. "We'll talk again later, yeah.... we'll do that." Turning on his heel he left Eastern submerged deep in thought.

Fully aware of what Simmons had managed to glean from the resident 'snout' (informant), by definition alone, Eastern's handicap would have been one of time. Further major problems he readily noted, could arise via the arrival of a Parole Board, who were scheduled to appear within the next two weeks, primarily to review Brezznov's immediate future. Dependant on the outcome, the Hearing as a whole could paint a canvas of gloom, should a decision to engineer his release rule in his favour. "I'll leave Rogon, that one to figure out." He told himself.

At least, wheels were turning from both directions. Certain information regarding his alleged 'form', (history) had now conveniently milked it's way into the system via Governor Whiting, and infiltrated through to the right sources. (although Eastern himself wouldn't have been made aware of it at the time). Twenty four hours later, it was as much as Eastern could do to contain himself.

"At the time, I felt like I was walking on bleedin' broken glass." He related to Simmons when in conversation prior to 'lights out', and continued, "I'm adamant that Brezznov, has taken the bait, leaving me within spitting distance of the man. What I can't afford to be, is appearing to be pushy in my approach. That could be dangerous. Once I feel that I've got his full trust, I can get to work on him, and hopefully open him up."

The expression 'nothing-ventured-nothing gained', is only as good as the time that it takes to realize it's full potential. In this case, leaving a pissed off Eastern to query the 'sell by date' attachment to said statement. A week on from his clouded altercation with

Brezznov, his invested interest enabling him to get his nemesis on side, had, literally, died a death. Apart from an enforced grunt of acknowledgment or a curt nod of the head in his direction while at work, any form of extended contact had evaporated....or so he thought!

Lying spread eagled on his bunk this particular evening, Eastern allowed his body to do the talking for him, as he relaxed in a semi-comatose state. With a six thirty am rise, and a day's split shift behind him, the only interruption he would have settled for would have been the welcome sound of the fire bell. As it turned out, the alternative option that presented itself minutes later, then convinced him that even sleeping was indispensable.

"Ruark! Are you awake?" On balance, the enquiry stank of bad timing, largely due to the obnoxious odour it brought along with it, alerting Eastern, to an immediate response.

"Fucksake! Can't a man have a five-minute break to himself? And while I'm at it, what the hell are you doing in here anyway? You little shit!" His explicit reference to human waste was painfully directed toward a furtive and pathetic-looking figure. Belonging to a seasoned 'con' along with added weasel-like tendencies, who had just sidled into his cell. 3118 Steadman, was the elected prison gopher, with a track record belonging to a career 'nonce' (child molester). That is , until the state reorganized his perverse attitude to life. That said, the stigma attachment involved, seemed reluctant to let go. This in turn, followed him around like a bitch on heat, along with his hereditary body odour as a trademark.

"Sorry, Mr Ruark" Steadman bleated, "I've got a message...I'm only doing my job, I swear." Wary by nature, cautious by demand now summed up Eastern's fast-growing interest.

"Message you say, what sort of message? I hope, for your sake, it's bleedin' kosher, you pathetic creep, otherwise you'll be reporting sick tomorrow morning...know what I mean? Just say what you've been told to say, and then piss off." Forced to cringe, Eastern got out of his bunk to confront him.

"Brezznov!" Steadman blurted out, "Mr Brezznov that is, wants a 'meet'. He said to tell you that he'll be down on 'A' wing in ten minutes from now...that's it...so help me." If ever Eastern had to think fast on his feet, that time had now arrived with a vengeance. The implication that possible grief could be lurking in the background, didn't figure in his strategy. Reasoning was suddenly at a premium, leaving his gut to say one thing while, at the same time, allowing common sense to run with the opposite. By untested word of mouth, he now found himself running the gauntlet to an identity crisis, the outcome of which could prove to be paramount. And it all hinged on the mutual respect he had gained thus far. Having committed himself into playing hard to get, he also needed to keep the impetus alive by dictating his own terms. The onus would now shift toward Brezznov to prove his own worth. With that in mind, it was left to his whipping boy to make the running as Eastern marked his card.

"I've got news for you, Steadman, so listen up. You get back to Brezznov, a bit lively, and you tell him, that Mr Ruark said if he's got anything on his mind that he that needs to discuss with me, he knows where my cell is. As from now, I intend getting my head down so do me, and yourself, a favour and piss off before I get nasty, you perverted little creep." There was no turning back now. Working under the assumption that Steadman would no doubt relay his reply, it all came down to the waiting game Any further thoughts on the subject inconclusive. And he threw himself back into his bunk. Minutes later, tiredness finally got the better of him and he drifted off into a semi-comatose state. Sometime later, he awoke with a start, fuelled by the presence of a third-party involvement.

"Sorry, Mike, I didn't realize you were asleep."

"Simmons?", He enquired drowsily. At least he had recognised the voice.

"Yeah, bad timing I guess."

"Ah, forget it, Benny. I couldn't sleep anyway.....problem?"

"No, I figured you might be in line for an update."

"Better late than never, mate", he assured him, "we need to share what we know, and hopefully have some SP for Rogon to chew over."

As part of their pre-plan, it was agreed that Simmons would solely be responsible for forwarding any relevant information back to Spooks HQ. His intended role was also held to be acting merely as a low-key observer. By, exploiting a possible motive or disclosure to the origin of Brezznov's alleged 'scam'.

Having aired their collective information, they arranged an after-supper meet mainly to discuss any relevant feedback from HQ. Some time later, Eastern found himself alerted to Simmons body language as he sighted his approach from a lower landing adjacent to their cell. "I could be wrong", mused, Eastern, "although he's definitely got something on his mind. His face has got Rogon written all over it." Moments later, on closing the cell door behind him, Eastern reminded Simmons that they only had twenty minutes, at best, to converse before lights-out came into play. The latter then took the high road as Eastern listened intently. "Rogon sends his regards and........"

"Fuck the sentiments, Benny, I'm looking for facts", Eastern interjected impatiently. "The last thing I need right now is that assole Donavon banging on the door for a threesome." Simmons swiftly drew his attention to the recent spate of anonymous calls made to Division, highlighting Brezznov's alleged 'scam'.

Apparantly, the forensic report on the evidence gathered at the last scene of crime, confirmed a DNA match consistent with one, James Moran. It seems he was wanted by the police for money-laundering and fraud."

"Well, that's a start anyway. All they've got to do is to apprehend him, surely?" Unfortunately, his enthusiasm didn't appear to wash off on Simmons. And it reflected in his reply.

"Oh yeah, the Brighton police did that alright", expounded Simmons. "They fished the poor bastard's body out of a builder's skip, round about midday yesterday."

"Shit! There, goes my bleedin' theory. What about location I presume we are talking as being in the City itself?"

"No question about that. The skip itself was sited in a back street of Powis Square. Although the police have made it clear that it's too soon to say that the street itself is the actual SOC. We'll just have to wait until a pathologist's report confirms their findings."

"Just our poxy luck", vented Eastern. "The victim could have been so useful to us. Saying that, I think we can be sure of who held the rights to his execution. What's your feeling?"

"Pretty conclusive you have to say."

"Silly question."

"Go on."

"I assume there's no doubt that Moran, was in fact murdered?"

"Absolutely no question about it, Mike. The two 9mm bullets the pathologist dug out of the poor sucker's head, bore all the hallmarks of a professional 'Hitman'." Swallowing hard, Eastern reminded himself that Brezznov himself was only a floor away, forcing him to realign his own fragile welfare.

"It leads you think just how much power one man can yield to influence a 'hit' of that proportion, especially when still resident on the inside. At least it now answers the question to Moran's motive when he implicated Brezznov", he was quick to point out leaving Simmons to sanction his claim.

"Precisely! His murder now puts everything into perspective. If you're saying his silence came by way of a long term grievance, then I fully agree with you. I don't honestly think for a minute that he knew anymore about the alleged 'scam' than we do at this moment in time. To my reckoning, Moran was way out of his league. He was always going to be a loser." From then on, any immediate debate centred around Eastern's estranged stand-off with Brezznov, remained on hold as he stole a glance at his watch.

"I reckon it's time we got our heads down, mate. This discussion will have to wait until tomorrow. Right now I'm feeling bushed." Sleep that night didn't come cheap, leaving Eastern to pay the price for their earlier spontaneous meeting. An hour or so later before he did finally succumb, he found himself wrestling with his beleaguered conscious, regarding the commitment involved on a personal level.

What had now transpired, only enforced his belief that the operation was now reaching a critical stage. The only one remaining comfort he recognised, was the fact that that he could abort the mission, should his covert position ever become compromised. Notwithstanding the danger element involved, although fully aware of his 'maverick' tenacity, even Rogon, wouldn't struggle to find the answer to that dilemma.

CHAPTER 4
A BREAKTHROUGH OF SORTS

Eastern had just returned from 'slopping out', while coming to terms with the dregs of a restless few hour's sleep. "A shit night followed by a shit morning!" as a personal endorsement, reigned supreme as being the thought for the day. Moments later, disgruntled as he was, he prepared to exit his cell to head for the shower room. He wasn't even allowed the grace to suffer in silence, as a voice from behind, demanding his attention, momentarily caught him off his guard, causing him to whip round and take short notice. Framed in the doorway stood the menacing figure of Asst Chief Warder Price, Purposefully intent on offloading an internal 'domestic' onto him. "Rumour has it that you're making hard of settling down in here....making waves....that sort of thing. And there we have the makings of a prime problem", he accentuated. Stopping short, he gave a derisive smile before continuing in a derogatory manner, "or, rather, you are that problem", which makes Mr Donavon, a very sad person and in turn I get to inherit his unwanted crap." Venturing further into the cell, Price continued to rave in the same verbal vein.

"pecking order!....fucking pecking order, Ruark! That's the secret when dealing with scum like you." His voice rose in strength, almost to the point of screaming, as he continued to highlight his singular opinion. For his part, Eastern could now be found locked into a bubble of controlled emotion, content to mentally override his threatened space. Goaded by the latter's alien persona, Price found himself losing his identity fast, as his voice now reached fever pitch, "you know how the system works, Ruark. You think you're one fucking clever bastard, don't you!? I've been watching you and I don't like what I see...asking questions ....and more questions...and that", he broke off suddenly, to allow himself a sneer to bolster his alter ego, "is what really bothers me."

Diplomacy while under duress is one thing, whilst voluntary participation becomes non-negotiable, Eastern reminded himself, and left him having second thoughts about his covert role. "I don't need this crap. It's beginning to get a bleeden' habit and encores aren't my thing," he exerted, the past reference alluding to Donavon's recent welcoming address.

Meanwhile, a repentant Price, was still in Eastern's face when releasing his parting shot, "I intend watching you very closely in future, Ruark. In fact, I'll be that close I'll be wearing your fucking shoes! Do I make myself clear? ...Good, I'm glad that we understand each other at last. Like I said before, Ruark, think pecking order." Turning on his heel and wearing a smug look of satisfaction, Price exited the cell., leaving Eastern to pick the bones arising from an unprecedented verbal backlash.

Satisfied that Price was out of earshot, he lost no time in venting his own brand of pent-up feelings of frustration. Simultaneously, back at Spook's HQ, even Rogon's ears found themselves onto a hiding to nothing regarding a personal level, as Eastern dissected the positive from the negative. Personalities apart, his chief concern lay at the feet of Price's solid implication that he'd been, quote "Asking questions and more questions." For his part, there was no suggestion in his mind that he'd been anything but meticulous in his approach for covert information.

In fact, on merit alone, Simmons constant delving into his mind would have been the subject, if any, of a 'Stewards Inquiry' in real terms. "No!. Unless I'm missing something, there has to be more to this", he considered. "Besides, I'm nearing the end of an alleged ten-year 'stretch'. Why the hell would I want to sacrifice my parole, in exchange for being labelled a nosey bastard? It's almost as if I'm being set up and" he declared in typical Eastern fashion, "I'm beginning to feel seriously pissed off!" Checking the time didn't do anything for his present temperament either, as he soon realized that the altercation had cost him his shower time, and more to the point was now threatening his working attachment in the kitchen.

"Oi!...yer flaming well late." Like it or not, Fuller, was on his case the moment that Eastern entered the facility, testing his enduring patience to the limit. "You think you've got some sort of a poxy arrangement, Ruark, walking in ere when you bloody well feel like it? I'd think again if I was you. Mr Brezznov aint gonna like it when he finds out yer...."

"When he finds out what, Fuller?" Well within earshot, Brezznov had suddenly emerged from behind him, unannounced, and, in the process, left Fuller to consider the availability of a swift exit as an option.

"Nothing...nothing at all Guv, it can wait." Fuller blurted out.

Completely dismissing him out of sight, Brezznov focused his attention toward Eastern, leaving Fuller to slink away. His sudden intervention had now impacted into leaving Eastern short of a pre-meditated script to work with. Acting on impulse, he declined the offer to pursue a likely confrontation, electing, instead, to give his brain an overhaul. Fortunately, his nemesis decided to get busy by taking the initiative.

"You can forget the likes of Fuller, Ruark. People like him are indispensable. That assole couldn't even walk my dog on the outside, besides which he's got no class. Thinking with his poxy mouth, as he does, is fucking unhealthy, and that leads to a bad attitude.....need I say anymore?" Caught flatfooted, Eastern acknowledged his timely response with a robotic nod. At worst, he'd anticipated a verbal war as a consequence of his belated opinion from the previous day.

'Patronizing bastard, I don't get it', became his first legitimate thought, but he decided to go along with what was on offer. "I hear what you say, although losers don't happen to figure in." Cutting him short, Brezznov hurriedly switched their conversation to suit his own design.

"By the way Ruark I got your message."

"Message, he queried. Hedging would hopefully give him some thinking time.

"Yeah, the one that Steadman, the 'nonce' delivered. We obviously need to talk some more, clear the air, know what I mean? I'm beginning to like your style, Ruark." He went on, "you've got the bollocks to say what you think, and I respect that in a man. Between us, I reckon we could work something out."

From then on, any further outcome quickly died a death. Engrossed as the pair we're, they failed to spot a fast approaching 'screw' bent on issuing authority. "Hey! Break it up you two, this isn't a bloody meeting house, you're here to fucking work…now move it.!" Eastern had no cause to complain as he headed back to the preparation area. Choosing to remain retaliatory had paid dividends. Brezznov of all people had now sanctioned a future working dialogue. 'Flavour of the month' was know a recipe he could live with in his efforts to get closer to the man.

The distinctive sound of the internal lighting system shutting down caught him unawares that evening as he lay stretched out on his bunk, reflecting on another day of having served the State. It did little to ease his current temperament in knowing that nine pm City centre time in Brighton, life, as he once knew it, was only just socially adjusting to a new chapter. He recalled that a full week had now elapsed since Rogon had procured his services. Or, in biased terms, a controlled nightmare! His thoughts then switched to sentimental values as an image of Joan made use of his sub- conscious. This in turn caused him to rebuke the fact that he'd allowed alien circumstances to infiltrate his personal life, thus creating a lapse in contact.

"I really must take time to catch up with Joan, tomorrow." Seemed, an appropriate thought, "and while I'm at it, I think I'll plague Rogon, as well." became his last remaining thought. With another morning, shift under his belt, Eastern lost no time the following morning by securing the use of a phone booth. On ramming the phone card home, he dialled an exclusive 'hot line' number. Full of apprehension, he prepared himself for a reply. He wasn't about to be disappointed as Rogon exploited his own charismatic manner.

"Mike? I was wondering how long it would be before you decided to get in touch. I presume this isn't a social call? Simmons has informed me, saying that it hasn't been easy for you in dealing with the adjustment."

"Yeah, well I'm bleedin' sorry about that, Rogon. 'Maybe I'm not as smart as I though I was,' Eastern fired back. And proceeded in a sarcastic manner, "On hindsight you should have booked me into the Waldorf suite knowing the staffing problems I'm having to deal with." Pausing to collect his thoughts he continued, "I assume that Simmons mentioned the ongoing grief aimed in my direction? Notably from particular warders. As was to be expected, Rogon wasn't found wanting when it came to manufacturing answers at a personal level.

What ensued, forced Eastern to wince at his current solution to disguise a hidden agenda. 'Warders!?, Rogon questioned in a symbolic manner, "Surely you must have realized, Mike that your mission was never going to be a 'Vicar's tea party'? That's why you were seconded for the role in the first place. Having said that, things do tend to get mucky if allowed to at this stage."

"Why do I get the distinct impression that this conversation is being edited?', Eastern considered inwardly. And added a wry smile, as Rogon, pursued the obvious.

"Hello....you still there, Mike?"

"Yeah, you were saying?', He responded in a casual manner.

"Basically, there is no error of margin to fall back on. In fact, it's imperative that your cover remains in situ 24/7. Should Brezznov at any time be allowed to form the slightest indication that you are anything but 'kosher', then the mission as a whole is blown apart. Like it or not, Mike, the buck ends with you getting a result. And as such, the agency needs to be aware of your inner strengths while acting under duress."

"So what the hell do you want from me Rogon...a poxy health-and-safety stress reference?" snapped Eastern in a jocular fashion, "besides. I like to think that my track record show's that I'm more than capable." With their conversation now showing signs of getting heated, Rogon acted positively to diffuse the situation.

"Your integrity has never been an issue, Mike. In fact my agency counterpart, namely Commander Paxon, speaks highly of you."

'Paxon!? who the'. His enquiry folded as Rogon swiftly interjected.

"My apologies, Mike. I should have said Price, whom you met recently...Asst Chief Warder Price that is." A sustained cold silence followed, allowing Eastern's distorted brain to complete a full 360%. And not before launching into a spontaneous verbal assault.

"You've got some fucking nerve, Rogon, setting me up again. Nothing changes, does it? But then we've been down this road before if you recall. Same shit...different day. You pluck me from out of my own comfort zone, sweet talk me into a situation, and then have the bloody gall to put me on trial, while compromising my neck, at the same time. You bleedin' bureaucratic cretin!" Typical of the breed, Rogon remained unmoved by his outburst and went for a patronising stance.

"Your frustration is duly noted, Mike, and you can rest assured that your valued input won't be wasted in the long term." He then added graciously, "Knowing that Commander Paxon is now off the case, it must afford you some relief I imagine?"

Eastern chose to remain unbowed as a mental picture of Warder Donavon entered the equation . And in doing so, prompted him into thinking out aloud.

"Pity you couldn't get that other animal off my back, Rogon. I reckon I could settle for that." Minutes later, having settled for the satisfaction that Joan's well-being continued to stay secure, a subdued Eastern made his way back to his cell.

Once inside, he promptly threw himself onto his bunk with a view to gaining some respite, knowing that in less than an hour he'd be back mixing it with the likes of Brezznov once more. In no time at all, his gut instinct came to the fore as he tentatively made his way into the kitchen gallery. Conscious of his presence, Brezznov lost no time in establishing a forced rapport. "Ruark!... over here." Eastern averted his gaze and acknowledged him with a casual nod of the head. There was no denying the air of hidden confidence his body oozed. Casually, he made his way towards his nemesis.

Not seeking to take any prisoners, Eastern took the initiative enabling him to force a dialogue. "So, what's it to be...business or pleasure?" he demanded brusquely. In response, the contentious glare that appeared on Brezznov's face , alerted Eastern to the fact that, like it or not, appeasing the man seemed a sensible move.

"Pleasure, Alex!? I don't do fucking pleasure. I'm a business man, and when I'm not, then I'm still working on it...can you understand that? Or putting it another way, in simple terms you could be short of a pound, whereas I could be short of a million pounds. So now you can see the difference between me, and a room full of fucking losers!" Forced to bite the bullet, Eastern nodded robotically as Brezznov clinically chewed him out. For the time being, he decided to keep his own feelings under wraps, sensing that the designer sermon he was being subjected to, carried a hidden agenda.

He wasn't about to be kept waiting on that score, as a further verbal wave came into play, "but then I take a further look around me," Expounded Brezznov, "and all I can see...is you and me, Alex!"

"And your point being?" Eastern enquired cautiously.

"You're an asset my friend. I recognise potential when it's gifted to me, and in your case that tells me we both share a common bond. The bottom line being that we are both business men in our own right." Pausing briefly, he checked himself by placing an onus of superiority on a personal level, shielded by a smile that belied his patronising comparison. "At varying degrees of course, but then I'm sure that you're aware of that anyway. Besides, I like to think that my reputation precedes me." For somebody of his size and stature, Brezznov's disciplined ego extended beyond the point of debate, by hovering somewhere between sheer nerve and a chauvinist male Prima Donna. Consequently, leaving Eastern to remain a staunch spectator, as self-elected 'little Caesar' continued to extol the virtues of a career-minded master criminal, "given a couple of weeks," he stated, "this place will become history as far as I'm concerned, Alex. And my life will be back to business as usual. Not that I've ever been off the case you understand," he swiftly emphasized, "on the contrary, the State might have controlled my person for the last fucking twelve years, but my head belongs to me, and that's the difference between their loss and my gain."

"You've obviously not allowed the time you've put in, to interfere with any plans you've got on hold?" Eastern concurred hurriedly, on the off chance that Brezznov could possibly open up and disclose important information, Implicating himself as being the major player in his forthcoming alleged 'scam'. The outcome arising from their illicit scenario suddenly evaporated, due to a nearby distraction made by the other prisoners arriving, accompanied by a 'screw'. A moment later, Brezznov became the first to vent his frustration, "Poxy system. I've had a bellyful of it. You would think that after twelve fucking years a man could have some privacy!" he snarled.

"Brezznov!....Ruark!" The 'screw' was demanding their attention. Completely ignoring his request, Brezznov made it clear that they needed to talk further.

"Leave it with me, Alex, I'll get a further 'meet' sorted, this discussion isn't over yet. Trust me, you'll be hearing from Steadman very soon." Turning on his heel, he left Eastern to contemplate on a brief measure of success, albeit high-jacked alluding to bad timing.

"Shit! Another few minutes and I would have had the arsole eating out of my hand. I can't believe that I got that close to cracking him." He fumed. Meanwhile, his present enigma, the 'screw', was busy concentrating on balling out Brezznov.

You can forget the rest of your shift, I've been informed that you're on Governor's report list in ten minutes, and!" he added, "with a bit of luck, it could be to do with your ticket out of here, leaving us with one less scumbag to worry about." Apart from a brief contact to sanction a 'meet' with Brezznov in the recreational hall later, the rest of his shift proved to be a mundane affair. Made even more noticeable by the acute absence of Steadman in the canteen. Reflecting on the quality of the food, he quickly dismissed any concerns he may have held on the matter, and put it all down to personal taste. An hour later, Simmons acknowledged his presence and gestured toward a convenient corner table to establish a low profile. In no time at all, the two were soon engaged in diplomatic banter. Momentarily, Eastern left off to express a dormant opinion. "I've got to hand it to you, Benny, you've certainly put yourself about, considering the time that we've spent in here. " Clearing his throat he continued, "Seriously though, have you at any time considered giving the agency the elbow? You and me 'firmed up' could make a bleeden' good killing on the outside, wouldn't you say?" He should have known better to ask. Simmons held the rights to insidiousness and the exclusive smile linked to his face said it all.

"It would never work, Mike. Your idea of a killing, as opposed to mine, is that my clients remain permanently stiff after I 'hit' them....right?"

'In the same manner, that you probably already knew, that Commander Paxon, and Price, were of the same person no doubt,' he consciously reminded him. Shrugging his shoulders as a form of confirmation to the question, Simmons decided to come clean.

"You're absolutely right of course, although the agency and the bureaucratic shit that it dictates, would argue the case. Having said all of that, Rogon himself wouldn't have it any other way. After all he is State-owned property, and as such holds the casting vote. But let's face it, I'm sure that you knew that anyhow through your own experience of late." Summing up Simmons reply, Eastern declined the offer, to agree not to agree, and pursued an alternative train of thought.

"Tell you what, let's talk 'faces' (villains) for a minute."

"Anybody in particular?"

"Yeah, as it happens I'm thinking Steadman, for instance., apart from the bloody obvious. What do we really know about the creep?"

"That's strange." A bemused Simmons questioned, "Of all the people you have picked on, you decided to settle for a 'nonce'. But then I'm a cynical bastard myself, which leads me to believe that you have an ulterior motive."

"Uhm...possibly, so let me run this past you. We are here to primarily extract information with the prospect of bringing Brezznov down....right?"

"And, given the time, I'm confident we will bring the assole down," affirmed Simmons.

"That's what's bothering me, you need to check with Rogon regarding Brezznov's Parole status. The grapevine is telling me that he's up before the Board sometime next week."

"Call me stupid, Mike, but I get the feeling I'm missing something here."

"No, Steadman! Like I said."

"You're still not making any sense, are you, suggesting that there's a link between the two?"

"It's occurred to me that he's the one person that we should be targeting. To my mind the guy is a walking encyclopaedia with likely connections to every 'con' in here...c'mon think about it?"

"Yeah, suddenly it all begins to make sense. No wonder he's managed to survive as long as he has without any grief. When you stop to think about it, he's one clever bastard and I'm forced to agree with you. As you so rightly suggest, he must have the SP on every con in here. And there's me thinking the guy is a right tosser!"

"Exactly" And that's my point. I'm willing to bet he knows what Brezznov's brain is up to on an hourly basis. And that's one hell of a lot I'd like to be a party to." With their meaningful conversation drawing to a close, Simmons suggested that it would pay to concentrate on attempting to set up a rapport with Steadman on a one-to-one basis. Hopefully earmarked for the following day. Detailed planning, as always, is perfectly acceptable. Unfortunately, reality is a factor that goes hand in hand with fate. Although nobody, apart from the perpetrators, would have recognized the significance it would have to bear as a result.

As far as Eastern and Simmons were concerned, the very idea of taking action at that time, as opposed to the luxury of being wise after the event, technically became the difference between night and day. In Steadman's case, it would culminate in his ignominious ticket to freedom, consistent with a Government-issue plastic body bag. And thereafter placed in a private ambulance, en route to the City morgue. Having failed to 'slop out' that particular morning, following Eastern's intentions to approach him, the prison staff's suspicions were immediately aroused, resulting in an internal investigation being launched. In no time at all, his lifeless naked and heavily blood stained body, now resembling a misshapen torso of what was once a living body, lay strewn on his bunk. On further examination, a pillow could be found covering his face. Consequently, a verdict of death consistent with asphyxiation was then pre-recorded by the prison medical staff. (this was ratified by the SOC Pathologist shortly after his arrival.) On close examination, it became apparent that the victim's testicles had been savagely removed from the lower body. Probably by a shard of glass recovered from a nearby broken shaving mirror.

This also accounted for the many random lacerations to the torso, clearly visible at the time. The severed organs were found to have been forcibly stuffed inside the victims mouth after suffocation occurred, by person or person's unknown. As is the norm, a study taken of the coagulation, estimated that time of death was likely to have been some twelve hours earlier. This in turn, coincided approximately before 'lights out' the previous evening. Forty eight hours on, the severity of the murder still remained the main topic of conversation amongst the staff and inmates alike. With the overall consensus blackballing a Steadman sympathy vote.

"As 'banged up' paedophiles go, the geezer was a dead man walking, somebody did the World a fucking favour." One old 'lag' was heard to remark. And as opinions come and go, went some way into finally bringing about a seal on the whole macabre episode. Shortly after the victim's body had been removed, the MIU (murder Inquiry unit) were far from convinced that the motive for the crime had been played out to resemble a 'justice' killing. With little or no evidence to substantiate a claim, their enquiry ground to a halt. It was eventually abandoned per se a week later. At that time, nobody could have been more relieved than Eastern.

"Bad enough that I'm 'banged up' anyway, let alone having to put up with the added grief of having been subjected to a ritual grilling process." he quibbled, "and then terminating into a full blown recreational ban." Fortunately, his time spent working in the kitchens had allowed him some respite from his cell. Regrettably, through circumstances, his time progressed from bad to worse. Due to an upgrade affecting internal security, personal contact of any kind remained stalled at a low premium. With no known antidote available for frustration, he found himself beginning to feel the pangs of an innocent man serving life! The realization that he was now fast becoming a lone and spent force became intolerable, due to the overriding absence of Simmons strange and sudden departure in the last seventy-two hours, noticeably consistent by the man's mysterious inclusion from his duties. And, even more defining, the use of the dining hall. Conjecture, as a pastime, is for mugs, and he didn't envisage buying any shares on the subject. Gut instinct in Eastern's case was an inborn commodity and one that he's always carried a potential reserve of. With 'lights out' a few minutes hence, Eastern lay at full stretch on his bunk , jostling with his memory by playing out the scenario issuing from the last week. Starting out with Steadman's murder.

The facts as I see it," he reminded himself, "just don't seem to add up. Apart from the obvious , the motive itself doesn't seem to fit the overall situation. Apart from the fact that he was a classified 'nonce', the man himself was a complete and utter nobody! Not only that, any personal gain at that level, and executed in an open prison, doesn't, to my mind, hold water. There's no future in it. No, as far as I'm concerned. The killing was too well-organized for my liking."

Also prominent on his mind, led him to believe that his former suspicions surrounding the victim's activities, "in that Steadman had access to damning information via his role as prison 'gopher', now bore a margin of substance. His theory being, that prior to his murder Steadman was possibly on the verge of going public, by disclosing certain covert knowledge that he'd been privy to. "Yeah, on that basis, it's all too bloody convenient as murders go," he assured himself, "and that just about sums up the whole damned rotten mess, although," he concluded, "the question still remains. What person, or persons, stands to gain the most from his timely death?"

CHAPTER 5
AN OUT & OUT RESULT

Slowly, and when it suited the system, the blanket of harsh regime existing in Foredown had now at last begun to lift slowly. As a result, the process now succeeded in making life more tolerable, to a degree, for Eastern, including the rest of the inmates. One 'con' in particular had plenty to crow about. Having survived the rigours of a visiting Parole Board, Victor Brezznov was finally given a release date. His good fortune, in turn, now created a knock-on effect in reverse by leaving Eastern out in the cold. Simply to chase shadows riddled with doubt.

The relationship between the two, right from day one, had never been anything less than strained but, at worst, a trickle of common ground had at least been established. Unluckily, either by design or prevailing circumstances, there it had remained, leaving an aloof Brezznov pulling the strings and allowing Eastern to rue a strategic 'meet'. That, due to misplaced fate, was now never going to take place. Indeed, time now was beginning to run out rapidly for any form of a breakthrough. In forty eight hours time, Brezznov could well be relishing the freedom of a civilian under licence.

A seriously pissed off Eastern, now found himself holding a non negotiable complaint, only made worse, when you've nobody to complain too, "And where in the hell is blasted Simmons? Now that I need him," he exploded yet again in anger. "I'm beginning to think that I'm the only person on trial here. For all I know, the mission, as a whole, could well have been aborted!" In some cases, negative thinking has a way of contradicting itself. Needless to say, in his case there remained more background activity going on then he could have ever envisaged.

That same day, Brezznov, either by design or cordiality, made a complete and unexpected move on him in terms of mutuality. The consequence of which, gave rise to beneficial progress firmly placing him back in the frame as the running man. Caught unawares, as his nemesis approached him, Eastern nevertheless managed to remain calm and collected as the latter thrust a small piece of paper into his hand before speaking in a direct manner. "Memorise this number, Alex, and then dispose of it. Once you're out of this 'karzy' (toilet) and the time is right, you can use it to contact me," and finished by insinuating that, "rest assured, you can do yourself a bit of good." good my friend." And then he was gone before Eastern had a chance to challenge him. Not that he was about to give a damn, . In future, any prevailing negativism surrounding his own covert role, could now be listed as redundant. The mere idea that, by default, Brezznov had unwittingly given him the key, enabling him to open up 'Pandora's box'. handing him back the grief that went with it, was something to relish. Milking the moment only became an added bonus, leading him to sound off.

"Don't worry, I've got your number in more ways than one you inglorious bastard! You might just as well hand me your dysfunctional head on a platter. Take it from me, this is only the start of you're worst nightmare!" Casting aside the fact that Simmons' untimely absence was still an ongoing problem, left him in no doubt as to his next move. "Rogon?...Rogon...shit! I need to contact him, and it won't wait. This latest development has opened up a whole new ball game....and", he stopped short to consider a more personal issue, "not only that! but the question, regarding my ticket out of here needs to be taken into account."

That, and a few other unanswered questions were temporarily

put on the back burner, as a further surprising move overlapped his predicament a short time later. At least, this latest hiatus allowed him a short-lived anonymity from his current problem. Trouble is, Warden Donavon had that effect on everybody he came into contact with. Just for once, his exclusive verbal charm at least became wasted on Eastern, as he sought to direct his usual inbred hostility toward him.

"Get yourself straightened out, Ruark, you're looking a fucking mess. You've got an appointment with the Governor in fifteen minutes, so I'll be back in ten. Don't make me have to wait. My patience is wasted on shit like you as it is!"

Stifling a "And you can go to Hell too," a slightly fazed Eastern then proceeded to make his way back to his cell. His brain could now be found working on overtime as he attempted to claw back some self discipline. "First of all, I've had Brezznov unloading onto me and now the Governor wants a part of me. I figure that any contact with Rogon is going to have to wait for the time being," he told himself. Preoccupied as he was, dealing with some paper-work on his desk, Governor Whiting didn't even bother to look up and acknowledge the two, as Donavon ushered Eastern into view.

Killing time, Eastern quickly surveyed the space around him, randomly gathering this addled thoughts as he did so. Satisfied that Whiting appeared to be heavily engrossed in paper-work, gave Eastern the chance to snatch a glance around the room. Almost immediately the idea became redundant, as Donavon swiftly reprimanded him. "Face the front, Ruark. You're not here on a sight-seeing tour." Placing his pen to one side, Whiting glanced upward and eased himself back in his chair. The cryptic look that he was wearing gave no indication as to his present thoughts.

"So, Ruark isn't it?" he enquired loosely. With Donavon hovering in the background Eastern elected to stick with protocol when replying.

"Yes sir, prisoner number 306..." Whiting promptly flapped his hand as a measure of disregard, cutting him short in the process.

"That won't be necessary, Ruark." Breaking off, he rapidly switched his attention to another line of thought. "That will be all for the time being Mr Donavon. I'll ring if I need you and it's crucial that I'm not to be disturbed for the next hour, is that clear?" Nodding briskly, a deflated Donavon exited the office with more on his mind than when he first went in. For his part, Eastern's mind had taken up a position midway between intrigue and disarray.

"I wish to fuck somebody would tell me what the hell is going down?" he confided in himself. At that point, Whiting indicated that he might have read his thoughts, by beckoning a bemused Eastern to sit down. Conversing as he did so.

"You're obviously wondering, and quite rightly so, that there's more to this intrusion than meets the eye? In short, what I am permitted to say, without any justification, is that you will not be staying another night here as an inmate. Basically, you're a free man...Mr Eastern!" A sustained silence ensued as Eastern's brain struggled to play catch-up, in response to Whiting's explicit disclosure and familiarity.

"This has to be somebody's idea of a sick joke" he retorted at length. "Somebody needs to start giving me some straight answers before I get really pissed off!" On hindsight, he should have got up and walked away there and then. The offer on the table in anyone's language appeared to be beyond consideration. Unless your name just happens to be Mike Eastern of course. From the minute that he had entered the office, his razor-like perception had been working overtime. Events were moving far too quickly for his liking and in doing so, had removed any assumed conclusions he might have held, relegated into obscurity. Sensing the possibility of a situation arising, Whiting decided to break his own silence.

"I apologise that I can't be more specific, Mr Eastern. Unfortunately, my hands are tied. What I can tell you for sure, is that plans are in motion, as we speak, to effect your immediate release. In fact, as far as this instillation is concerned, our records will show that you never existed."

"Uhm, your beginning to sound like you have the same attitude as somebody else I know" came back the reply, and continued, "So explain this for me. How do you intend glossing over my connection with the resident inmates and my sudden departure.? Don't tell me that the last six weeks have been all for nothing?" demanded Eastern, "oh, and one other thing. Seeing as you're so familiar with my covert involvement, you do realize that by pulling the plug on me at this stage, you've jeopardised any strategic relationship that I managed to build up with Brezznov."

Shrugging his shoulders in an untried sympathetic gesture, Whiting replied in the same vein. As I stated before, Mr Eastern, all the facts surrounding your current position will be conveyed to you in due course." From start to finish, their estranged conversation, so far, had only given him grounds, by increasing his inbuilt doubts as to their origin. "The cut-off point is too neat and tidy. And there's Simmons' of course. Why the hell isn't he here? He's up to his neck in this charade as much as I am," he reminded himself. His patience, it seems, had finally dissolved, and he was now looking elsewhere for some form of confirmation. In desperation, he turned on Whiting. "The phone...I need to use your phone!"

Caught up in his own private war, had made him oblivious to the fact that the office had now opened to reveal an interested third party.

Keen to make himself heard, "That won't be necessary, Mike, although I do owe you an explanation." Despite being heavily engrossed with Whiting and his negative approach, Eastern would have recognised the exclusive overtones of that particular voice everywhere, as it cut through his immune system. The sheer timing alone was as predictable as the man himself. Putting persuasion to one side, his thoughts shifted up another gear as he swung round to confront his demons. He wasn't about to be disappointed and lost no time venting his feelings on the situation. "Rogon!" He bawled, "I'm not even going to ask what the fuck are you doing here? Although seeing as you are, I hope for your sake that you've left any bureaucratic shit you might want to throw at me, back in your office." True to form, Rogon appeared to be unmoved by Eastern's outright demand, and kept his demeanour focused solely on the latter's welfare, after shaking hands.

"Good to see you too, Mike. It's refreshing to see that the system hasn't diminished your personal attributes. I presume Mr Whiting has explained the unforeseen turnaround regarding your internment?"

"I figured out you already know the answer to that one, so let's cut to the chase Rogon. And we can start by you dealing me with some hard facts as to why the operation has been so conveniently aborted." Clearing his throat, Rogon stated his case.

"Basically, the agency, while acting on a directive from Whitehall, prompted me into making a swift decision, just over a week ago, prior to Steadman's demise." He explained tentatively.

"Steadman!?" echoed Eastern. "How come a low-life like that be allowed to influence the operation? You'll be telling me next that the arsole was a leading player in your little game." A bad attempt at expressing a meaningful smile followed, as Rogon picked up from where he had left off.

"Until I knew any better, Mike, I had a problem, myself, in thinking that Steadman could be of little or no importance. But the ironic truth of the matter, is that he was the one person, above all else, who instigated the conclusion of the operation." Glaring, Eastern motioned him toward a nearby chair.

"If I didn't know you any better, Rogon, I'd have to say that this whole bloody charade could take some time to unravel." Having made himself comfortable, Rogon then went on to explain the justification for his former decision to abort the mission.

"We need to thank Simmons', or should I say 'B', into kick-starting the fact, that, Steadman was not all he appeared to be."

"I can recall testing that theory with 'B' at one stage," asserted Eastern. Nodding briskly, Rogon continued. "Yes so I believe. Anyhow, acting on a premise I authorised a thorough search of Steadman's cell to be carried out, the consequence of which, resulted in the discovery of a diary, containing pages of guilt-edged information. Relating to certain inmates, to surface."

"I wouldn't mind betting that Brezznov figured highly on his 'hit' list" suggested Eastern. "The creep used to hang around him like a bitch on heat."

"Apparently, more than most Mike almost to the point of a full-blown dossier, in fact. But more importantly, and this is the crux of the matter, part of the information also stated that he was about to go 'public' with the inside knowledge that he'd accumulated, as a trade-off in pursuit of an early release."

"Christ! What the hell was the silly bastard thinking of? Whistle-blowing at that level is on a par with assisted suicide. Rogon shrugged his shoulders in a carefree manner before replying.

"We'll never ever know the answer to that, will we? But from Whitehall's prospectus, they would have ensured that Steadman's volatile scheme would never have been allowed to materialize. Simply, if Brezznov had found out that we had pre-knowledge of his intended 'scam', he would have most certainly pulled the plug on it, and all our groundwork would have been in tatters." Eastern's head was now at full stretch as he manoeuvred his brain from one scenario to the other neither of which seemed compatible with Steadman's sudden and unexplained demise....unless. A random thought then struck him as he digressed.

"Correct me if I'm wrong, Rogon, but just how far would Whitehall, or yourself for that matter, have gone to maintain his silence....murder possibly?" Rogon's face remained unflinching, even though Eastern had put him directly on the spot. Although, what Rogon couldn't disguise in a confrontation, lay in his body language and, as such, became a weakness that Eastern had been well accustomed to from their early association. Almost immediately, alarm bells began to sound off, reminding him that there was more to his enquiry than he could have imagined.

A cold silence ensued before Rogon finally broke the ice in his own indomitable trademark manner. "I'm not here to justify my reasoning to you or, in fact, to the very people to whom I'm answerable to...but murder? I think not, Mike. As a high profile agency we find that word most disturbing and, dare I say, old fashioned? No! We prefer to use the term 'put down'. It sounds that much more final you have to say. and, indeed, trivial, when you consider what is at stake here." Inwardly, Eastern could be found seething at Rogon's blind arrogance and more than determined to have his say.

"Why don't you come right out with it, by admitting you had the poor bastard assassinated? You just don't get it do you? In my book, you've managed to mess up big time you and Whitehall together. It's not just a 'nonce' you've managed to 'put down', but also the fucking golden goose for Christ's sake!"

"I totally disagree, Mike." Rogon fired back, "Once we were in possession of the diary, we had everything we needed to know, in black and white. What more could you want!?" Eastern was now resigned to shaking his head, more in despair than in anger.

"I can't believe you just said that, so I'll spell it out for you. What you so badly wanted and haven't got, is the evidence that Steadman took to the grave with him. When people like him are calling the shots, they inevitably, keep to themselves as a means of bargaining. If the truth was best known, the man was a walking encyclopaedia. At worst, you could have struck a deal with him. The agency had nothing to lose and everything to gain." Pausing to collect his thoughts, he continued. "By the way, what's Simmons take on the outcome as it stands?"

Eastern had undoubtedly touched a raw nerve with his opportune request, leaving Rogon to squirm unconditionally in his chair before replying in a brusque manner. "Simmons!" I'd much prefer it if you referred to the man as 'B', if you don't mind. Like yourself, his covert position no longer exists." Eastern hadn't finished with Rogon just yet and likened himself to a terrier with a rat between his teeth.

"He did it, didn't he?"

"Did it? I'm sorry, Mike, you're not making any sense."

"Steadman! You got 'B' to do the dirty work for you."

"I don't have to justify the answer to that question, except to say he gets well paid for what he does."

"Yeah right. I had this feeling all along, especially with regard to the fact that he'd gone missing the day after the murder. Now it all makes sense." Leaving off briefly, he allowed an irritation of sentiment to enter their conversation.

"We come from different worlds, Rogon. You and the agency including those fucking pin-striped puppets who constantly pull your strings. They tell you when to jump...and me? I get to sleep at night even when I'm on the inside. How about you, Rogon, what do you do? I reckon you lie awake half the bleedin' night dreaming about dossiers and sanctioning Government 'hits'! God help you when you retire to the real world, you're going to be one sad old bastard that's for sure."

For whatever impact his feelings may have been provoked by, was lost in translation, as a repentant Rogon sought to take the meeting to another level, simply by averting his attention back toward Whiting. "Well George, I think that just about wraps up our business up for the time being. I'll leave it with your people to retrieve Mike's, personal effects. We can pick them up on the way out. In the meantime, thanks for your co-operation. Incidentally, you won't be seeing me again." Shaking hands, Eastern followed suit but not before he took one last swipe at the system.

"Give my regards to Mr Donavon for me, if you would Governor, and tell him he didn't qualify for a 'Michelin star' this time around." Smiling discreetly at his parting shot, Whiting swiftly put a seal on their bizarre contract.

"Under the circumstances, Mr Eastern, your request would be highly improbable. Although, as far as guarantees go, and the inmates are concerned, you're on a transfer to Wakefield gaol. As for the prison authorities, any form of co-existence between themselves and you, has never been registered. Half an hour later, a much relieved but frustrated Eastern found himself detained in an agency car, bound for what could well be a hotly disputed debriefing session.

On the positive side of things, he took close comfort in knowing that his social life would at least be back on track once again. Long before their arrival at Spooks HQ, Eastern had already made up his mind, up before the inquisition had started, that he was prepared to sit back and allow Rogon the time to justify his actions. In retrospect, his unfailing tuition should have told him differently. In contrast, keeping an open mind could well have been the way forward. Slowly Rogon lowered his coffee cup before speaking, Choosing his words to appease Eastern would be paramount, when deliberating on his next move to carry the operation forward.

"So, Mike, I believe this is where we first came in. Now, along with added hindsight, the situation that we are now left with isn't one that I could have visualised. Trouble is, that happens to be the business that we're in, I'm afraid. Personally, I would like to think that a margin of success has been achieved, inasmuch much as

Brezznov, has no reason to suspect that Steadman's, unfortunate death was due to anything, least of all being outside interest. The plain fact is that life goes on, and with Brezznov's release now imminent, we are now in a position...." He paused to emphasize his next gambit, "That! Thanks to the information that Steadman was able to procure, the agency now have a gifted opportunity to infiltrate his organization."

Eastern's patience had now outreached it's performance. Rogon's blaze' attempt to whitewash over what he himself considered to be, an 'Illegitimate murder', was proving to be a blunder too far. "Don't patronise me Rogon. That negative crap doesn't wash with me anymore. You seriously need to explain your motive for withholding Steadman's death from me for a week. Or was that a code red? 'B' was the designated go-between, which became very convenient for you to string me along, and then to remove him entirely from the picure when it suited you. Stopping short, he made a sudden token look over each shoulder, and returned to level Rogon with a fixed air of expectancy. "Talking of which, where is your precious 'hitman'? You've always led me to believe that 'B' and myself were on a joint mission. Seeing as this is a debrief, where the the hell is he, I ask?"

"It's not my wish to prevaricate on the situation, and I can only apologise in his absence, Mike. But State-related circumstances have dictated that his services have been directed elsewhere. In fact....." Breaking off suddenly, Rogon consulted his watch before continuing, "I can say with some amount of certainty, that less than 20 minutes ago GMT, the world as we know it, is now rid of one more despot." Shrugging his shoulders in a care less attitude, Eastern dismissed his keen sense of State interest out of sight, and veered his attention to focus squarely on the Brezznov affair.

"That being the case, then we'd better press on, and start by sharing what evidence Steadman supplied us with and what we intend doing with it." A look of relief clouded Rogon's face as an offering.

"I don't have a problem with that, Mike, in fact...." Breaking off, he delved inside a nearby leather satchel. "Here, what do you make of this?" Producing a small booklet, he placed it in front of

Eastern for scrutiny. "Well! What does that do for you in terms of positivism?" he enquired. as Eastern proceeded to flick the pages over at random.

"Uhm, Interesting...yeah interesting," he remarked glibly. One page in particular seemed to dominate his thoughts, by causing him to smile discreetly. In anticipation, Rogon was quick to pick up on his body language.

"Is it something you wanted to share, Mike?" Shaking his head, Eastern strove to put his mind at rest.

"You wouldn't appreciate the irony of what I'm thinking right now."

"No? so try me." The question is, how do you begin to humour a State 'robot'? In Rogon's case, it becomes a 'no-brainer', which left Eastern to reply anyway.

"Looking at what I've seen of the contents implies that I wasn't the only one who figured that Donavon was a nasty bastard.!" The implication as expected, sailed clean over Rogon's head, who's integral priorities, for selfish reasons, lay elsewhere, leaving him to pursue his findings.

"So, what do you make of Steadman's reference quote..."That money breeds money, but the difference is it won't be mine that I'll be investing?" You'll find it on page fifty-five I believe."

"Well, if Steadman heard it right, and I suspect he did, it obviously relates to a monetary 'scam' purely by definition."

"Precisely my feelings. In fact, every snippet of information he's logged, I find relates to finance in one form or another."

What about diamonds, is there any suggestion to suggest that his interest lies in that direction?" Rogon was insistent when replying.

"I'm afraid not, so we can rule that one out." Eastern decided to turn his attention back to Brezznov's claim that he would be using a third party benefactor, to subsidise his alleged investment. "If I didn't know any better, I'd have to say we could be looking at a Bank 'heist' (robbery). Probably on a massive scale, followed by a shares monopoly. What are your feelings on that Rogon?"

"Off the record, I tend to agree with that theory, Mike. Having said that I do have reservations in that area."

"You do! In what respect?" Challenged Eastern.

"I'm finding it damned hard to believe that Brezznov, bearing in mind the fortune he's amassed, would want to undergo the grief attached to an organized 'heist'....." He stopped abruptly to consider a hidden option. "Unless of course we are looking at a monetory fraud on a major scale, via a world-wide banking network, escalated by the present internal computer system." Eastern's eyes lit up to signify his approval.

"In other words, a monumental Cyber 'scam'. I like the genesis of that Rogon, it ties in with his claim to a 'paper money' investment."

"Exactly! Assuming of course he could hack into any one system, and that way he hasn't laid out a penny of his own money on his alleged return, and therefore adding credence to my original theory." At this point he continued to study Steadman's diary for any possible lead he might have missed.

"Anything look familiar, Mike?", questioned Rogon.

"Well, assuming we have hit on the right format, we now need to consider our, next move. It's imperative that we endeavour to get in at the beginning. As sharp as Steadman may have been, there's not one single concrete entry in his diary that lends itself to reveal when and where Brezznov intends putting his alleged 'scam' into operation. All we have at present is pure supposition to go on."

"You're entirely right of course," Rogon added "so now I'm saying to myself, at least you had a repertoire with the man, which is a huge bonus. And one that we need to capitalise on. I'm thinking, there might possibly be a way for you to come through the back door, so to speak. If so, there's a chance you could pick up where you left off."

"God! You make it all sound so bloody easy. It means that I'll be back under-cover and working on the outside. Contact! How do you propose I......?" The pressure alluding to the last few days had almost seconded his overworked brain into retirement. It was only now that he realized the full potential arising from the trump card that had momentarily eluded him. Now was the time to deliver his coup de grace, as he swiftly adjusted his reasoning. "Let me ask you something Rogon. What do the numbers 01273181933 mean to you?" His enquiry being spontaneous, led Rogon to sideline what could be on offer, by dismissing it out of sight.

"Are the numbers relevant Mike? If not, the answer to your question is no." "For whatever reason, Eastern appeared to be unruffled by Rogon's negativity and increased his eagerness to offload the information he'd managed to secrete thus far. And given to him as a future gesture by Brezznov himself.

"I didn't think for a moment that the numbers would do anything for you, but just for the record, they represent my calling card as a means into contacting Brezznov himself. Alternatively, if you have a stronger lead than mine, then I'm willing to listen."

"Touche,Mike, you kept the best to last it seems, which I can't compete with, so I suggest that you take some time out and get your head around what's going down. As things stand, I can't imagine Brezznov deciding to make a move just yet. His alleged 'scam' is far too complex and would entail a vast amount of planning. Besides which, he is still under licence...right? He can't afford to mess up." Having established a pre nuptial working relationship based on assumption, Eastern remained at Spooks HQ for the following hour mulling over strategy procedure, the logic being his proclaimed phone connection with Brezznov in mind.

It was also agreed that a two-month cessation would be put in place forthwith. This would grant the agency access to some borrowed time to deal with Eastern's alleged release from internment. Their motive being to ensure his covert identity remained intact within the 'underworld', should it ever become a topic of conversation. As for the strategic discontinuation, it was never intended to be spent as a 'category A' holiday.

Eastern was fully aware that his mission as such, hadn't even got out of the starting blocks. From his point of view, it was a time to regroup and capitalize on his ground resources. The following few weeks would severely test his durability and patience, right up until the moment he felt that his timing was right to place the call. That would hopefully reunite him with his nemesis, Victor Brezznov.

CHAPTER 6
A CALL FROM THE WILDERNESS

Removing a wild animal from its habitual comfort zone, and then suddenly relocating it into a controlled environment, could mean you possibly winding up with somebody resembling the likes of Mike Eastern! His designer world, ranging from dusk until dawn, now seemed far removed from what could now be regarded as being the norm. The last eight weeks lapse that he had managed to stumble through following his interment, had long taken its toll, and reduced him to the dormant role of the man-in-waiting, who, at best, could be found to be intoxicated with utter frustration. But now, 'cometh the hour cometh the man', and all he had to do to justify his time spent in exile to order, would involve making one lousy phone call.

No pressure there then? His mobile almost slipped out of the sweat-lined grasp of his hand, as he tentatively thumbed the required digits as a means to a connection. The adrenaline rush he now found himself experiencing was par for the course at any time, when sanctioning that certain 'buzz'. This time around, though, this call would be different, due to the onus leaning heavily on a major breakthrough at one end, and the realization of a reunion with Brezznov, no less. Eastern heaved an unrehearsed sigh of relief as the dialing jingle kicked in. "At worst" he told himself,

"The contact number he's supplied me with is at least kosher." So now we arrive at the waiting game, and patience as far as Eastern was concerned, now began feeling it owed it's allegiance to a pack of cards.

"C'mon...C'mon, just pick the bleedin' phone up why don't you? He asserted. His short lived diligence appeared to have paid off, but was quickly defused by the distinctive tones of a woman requesting information.

"Hello, you have reached the main office of Europa International Holdings. I'm sorry there is no-one available to deal with your enquiry. If you would like to leave your name and number we will endeavour to get back to you as soon as possible." Eastern could now be found struggling to accept the consequences of what could be a miss-dial on his part, or a sick joke instigated by Brezznov. The latter, at this point, seemed to tick all the boxes. The mere thought that four months of intense graft had evolved into a pre-meditated 'scam', now dogged Eastern's mind.

Eastern immediately set about back tracking the number and checked the digits that Brezznov had supplied. "There is no way I could have entered them incorrectly, there rubber stamped on my poxy mind for Chrissake!" His bottom lip then took the brunt of his frustration as his top teeth systematically clamped down on the soft flesh and, in the process, drawing blood, which he spat out when venting his anger. "The bastards set me up and hung me out to dry, unless of...." A glimmer of hope emerging from behind a wry smile now suddenly ambushed his thinking by registering a further option, and forced him into a reverse psychology mode of reasoning.

"Put yourself in his shoes and attempt to infiltrate his mind as to his thinking. Alternatively, the alter ego change in persona he now finds himself having to adapt to," he urged himself. "Of course! I should have known better. The number he has given me is more likely to be a security cover. Yeah, the game would be to stick with the voice mail request." Once, having repeated the call and divulging his details, he found himself floundering in no-man's-land, while anticipating a call that might never happen. Or so thought. Some forty eight hours later, while relaxing in his apartment, he found himself distracted by the familiar overtones emerging from his mobile.

A rapid glance at the numbers on show were clearly unfamiliar and as such implied that he needed to revert back to his covert non de plume. One false slip of the tongue would mean game over . With that in mind, he stamped his authority by kicking off. "Alex Ruark speaking." It was basic but nevertheless believable.

"Alex...it's been a while...Victor Brezznov. I recognized your voice. I'm pleased that you got back in touch. The truth of the matter is that we need to talk in depth and fairly soon. Incidentally, about the number that I left you with. It's a routine I use to give myself an edge. I like to know who I'm dealing with, but I guess you worked that one out for yourself. Congratulation by the way, the word on the street tells me that you're out the fucking system at last. Now that's what I call influence and I admire your style. I've got plans...big plans! And it's no secret I want you along for the ride, so in the meantime keep your nose clean Alex. One other thing, the number that's registering will become void when we finish this conversation. I will get back to you soon." And then he was gone, leaving Eastern to pick the bones from out of a situation, that would rank priceless to obtain. Even from the best 'snout' in the business. Suppressing his good fortune, also reminded Eastern of the pitfalls his future role could evoke. As from now he would be running the gauntlet, set in a world synonymous with fear and murder as a companion, compounded by the conclusion that his precarious cover could be blown at any one time. With Brezznov now firmly set in the driving seat, Eastern was given the impetus to reflect on his domestic affairs. To his mind, for security reasons alone, his apartment in Brunswick Square, should remain incommunicado as opposed to a working base.

Time being of the essence, he lost no time in contacting Rogon at Spooks HQ, requesting that he should come in to discuss the latest surge of information. And more importantly, to organize the necessary use of a 'safe house'. Firmly seated in his chair, Rogon expressed a short plastic speech of gratitude. "Mike, I congratulate you. It seems that together we have achieved more in the last hour compared to the last three or four months! I don't have to remind you how well this is going to look once my progress report hits Whitehall." As self appointed opinions come and go, Rogon appeared to be in a class of his own, leaving a fuming Eastern to remind Rogon that one plus one only equates to two in mathematical terms only.

"I'm not so sure about the bleeden' 'we' business. I suggest that you might want to add a third party rider to in your bloody report Rogon. That while you and your Government tossers were out on the golf course or 'lording it up' in the West End. I just happened to be fucking 'banged up'! simply, for their convenience in order to make that report possible. Am I getting through to you?" As usual, Rogon was unbowed by his prompted outburst and attempted to gloss over what he classed as, "An official error." He then concluded by stating. "That won't be necessary, Mike, the top brass are well aware that the lower ranks are the real bread-winners."

"Bloody amen to that!" retorted Eastern. "Now, about this 'safe house'? As I'm still paying rent on my existing office, I suggest that we could use the premises as a base of convenience, operational as from tomorrow." Heaving a sigh of relief, Rogon nodded his approval before replying.

"For once we are solidly in agreement, Mike and I'll push to get your electrics updated, new hot line...numbers etc, so I'll need a key." He paused briefly to digress.

"I note your firearms licence still remains tenable. Should you feel a situation arising whereby you require that extra touch of security, then Metcalf will look after your needs. You'll find him down below in the armoury. Well, that just about sums it up from where I'm sitting, Mike. So, on that note, good luck and good hunting. Oh, and remember, I'm always here should you require anything." Rogon's fragile attempt to bolster a form of unity via expression, obliterated as Eastern rose to the occasion.

"So what you're saying is, should the situation arise where I find myself staring down the barrel of a gun, waiting to have my bloody brains blown out, I can tell the asshole who's pulling the trigger to wait until I've phoned you first...is that right?"

"Your sarcasm precedes you, Mike. I can only say in my defence that today's worldly criminals are much more avant-garde in their approach to persuasion." Eastern had heard enough and indicated that he was about to leave, but still determined to get the last word in.

"I don't have a problem in knowing that your theory regarding the criminal fraternity is true. In fact, next time I see Brezznov I'll tell him that your his number one fan. He'll' appreciate that." Smiling broadly to himself he left hurriedly, leaving Rogon scratching his head while seeking a suitable meaning to his logic. Some time later a State Limo dropped him off at Brunswick Square and left him to his own devices. Once inside his apartment, he threw himself into the nearest armchair and flopped out in disarray. The next voice he heard was the dulcet tones of Joan as she emerged from the dining room.

"God! You look as if you could use a drink, Mike. If I didn't know you any better I'd have to say that creep Rogon is responsible." They say, and I quote, 'that time is a great healer'. In Eastern's case the time in question terminated beyond three glasses of Scotch later. Being somewhat relaxed and fully at ease with himself, made it possible for him to unwind. It was also an opportune moment to put Joan in the picture following his debrief.

"So you see darling, as from now, the name Alex Ruark, for obvious reasons, is dead and buried. As far as you're concerned the guy never existed. He then went on to divulge (within the bounds of security requirement), that his future hinged solely on the strength of a pre-arranged phone call collection date unknown.

Whether or not the time exclusion was deliberately intended to become a personal test of nerve, or for undisclosed reasons, Eastern was left in no doubt as to who was pulling the strings. The call, when it eventually came through a week later, was concise in nature. And to all intents and purpose had obviously been taped, thus allowing him no recall. "Alex! Be at the following address no later than 10.30 am Friday next." On investigation, the designated address turned out to be an apartment, set in a block of flats situated in Wilbury Road Hove. Putting the importance of the call to one side, Eastern typically reviewed it from another angle, "Yes Sir!...no Sir! Three fucking bags full Sir. Compared to you

Brezznov, Napoleon was a nothing man. What I can say, is that as from now I'm on your bloody case twenty four seven. And I warn you that I only sleep when I'm paid to."

As expected, the next few day's, found him hell to live with. Finally Friday arrived. Selecting a bay at the rear of the flats, Eastern parked up and made his way to the entrance. Once inside he took the lift to the fifth floor. A quick time-check clocked him in at ten twenty six Taking a deep breath he rang the bell and hesitantly waited for a reaction. "It wouldn't be the first time the asshole has set me up" he muttered. Any further allusions he may have held, were then kicked into touch as the door opened to reveal the imposing figure of Brezznov himself, framed in the doorway.

When considering the facts relative to their past relationship, it became apparent that Brezznov still managed to retain an in-built bluntness in his manner. "Glad you could make it Alex. Step this way, there's a couple of 'faces' I'd you to meet."

"The man's colder than a bleeden' block of ice." Eastern told himself. Full of apprehension he tentatively made his way inside. The sight of two dubious looking figures, both of them by design, were strangers he noted, were heavily locked in conversation at the far end of a spacious and plush bespoke lounge. Completely ignoring them out of design, Eastern directed his attention onto Brezznov, and went for broke as a ploy to gain some ground. "I've got to hand it to you, this is what I call a class 'gaff' (building). . Bit of a leg up from poxy Foredown you've gotta say. Even that asshole Donavon would have to agree on that score Victor."

"Yeah, fuck em all" responded Brezznov, "that's what I say, It's about what's happening now that counts. A drink....c'mon... let's have a drink to freedom yeah? and then we can talk some." Having fuelled their glasses from a well-stocked corner bar, it was left to Brezznov to do the running. Beckoning the two strangers over, he proceeded to put introductions into place. "Alex, I want you to meet Tommy Brandon, or 'Wheels' for short. I'm telling you now, this guy is the best driver in the business." A rehearsed but questionable look crossed his face before continuing. "So now you're probably thinking to yourself, what the hell makes you think that? So I then say, right up until the silly bastard took a 'bung' (backhander), he was attached to the 'Sweeney' (Flying squad). Anyhow, their loss my gain....Alex meet 'Wheels'.

For a split second, Eastern's heart beat dropped like a stone. Coming face to face with a 'bent' cop could result into his worst nightmare. "Shit! If the guy recognises me it's fucking game over, accelerated his brain. Without hesitation, thinking on his feet, he swung into play and decided to call the guy's bluff. "So, what 'Manor' were you working when you were with the 'Bill' (police)?" asserted Eastern. At least Brandon's face wasn't familiar, he noted.

"Manchester...I was based in Manchester for a few years. Then following a stint in Birmingham I was relocated to London....why do you ask?"

No reason...no reason at all, just being bleedin' nosey. Know what I mean?" Smothering a huge sigh of relief, Eastern realized that he had wriggled out of a potential life-threatening situation. The twisted gut syndrome and sweaty palms he'd now inherited, he now regarded as a bonus. Brezznov then fortunately intervened by introducing the second stranger.

"Alex, take a good look. This is the guy who invented Cyber. Trust me when I say he's a fucking legend with a set of Tabs. As hackers go he's the best in the business. Putting it mildly, he's the biggest asset I've got, so I intend getting a kosher return on him. He answers to the name of Aubrey Thorpe Millington. Just out of interest he's a by-product of Eton and as his initials are ATM we call him 'cash' for short, seeing as how he's got this nasty unique tendency to obtain money, without holding a genuine account." Eastern likened his handshake to that of a defrosted sausage and delayed his grip before disengaging.

On a personality rating, he instantly loathed Brandon more than he despised Millington. The stigma attached to a 'bent' cop could be found etched in granite and remains so, as an epitaph, even after death. "A right couple of 'tossers' (idiots) I've been landed with" grated Eastern to himself. "If I'm fortunate enough to come out of this poxy fiasco alive, the only reunion I'll be going to will be one held in a downtown morgue. And it won't be mine!"

On the plus side, the extreme pleasure of informing Rogon that his theory regarding a possible Cyber crime, could be considered a reality and, as such, not one to be dismissed. "The prospect of witnessing Rogon actually smiling, would be a commodity that even money couldn't buy", became his overriding priority. His inner thoughts were then dismissed, allowing Brezznov to interrupt his private space once again.

"Alex! ...a refill my friend? And then we can get to grips as to why wer'e all here." As far as intrinsic computer science goes, Eastern would have been far better placed lecturing on tribal Swahili. Millington, on the other hand, as Brezznov predicted, reigned supreme in a class of one, by confidently outlining an initial instalment plan, setting Brezznov's Cyber-fraud into operation.

"Like I say, Victor, the choice of banking facility you decide to 'hit' rests with you. I can only recommend that it be highly rated European Corporation based in the City. The risk of success does of course apply at every level, so I'm suggesting that we go for broke on this one. Do you have any reservations with that in mind, Victor?" Brezznov chose to demand a stone wall approach when replying.

"I don't have a problem with your logic. I'm paying for the best, so now I mean to have full control of the fucking best!" A much relieved Millington was also adamant in return.

"Trust me, and you will have given time. If we manage to pull this one off, then I won't be able to live long enough to spend my cut." Eastern on the other hand had other ideas regarding Millington's pre-formed objectives on life expectancy, and as such committed himself to remain alienated.

"I wouldn't have any qualms on that score sunshine. I'll be making damned sure on both counts that you won't!" he told himself. Brazen as ever, Millington continued to exploit his designer format.

"Once you're in a position to expose which Bank we intend to 'hit', and you have quantified the fact, I'll then be in a position to start thinking about installing high profile key logging software onto the appropriate PC's. That, and I emphasize the fact, will be the easy part. Assuming of course Victor that you've got alternative designs on using a third party on the payroll as a middle man. If not, then your planning is totally flawed. It's far too risky." Tensing himself, Eastern looked on, anticipating a verbal backlash from Brezznov as a response to Millington's seemingly negative but direct conclusions.

Any suggestion of an anti-climax swiftly evaporated. As if on impulse, for reasons he held in check, Brezznov rose from his seat and swaggered across to the bar, intent on replenishing his glass while refusing to make any comment. His actions seemed to take for ever almost as if the scene itself had been pre-planned. From where he was stationed, Eastern could almost reach out and touch the aura of arrogance that Brezznov was now radiating. "I swear the devious bastard is holding something up his sleeve, I just know it," he told himself. "Any minute now and he's going to open up." His perception fell way short , resulting in a learning curve for him to take on board.

You cannot rush people like Brezznov. It was an inner trait that went hand in hand with his stature. Any attempt to upstage him would inevitably prove fatal in anybody's language. To listen and watch only became a reason for living. The tension in the room began to mount and thicken as Brezznov continued to demand the stage, simply by rotating the brandy glass in his hand, ceasing only to savour the aromatic bouquet it expelled. As stoic as he was, Eastern began to inhabit the pressure, forcing him to examine his own inner feelings. "If the air in here get's much thicker," he mused, "you could use it for carpet underlay."

Without warning, the charade came to a dramatic climax as Brezznov removed himself from the bowels of his glass, confronting his audience head on. "Gentleman! Your patience is commendable and duly noted. For that reason alone I can confirm that as a collective 'firm' (gang) , we are now operational and poised to rip the heart out of the world's financial banking system." A sustained silence ensued, long enough to allow any remaining tension to evaporate, while at the same time giving his rapt audience time to digest the impact issuing from an over-zealous statement.

For his role, Eastern had no immediate designs to market his own conclusions to Brezznov's rehearsed script, and elected to remain low key. To his mind the moment had become surreal. On the one hand, he'd now become privy to a high level of SP and therefore had a reason to be mindful of the fact. On the other hand, a sense of impending anxiety that the confident rant of a specialist international criminal, could become a reality."

His thoughts were jarred as Brezznov continued to milk their private space. "Flawed!? You mentioned the word flawed Aubrey, and there you have me. That word doesn't exist in my world, so this time I'll forget your dumb ignorance in choosing it. Instead, let me enlighten you with some extreme facts. About three years ago the 'scam' that we are about to embark on, started out as a seed of an idea. Since then, due to innovative planning, it has now enabled that idea to mature into a fool proof scheme. And a personal time for me to stamp retribution on an incorruptible system." Pausing, his face took on a fresh mask of calculated confidence, before continuing.

"So you see gentlemen, my time spent in the wilderness has proved to be a lesson in conviction, if you will excuse the pun. As you're all now fully aware, I haven't been idle and I can assure you all, here and now, that given the right co-operation, I will succeed on the sheer basis of audacity alone.....any questions so far?" Excluding himself from the offer, Eastern averted his gaze towards Millington, anticipating a reaction to his earlier logic. He wasn't about to be disappointed as a fired-up Millington took it into his head to walk a verbal line, bordering on allegiance and self- belief, when contesting Brezznov's claim to superiority.

"Up to this point Victor, I still hold overall reservations. I'm not totally convinced that the 'scam' is workable. The case that you are making looks far too gift-wrapped for my liking, and that's what bothers me. You've forgotten to mention the key aspect of how you intend to gain entry into the proposed banking facility you might have in mind. From a positive approach, I would like to think that your definition of co-operation stems from my view, that without the use of a 'bent' security guard on the payroll, the heist would prove to be a disaster. What then started out in life as a forced smile, swiftly dissolved into a defiant leer as Brezznov sought to exploit his own version.

"Facts! you want fucking facts? I'll go one better than that my friend, and hand you out a lesson in reality, by making you mindful of the fact, that subject to the bloody Stock Market going belly up in the coming fortnight, my designated target along with it's internal security, will be in a state of open house. Putting it mildly gentlemen, we will be in business holding a franchise monopoly on nominated accounts and stocks." He stopped off briefly before delivering a hidden and explicable coup de grace. "Or putting it another way, ensuring that other interested investors will be out of business in the process!"

"And the Target itself?" Millington questioned, "When do we get to..."

"....you don't!" interrupted Brezznov sharply on a pre-assumption, "that is until forty eight hours before we make our move, then, and only then, then will you all be made aware of out intended target. In the meantime I suggest to you that this meeting never happened, and basically you need to chill out until such time that I contact you again." As before, the astute look on his face, portrayed the epitome of confidence as he left them reflecting on a verbal afterthought. "I can assure you that every minute spent in waiting will be more than compensated. And comes with my own personal guarantee."

If Brezznov's prophecy was intended to make Eastern feel that an illicit monetory injection could ease his timing, then he couldn't have been further from the truth, as he explained his mounting frustration to Rogon later on that day, after contacting him at Spooks H.Q. "Believe me when I say that the man is a fucking island of intrigue, should you feel the need to discuss bleedin' mind games!"

"On that basis," concluded Rogon, "I can only assume that you haven't any fresh detailed SP as such, enabling us to move forward" Shaking his head negatively, Eastern then went on to explain that Brezznov's cat and mouse approach toward the alleged heist, had virtually wiped out every chance of putting into place, any contingency planning.

"At best," he explained, "we have a time span of about forty eight putting into a place, a preventive task force. Having said that, if Brezznov chooses to keep the location under wraps until the eleventh hour, there's every reason to suggest that his strategy, could possibly leave us up a blind alley chasing shadows."

"Damn! That means pretty much anywhere in the City," concluded Rogon. And went on, "To say the man is an enigma, would be letting him down lightly. He's obviously learnt from his past mistakes . It seems that from what you've managed to glean so far, Mike, that even he has to move with the times. I refer of course to the elaborate and sophisticated method of criminality he now chooses to employ. Nodding with intent, Eastern was adamant as he replied, "Yeah, it's ironic when you stop to analyse the facts, because in retrospect you could say that the establishment have shot themselves in the foot."

"I'm sorry, I don't follow you," a bemused Rogon questioned.

"Simply by putting him out of circulation for a lengthy period, I figure that the time he's spent, from his point of view, hasn't been wasted. All it's done is to give the man a lifeline in which to further his egotistic career." Their short and unproductive conversation then ground to a halt. As an afterthought, Eastern was quick to assure Rogon that his covert position had in no way been jeopardized, and that any future contact would remain in situ.

CHAPTER 7
THE WILDERNESS SYNDROME

The following forty eight hours proved to be a war of nerves for Eastern, as a frustrating air of expectancy hung over him, akin to a pregnant rain cloud waiting to unload. As a selfish contrast, the rare privilege issuing from an unrehearsed moment of clemency to acquire a form of sleep, never seemed to realize it's potential. Eastern awoke with a start. Almost immediately he instinctively became aware that there was a certain infinity about the ring tone on his mobile. One swift glance was enough to convince him that his gut hadn't lost it's flair. Robotically he made the connection.

"Alex?"

"Speaking." Relief masked his face. "What's occurring, Victor?"

"That's for me to know and you to find out, Alex, my friend, but that comes later." Brezznov replied guardedly." A minute into their conversation and already Eastern found himself having to bite the bullet, as Brezznov's exclusive controlling attitude seconded him into playing the running man. A patronising stance seemed to be the way forward.

"That being the case, Victor, I presume my services are at your disposal. When do you envisage us getting together as a 'firm'?" Brezznov was quick to validate Eastern's obvious need for action.

"Your impatience precedes you Alex. And in time will be

financially recognised. In the meantime I've arranged for a cab to pick you up at seven thirty tonight, and drop you off at a specific address, prior to meeting up later in the evening." Without hesitating, Eastern fired back in the likelihood he might catch Brezznov off guard.

"Out of interest, do I get to know the drop-off point Victor?" The latter remained unmoved by rejecting his probing enquiry out of sight in a brusque manner.

"As far as you're concerned, that's between the driver and myself Alex, due to an added security issue. I'm sure you understand?" Reproaching himself, Eastern felt his reply held an underlying and personable ring attachment to it, and readily decided that under the circumstances he needed to curtail the subject. By default, he was now reconciled to being on the outside looking in. A fresh approach to gain a foothold of trust and solidarity would be essential., even when surrounded by people

For his part, his nemesis stood alone, basking in the glory that he was a self-made control freak who epitomized the term 'user' when dealing with individuals. Eastern's own version was not to be denied, as certain characteristics gate-crashed his take on survival. "Without question the guy is one evil bastard, reveling in a two-edged psychopathic attitude," but not before Brezznov had rubber stamped his credentials.

"I take it you don't have a problem with my strategy then Alex?" he enquired. Briefly, Eastern found himself wanting for a reply as he allowed his brain to dissolve the content of his inner thoughts.

"On the contrary Victor, I tend to dismiss the word 'problem' in exchange for one that's positive. Besides, who am I to argue? I'll leave that to my cut in the deal, to do the talking for me." Having been subjected to lying through his teeth in the face of adversity, now became a bitter pill to swallow. The white flesh exposed on his knuckles showed through like organ stops, as he fought to suppress a bout of controlled anger. Brezznov meanwhile continued to wallow in his illicit ideals.

"It's important that you think that way Alex. Because you will soon realize that the stakes surrounding this heist succeeding, are higher than you could possibly ever imagine. And I've no intention of coming in second again. Complacency is for fucking mugs! I allowed myself into becoming vulnerable once, and it cost me twelve fucking years of my life.....not that I wasted the time that was coming to me," he was quick to point out. "So for that reason alone, the operation will not fail. By the time this mission is over I will have brought the financial World down onto its poxy knees."

If Brezznov had purposefully set out on a grief trip, then he was doing a good job of seriously pissing Eastern off. As far as he was concerned their conversation had run its course. Inwardly he cursed the world at large, and placed Rogon at the top of his stockpile for playing the cheap role of an inveigler. And in return forcing him self to pay homage once again. "So much for my bleedin' CV," he chided. Having regained his composure, he retraced his thoughts back, which centered on, Brezznov's latest omission. "At least he's confirmed the fact that his illicit intentions lay in the form of a monetory 'scam'. The worst way, it puts the agency on the ladder, even if we can't see the top rung.

"Hello! You still there Alex?" For a split second he was forced to withdraw any further notions he may have held, as the relentless pursuit of Brezznov's intimidating voice ambushed his space.

"Yeah, just for a minute Victor I found myself wrapped up in your scheme of things. Now I can see where you're coming from in terms of commitment. The spin off from a heist that magnitude is mind-boggling. In comparison, it makes the word 'ransom' sound like a poxy vicar's tea party." By putting personalities aside it made sense to go with the flow, in the realization that a loose snippet of SP could become a reality. Their conversation then gathered momentum as Eastern ceased validating his views . And leaving his nemesis to continue echoing his own take on the intended heist.

"The secret of success in this case hinges on the timing, and I'm as hungry as the next guy." he declared. "But in the end, it's all down to patience and I'm a past master at that, thanks again to my 'previous'." (record). Switching his thoughts, he paused briefly to allow a secondary motive to surface. "That aside, it's not all about dividends Alex, as from now it starts to get personal...know what I mean?" For once, Eastern became stymied for an answer, in the knowledge that the system had inadvertently handed Brezznov poetic licence to carve out his game plan.

His own position as a rank outsider then swung into contention, causing him to readdress the strength of the volatile danger that he'd elected to undergo. It was then left to Rogon to once again accept the brunt of his current situation by proxy. "If I come out of this wearing a garland of shit you pathetic Whitehall android, then trust me when I say you'd better focus on an early retirement." he told himself meaningfully. Typically, he swiftly adjusted his thoughts in replying to Brezznov's initial position regarding a 'personal syndrome'. "I can well sympathise with you Victor on that count. I mean, a twelve year stretch fucking banged up in a Government health farm. You're going to feel well pissed off...and personal!? That's got to be an understatement." Brezznov lost no time in concurring.

"You know and I know that they eventually mess with you poxy head. You've done the time and now that you're back on the outside you realize it's all a one-sided fucking game! Trouble is, as you know, it doesn't end at that. The bastards just don't know when to let go do they?"

"You're only saying what I'm thinking already." replied Eastern, "But yeah, go on."

"Since being released, the 'Bill' (police) have been on my case 24/7. I can't even have a shit without them knowing an hour later... know what I mean?"

"Sure! You and me both. The system has an ongoing PDH in grief. Dealing with it while remaining legal takes consideration, but as I say we've both inherited the same shit of course. Results! It's all about fucking results. They can't wait to see you crack. Remember, they have all the time in the world, and the resources, which is why I like your stand on patience and security."

"You've got a good head piece working for you Alex and you're double smart with it. As I've said before, having a 'face' like you around is a bonus." A controlled and sustained silence came into play as Eastern deliberately held back. Hopefully to allow his nemesis time digest his patronising observations, including the off-chance that he might be cajoled into confiding in him.

Alternatively, had he ridden his luck too far when attempting to appease Brezznov by coming in through the back door? In the event, the latter quickly put him out of his misery in a clinical manner. "There's also something else you need to take into account, and that is my staunch independence. I've always been my own man. If you're in business I find that two people sharing the same ideals can be dangerous. So as from now, you'd better get used to the idea that I give the orders....understand!? Oh, and while wer'e at it there is one other thing that bothers me slightly. I can't figure out how come a smart guy with your credentials allows himself to take a fall like you did? You're nobody's patsy that's for sure. Could be that I don't know you as well as I thought I did."

Out of mind and out of sight allowed Eastern to smother his restless body language, as Brezznov's one-on-one character assassination drove a wedge between his personal opinions and reality. He had been forewarned in no uncertain terms, subsequently leaving him rattled. True, their relationship was always going to be strained full stop. But now this latest verbal revelation had literally pulled the carpet out from under his feet. From now on he would be resigned to walking on egg-shells in his approach. Moments later, to make matters worse. Brezznov, for reasons of his own, chose to abort their conversation sine die leaving Eastern hung out to dry.

As a means of compensation, he let it be known that, "I'll be off the 'manor' for a short while, on business, before I get to contact you again. In the meantime I need you to make some enquiries regarding a set of 'bent wheels' (stolen car). You know the score. Incidentally, this number will become obsolete by tomorrow." He then hung up, leaving a stone-faced Eastern to dwell on what might have been. A short while later that same evening, he contacted Rogon at HQ and arranged a 'meet' for the following day re: an update.

CHAPTER 8
HORSES FOR COURSES

Having downed his token cup of coffee, Eastern shuddered involuntarily followed by his carte blanche opinion to express his obvious distaste. "Hell, Rogon! Those coffee grounds taste like a by-product left over from the cold war. Either that, or you've got a guerrilla posing as one of the kitchen staff. Besides which, I can't see those bloody playboys over at MI5 standing for this crap!" Rogon appeared unmoved by Easter's blistering attack on the in house-catering. Instead, it was left to his regimented absence of humour to be found wanting in reply.

"The last agent who complained about it, found himself shipped off to a Lithuanian outpost for three years. And just in case you've forgotten, Mike, I'll remind you that this room is 'bugged'. Now, if you don't mind, can we proceed with the Government business in hand? More importantly, I have to tell you that Whitehall are leaning on me for SP, and the PM himself has taken a personal interest in this brief, due to the enormity of Brezznov's alleged banking coup."

Eastern remained unrepentant as he opened up, in knowing that besides the agency he would also be dealing with an officious third party to answer to. "Interest!? Utter bollocks and you know it, Rogon. Assuming that Spooks get a result, the PM will come out through the bloody back door on a gilt-edged vote winner, using my neck as the combination." And added, "From what I've heard, the guy's a diplomatic power- mad asshole!" For the time being, their addled conversation became temporarily shelved as Eastern's recent counterpart Spook 'B' entered the room.

"My apologies for running late gentlemen. I've since been engaged into breaking in a .44 Magnum Blackhawk Beretta on the range. I'd hate to think that I've missed something of importance. If I have, I'm sure you'll get me up to speed." Eastern rose and extended his hand for Simmons (nee 'B') to shake.

"So, we meet again my friend and, no, you haven't missed anything..." He paused as a wry smile creased his face, "Except to say, what more can you express about a moron that everybody already knows about? And consciously averted his gaze toward an uncomfortable looking Rogon. Together, they exchanged small talk for a few minutes, but not before a jaded Rogon wielded his superior authority.

"Gentlemen...if you don't mind, let's not forget what we are here for, there will be ample time for free talk later." Rogon then drew Eastern's attention aside to justify Simmons future role within the agency's strategy. "As of now Mike, 'B', you'll be pleased to know, has been reassigned to your brief indefinitely. His role of course will remain as a covert position by working in your shadow per se. Is that understood? Available as always should you require back up. I would expect you to liaison periodically dependent on your circumstance at any one time, understood? The minute you suspect that Brezznov is ready to make a move I..."

His tactical thinking was quashed as Eastern cut him short. "Before you commit yourself, I suspect that we could be in for a long wait, I'm afraid. The way things are shaping up at present, Brezznov is reluctant to put his bleedin' foot out of the door!"

"I take it we are talking legal harassment here, Mike?" enquired Rogon with an air of subtle conviction. Eastern made it quite clear that he didn't need a cue when replying.

"I'm surprised that you're not already aware of the local 'plods' (police) involvement. As far as Spooks are concerned, I'm left out in the cold, feeling pissed while waiting for something to happen. Meanwhile, the 'Bill' are getting off on a non- productive surveillance trip! Personally, I don't give a shit providing it doesn't interfere with my private life. Cards on the table. If you want to make this brief work, then you 'd better call your dogs off, because Brezznov is going nowhere all the time he's getting grief...I mean, would you? Give the asshole some credit!"

Without question, the moment became game, set and match as Rogon caved into Eastern's logic. "You're understandably right of course Mike, leave it with me and rest assured I'll deal with the situation. Is there anything substantial that you'd like to add?"

On reflection, he should have known better than to have asked, but Rogon, being himself, and politically insensitive, to a fault, had, in in another world, co-written a Government manual titled ...'The idiot's guide to the impossible' and could now be found to be co-habiting his disturbed brain.

Being subjected to the token role of intermediary while Eastern and Rogon were busy crossing swords, had extended one man's patience, by fringing on the age-old adage that 'Dead men don't tell tales', agent 'B' finally decided there and then to put their session in perspective, based on a 'license to kill' forum.

"It seems to me that this Brezznov guy is making a damned good job of winding up the pair of you and you're getting nothing back in return. Why the hell don't we put a cap on it by using some constructive initiative? Grant me a Whitehall sanction for a 'hit' Rogon, and I'll simply take the bastard out...end of story!"

As expected, Rogon's thoughts lay elsewhere. He appeared to be unmoved by the illicit proposal choosing to retain his rigid persona. "If I thought for a minute that there was the remotest chance 'B', I wouldn't hesitate to sanction it....but you know Whitehall and their cryptic guide lines. As things stand, it's paramount that the mission that we are undertaking, has to appear to be whiter than white in the run-up to succeed. Although in retrospect, the idea itself carries a lot of appeal by releasing the Government from untold grief, should Brezznov manage to achieve his alleged 'scam'."

At this juncture, Eastern's present reasoning ran on a parallel akin to Rogon's definitions, and dismissed the abysmal scheme out of sight. "I suggest that we all calm down and concentrate on some radical thinking, by drawing our attention to the fact as to why he's gone to ground full stop. Putting aside the 'Bill's' presence for a moment, I strongly suspect he might have smelt a rat. This makes my priority to get him on side fading out of sight."

"Damn the man's perception, this could end in game over at this rate." Rogon interjected.

"Yeah right, in more ways than one," agreed Eastern, and rounding up by quipping, "At the moment, I've got more chance of taking the Pope out on a bender than retrieving any SP." Agent 'B' then proceeded to make his presence felt by underlining a throwaway supplication.

"It's only an idea...but..." He hesitated briefly to convince himself that his plea might be considered even as a last resort. "Supposing, just supposing, we were to break with tradition by commandeering the local 'plod' to pull him in on 'suss'? (suspicion) Assuming of course, that you can establish a reliable source of contact, Mike? If nothing else, it's bound to piss him off...what do you think?" Shaking his head with added reluctance, Eastern was adamant in reply.

"That I'm afraid it is a total negative mate, when you consider the legal power he could lavish as a crutch. He'd be in and out of custody quicker than bleedin' Houdini. No, the way I see it is to catch him, 'bang to rights', and then let the law do a number on him." Rogon complied with a nod and referred to his previous statement.

"As I said before, this mission has to be executed by the book." Moving on, he drew their attention to another supportive although nagging issue. "It has occurred to me that we could be looking at Brezznov's alleged monetory 'heist' from the wrong

"I'm not sure I know where you're coming from, Rogon," replied Eastern with a blank look. "We can only assume his motive is based on the evidence he's entitled us to."

"Exactly, and that is what's worrying me, Mike," he fired home, "I think that is exactly what he wants us to believe. I'll remind you of the fact that he's changed his strategy once before in case you have forgotten. Who's to say he won't do it again?"

"Okay, so what line of reasoning are you now suggesting?" 'B' enquired. Rogon, in order to magnify the issue, took his time before answering.

"In a word, diamonds, gentlemen plain and simple. We could be looking at complete supremacy over the world diamond market, associated with an audacious fraud." Eastern's outward body language dismissed Rogon's views out of sight.

"The whole concept is crazy and lacks substance. The bare facts alone bear that out. I mean, think about it for a minute and consider this. The creep has just served life for his passion with stones (diamonds)." He broke off rather abruptly to process a further underlining thought laced with cynicism. "Surely the guy couldn't be that naive...could he?" Rogon had now unwittingly allowed a seed of doubt to surface, the proceedings and, in the process, was confronted with a can of worms to exorcise in the time designated for a debrief.

"You have to say Mike, that at the end of the day, diamonds generate extreme power when placed in the hands of an illicit franchise element. This in turn could well evolve into a massive monopoly investment." He paused, gathering his thoughts to stake his claim and continued, "just imagine the scenario in the hands of an ambitious and career criminal like our man Brezznov? You have to say the idea gives credence to my reckoning. Therefore, on that evidence, I rest my case." To make matters worse for Eastern, who still remained unconvinced, agent 'B', as an interested partner, then threw a stoic lifeline of allegiance to his cause, by upholding Rogon's logic.

"I'm with you on this one Governor," he remarked solidly, and averted his attention toward Eastern. "I'm sorry, Mike, but experience can't be ignored. My take on the subject tells me that Brezznov given the opportunity and timing , could be in a position to hold the world banking organization to ransom. As a remedy, I refer you both to my original strategy, that being and I quote... when confronted with a mad dog you put it down!" Needless to say, either by design or personality clash, the meeting quickly evaporated as an air of negativism took control.

The journey back to his flat a short while later, found Eastern in a somewhat turbulent mood. And resigned to the fact that he'd been systematically outgunned by the system. Alternatively, the added thought that his nemesis was still out there foot- loose and sharing his world was fast becoming a burden too far. Once indoors and overdosing on frustration he decided to seek some solace in a bottle. His efforts however, hadn't escaped the sensitive eyes of his of his partner Joan Travis.

"You can call me a liar, Mike, but if I didn't know you any better I'd have to say that it's obvious you've had a bad day at the office. That's the third Scotch you've down loaded in the last hour. Do you want to talk about it, or is it a State secret? In which case just forget that I asked." At any other time, a simple token nod of the head, one way or the other, would have sufficed as a means to an end. It would seem that Eastern was now in a state of denial as he appeared to be oblivious to her presence , and, indeed, to her enquiry for that matter.

"That's strange." Joan mused. Reaching out she shook his shoulder in a gentle manner, "Mike! Are you okay? You seem a little distant...did you hear what I said?" Whatever subconscious door she had been knocking on for a form of contact, suddenly opened as he spun round to face her. His distorted face morphed into a mask of realization , causing her to start as his blazing eyes steeled into her own.

"Of course!" he exclaimed in a pronounced tone, "how could I be such a klutz?...the answer has been there all the time in black and white telling me.

And to think I couldn't see it." By now he was almost shouting as he gripped her arms forcing her to listen. "Ruby!...Brezznov! It has to be." A bewildered Joan was left struggling with an irrational situation that was rapidly spiralling out of control. Confronting him with her own demons seemed the only way forward.

"Mike! For God's sake, you're frightening me. You're talking in riddles and not making any sense, besides which you're hurting me." Reverently, he air-brushed his grip on her arms apologising as he did so for his unwarranted outburst. Finally leaving off to reply in a slow and controlled voice.

"It has to be...Ruby and Brezznov! That's the connection, it's too much of a coincidence not to be." Meanwhile, Joan could be found still left floundering in a recipe of sheer frustration and total disbelief at his uncharacteristic display.

"Names...conclusions....what!? What the hell does it all mean, Mike darling? I honestly feel I don't know you anymore." Without prompting, he took her in his arms and consoled her before declaring his interest.

"It means baby, that I'm pretty damned certain I now know where Brezznov has gone to ground." Pointing at a nearby chair he indicated to her to sit down. "I guess I've got a lot of explaining to do Joan. Emerging from a wilderness of despair into one of sensibility, suddenly seemed like an easy act to follow.

"That's the most defining suggestion you've come up with all night," he gushed with enormous relief. On hindsight her timely observation had put the whole charade into perspective. Taking the nearby bottle of Scotch into account, she gestured directly at it. "I reckon you had better pour me a large one as well Mike. I have this impending feeling that we are both in for a long night." Having replenished their glasses he focused his attention toward a nearby newspaper by bringing it into play. Gathering his thoughts he explained his previous out-of-touch actions.

"Basically I owe it all to the Clarion (local rag), who indirectly handed it to me on a plate. Here, see for yourself," he drew her attention to the horse-racing section. "Tell me, what do the headlines do for you on page three?" Slowly Joan scanned the print looking for a form of recognition. The content that briefly caught her eye read as follows....top weight RUBY WARRIOR'S five wins in a row. Shaking her head Joan exchanged a meaningful glance at Eastern.

"I wouldn't even know where to start, Mike, unless..." she faltered to consider a possible connection. "Unless."

"Go on," urged Eastern.

"Well...stupid really..."

"I'll be the best judge of that, Joan," he interrupted. "Just take your time and say what you're thinking.." Joan gazed searchingly at the wording once again . Finally a flicker of recognition clouded her face, giving way to her thoughts.

"Obviously the word 'Ruby' becomes prominent. I'm now thinking precious stones...along with diamonds which in turn alludes to Brezznov's first love. There! How did I do?" she gasped. His body language alone was proof enough to show that he was totally rapt at her prognosis.

"Do!? Better than you'll ever know, Joan. The word 'Ruby' was the key into opening the door to my problem, and..."

"....I still feel that I'm missing something here," she interjected. "Namely the link between Brezznov and the word itself."

"And you've every right to, Joan. Let me explain. Sometime ago during a conversation I had with him inside, he inadvertently let it be known that he owned a country residence situated in the sticks, but within easy reach of London Gatwick International airport."

"Convenient for strategic purposes no less."

Precisely! I couldn't have said it better myself. But more importantly Joan, the name of the residence was prefixed by the word 'Ruby', as in Cottage or House."

"Right! I can see that it all makes sense now. So tell me, with that in mind, where do you intend going from here?"

"Ideally, it makes sense to get Rogon involved as soon as possible. It shouldn't be too much grief to pinpoint the location, I'd have thought, simply by scanning the Land Registry. Assuming of course, the property isn't logged under another pseudonym. If our hunch turns out to be kosher, then the spin off from that in terms of guilt-edged SP could turn out to be priceless." From then on, their evening reverted into one of spontaneous celebration., made possible by Joan's earlier submission. It could be a long night. Either way, nobody, it seems, could be heard contesting her theory.

CHAPTER 9
MISSION IMPOSSIBLE

Forty eight hours had now elapsed since Eastern's bespoke revelation alluding to Brezznov's 'bolthole'. His hunger for some positive feedback via Rogon, could be found running neck-and-neck with a roller coaster. Fortunately, Joan was on hand to offer a sympathetic shoulder as a get-out clause. Once again he forced himself up from out of his chair and began to pace up and down like a caged animal. "Two poxy days and still nothing! And all for a simple yes or no." Eastern fumed. "I can see now why MI6 keep their distance. I'm starting to compare Rogon to a chinless wonder."

Either out of sympathy or the need to intrude on his routine, the sudden interruption emerging from his mobile did at least offer him a spasm of relief. It only improved as he confirmed the origin of the caller. From then on, his impatience got the better of him as he went for the jugular. "Rogon! Where the ruddy hell have you been all my life!?" he blasted. "And don't even think about feeding me any of your bureaucratic shit." As a third-party reluctant observer, Joan was forced to cringe as Eastern continued to offload his pent up frustration. "This call had better be worthwhile my friend. I'll remind you that nothing short of a result will suffice. Do you understand?"

Question! How does one define the workings of a Government 'android' when under pressure? In Rogon's case the powers to be had ensured that a safety mechanism or bypass became a legal requirement, when confronted with an anger situation. "Hello to you too, Mike. It's comforting to know that your allegiance still lies with the agency. And vital that you keep an open mind on investigative SP. I also note your complexity in this matter. You can rest assured that your initial supposition regarding Brezznov's whereabouts have proved to be conclusive. I applaud your tenacity."

"Yeah, and I fucking love you too, Rogon," barked Eastern. "So give me the wider picture while you're on a roll." A short hiatus followed as Rogon gathered himself. He opened up by confirming that Brezznov's alleged 'bolthole' was indeed a reality. The SP itself came to light following a 10-mile radius sweep surrounding Gatwick IA. Listed under the heading of 'Ruby' cottage as supposed. Location wise, it lay some three miles east of the airport, set in a small hamlet known as TINSLEY GREEN .

And situated midway and flanked on both side between the M23/A23. As was suggested previously, the cottage itself was set in a prime position should the likelihood of a spontaneous exit from the country become a necessity." He went on to say that the Registration plates on a dark-coloured 4x4 Range Rover parked in the drive of the property, verified Brezznov as being the owner of the vehicle. Thus far, Eastern had every reason to be upbeat, given that the cast-iron SP was a creditable step in the right direction. Having said that, the temptation to have one last swipe at Rogon and his coveted 'lost' forty eight hours, was proving to be too hot to handle. Suffice to say, he didn't make any apologies for it's inclusion.

"I suggest that in future, your agency logistics might well want to consider an extended sabbatical, and reap the benefits of a refresher course, when dealing with theories." As was to be expected, his personal observations fell way short on direction, leaving Rogon to relish the final word.

"May I remind you, Mike, that time itself is measured in favourable results as opposed to verbal scepticism." Managing to stifle a chuckle at Rogon's prophecy, Eastern labelled it merely as being Government protocol. He then placed the latter on the spot regarding their next move. "Knowing where to find the guy now, changes everything, wouldn't you say, Mike? We are in a strong position to monitor his every move. With added caution you understand. And as you so rightly recommended, it's imperative that he is made to feel completely unaware of any alien activities."

"Absolutely! So, where do I fit into this latest scheme of events?" demanded Eastern with an air of longing. "Boredom quickly becomes a habit, a fucking bad one at that, and I'm used to working at the top end as you know."

"Unfortunately Mike, Brezznov, through circumstances, is dictating the run of play at present, in spite of our latest source of SP. Everything hinges on him contacting you again. As personalities go, you're better equipped to understand him more than anybody. No. I'm afraid we are back to the waiting game once again, and if that's what it takes to get a result I'd willingly settle for that." For once, Eastern was forced to admit that Rogon had got it right. Although he wasn't prepared to give the latter the satisfaction of divulging his own inner thoughts.

In winding up, It was also agreed that after some differences, agent 'B' would be responsible for carrying out a one-to-one surveillance at 'Ruby' cottage, until such times that a change in circumstances implied the need to negotiate his position. Right from the start, Eastern had cast doubt on 'B's' role while acting as undercover agent. A difference of opinion being, "You have to agree Rogon, the man is a loose cannon at the best of times. He'd think nothing of 'blowing' (killing) Brezznov away just for the hell of it. I just hope he doesn't jeopardise the state of play." Rogon then hit back by stating.

"After a lengthy consultation I issued 'B' with a waterproof proviso, and one which convinces me he will certainly adhere to." Seventy two hours had now elapsed since Brezznov's bolthole had gone public, leaving Eastern totally isolated. The only ironic consolation he could hang on to concerned Brezznov's health, of all things.

"At least 'B' has managed to keep his trigger-finger out of

the equation, otherwise it would be breaking news by now," he explained to Joan in conversation. And then three days slipped by and just as quickly became four. Only this time it carried an edge aligned with relief. It was a Friday evening when the breakthrough finally became a statistic. The Scotch he'd imbibed as a companion felt good, as it slid off his palate before hitting the back of his throat. But not in the same league as the ring-tone issuing from his mobile. A hasty glance told him all that he needed to know.

"Alex! It's been a while. Tying up loose ends you understand. I trust you're still available? As you are aware, I've been off the 'manor' for a short while, mainly for business purposes which will become clear within the next forty eight hours."

"Yeah! Tell me something else I don't already know you pompous bastard." (the reference being to his knowledge of 'Ruby' cottage), a smug Eastern told himself before replying in a casual manner. "Victor! Good to hear from you. Life has been pretty quiet since you've been away. And now you're back why do I get the feeling you're going to hit me with a proposition?"

"Because I'm aware that your hunch is my gain, and that makes me feel good. As from now, I can predict that nothing will be allowed to stand in my way to achieve what I believe will be the heist of a lifetime. And you my friend will be part of it. To come out of this 'scam' as a loser is an option I wouldn't even consider. Every aspect and every pitfall had been checked and double checked. Alex, I will emerge as a winner, not only financially but as the man who fucked the system. Now that's what I call a guilt-edged double to invest in. Especially if you're contemplating a lifestyle you can only dream about."

"You make it sound even more kosher, Victor, I've gotta hand it to you, your week in exile hasn't exactly been wasted, has it?"

"You don't miss a trick my friend. Lucky for me though, I didn't have the pleasure of the 'Bill' breathing down my neck 24/7. The time I've spent away has been a bloody holiday. Those suckers would give anything to find my little part of paradise." Eastern afforded himself a wry smile of guilty pleasure as a mental picture of 'B' on the end of a pair of binoculars entered the equation.

"Not half as much as you would for knowing what I know

right now." He told himself. "And you think your one clever bastard? Well I've got news for you asshole, make the most of your freedom while you can and dream on. Because at the moment you're getting by on borrowed time." Prematurely lost in his own small world had now left Eastern to deal with his agitated nemesis.

"Alex! You still there?" Momentarily he was off guard and found wanting.

"Yeah....Yeah, I lost you for a minute. " He lied through his teeth. "Poxy reception I'm getting...hang on...is that any clearer?" It quickly became apparent, as Brezznov continued where he'd left off, that he hadn't suspected anything untoward.

"Good! Now listen up, this is important. Seventy two hours from now, as a 'firm', we will be in business. Having said that, the strategy surrounding the mission remains with me. Now then. What I can tell you, is that it will all happen up West and..." Eastern hadn't bargained for an off-the-'manor' locale and pushed him for a reason why.

"London!?" he questioned. "Why the 'smoke' of all places?"

"Why? I suggest to you that the choice I've made is fairly obvious. When was the last time that you shit on your own door step, Alex? If I didn't know you any better, I would have to say you're beginning to under-estimate my potential. I can only presume that you're asking out of pure interest...am I right?" Inwardly, Eastern was left fuming for having allowed himself a rare moment of naivety for questioning Brezznov's game plan.

86

"Without question Victor, your judgment does you credit. It is your call after all, so I don't have a problem dealing with it."

"Good! I'm glad that you see that way, Alex. In the past, mistakes have cost me dearly, and that isn't healthy, so I don't intend going back down that road." Lowering his mobile, Eastern sighed with relief in the knowledge that Brezznov hadn't smelled a rat.

"That's for sure! So, where do we go from here, Victor? The thought of putting one over the 'Bill' on a personal level does it for me. Getting off on that alone gives me a buzz...know what I mean?"

"Yeah!, like yourself." responded Brezznov. I've had ample time to think about this one, which means getting a result is that much sweeter. Moving on from that we need to discuss some finer details surrounding the operation. Ideally it makes sense to use an out of City venue for a 'meet'."

"Couldn't agree more Victor. Not only that, knowing the poxy 'Bill', they've got this funny attitude about showing up when you least suspect it."

"Exactly my sentiments," echoed Brezznov, and continued to commit himself to the script. "Tell you what, we'll do it nice and private. Let's say the 'Duke of York' pub at Sayers Common, It's just off the old A23 this side of HICKSTEAD International Show Jumping Centre."

"I like your style Victor, so what day in particular are we talking about?"

"This coming Sunday night looks a good bet to me, say around 8 o'clock. That way it leaves you twenty-four hours to dwell on the idea." Moments later, he pulled the plug on their conversation, leaving a contented Eastern with plenty to think about.

"The only setback so far, as I see it. Is the lousy lack of SP revolving around the 'heist'." He relayed to Rogon that same day. "I can only hope that Brezznov will 'sing like a canary' tomorrow night. At worst, it will give us a clearer picture of what wer'e up against. To suggest that we are looking at an inner City bank job, and without a location to refer to, tells me he's got carte blanch to assign a target when and how he chooses to. He's waited a long time for this moment and that's why he's keeping any SP close to his chest. Any disclosure coming my way only relates to timing, and who's to say that's even kosher? Putting it mildly, Brezznov has got the State by the bollocks!" Eastern could have sworn that he heard Rogon wince, prior to concurring with his own thoughts.

"Just the inclination of it makes my blood boil. Even I hadn't envisaged the amount of ground that we need to cover. This could mean bringing the 'Met' boy's in as a back- up cover. I mean, how the hell do you police a situation like this anyhow? No! This has to stay within the agency. At best, I'll save what SP we have got until we know different. And I'll endeavour to hold off Whitehall as best as I can...and," he emphasized, "if the Prime minister thinks for a minute he's being dealt second-hand news, then I might as well put my head on the block."

At this point, Eastern found himself hard-pressed not to laugh at his mentor's self- assassination, by putting the complexity facing the situation into perspective. "As opposed to a personal indictment Rogon, I suggest that you face the fact in knowing that just for once you're in the real world as of now. And not in that starry-eyed glitz of bloody 'never never land'. So, to recap on the issue you have with Whitehall, I can't stress enough how important it is to keep the solution under wraps for the time being. If Brezznov gets the slightest sniff there's grief involved, he'll pull the carpet out from under our feet.." And went on, "On a personal level and having come this far I wouldn't be a happy man should that be allowed to happen. Besides, I can't imagine   life without you around. Now that would be dull."

Your uncanny use of words now leaves me somewhat confused Mike, so I'll act positive and take that as a compliment." His designer conclusion induced Eastern to chuckle when replying.

Strange, and here's me thinking that you didn't have a shred of feeling left in that body of yours. On a more serious note, it is always wise to remember that Brezznov himself is only human and therefore liable to make mistakes. In his case and looking at the alleged magnitude of his operation, it can only result in total disaster for him, should he become sloppy in his approach. In other words, he would become vulnerable and that, my friend, is the moment that we could turn this whole nightmare around." Far from wishing life away, Sunday seemed to arrive unannounced for Eastern. Impatiently he once again consulted his watch and readily noted that the time had only lapsed some ten minutes from the previous check. With the current time now standing at 7pm, his over-zealous eagerness to be on the road was finally beginning to get the better of him. As usual, Joan had picked up on his trepidation syndrome by adding her own version of events. "For God's sake Mike! Look at yourself. You really do need to chill out. If I didn't know you any better, I'd have to say you're giving the impression that you've got a date with another woman. I can only hope for your sake that's she's worth it."

Notwithstanding a domestic, Eastern also had to live with the fact that his alleged date with his nemesis in an hour's time, hopefully didn't have the makings of a bum deal. As it turned out, he was forced to succumb to Joan's perception by putting his body language down to a correlation stemming from his ongoing love-hate relationship with Rogon on the one hand, and his fragile allegiance to Brezznov on the other. "I'm sorry darling, I was somewhere else.....you were saying?" For someone who epitomised the genesis of demureness, Joan's exchange to his pathetic plea of absence could be found to be in a class of it's own.

"Just this darling. If you were to wake up one morning to find your 'balls' missing. I would like to think that I had done enough in persuading you to remember my initial observation!" Twenty or so minute later, Eastern exited Brunswick Square and headed for the A23 via Dyke Road. He was still scratching his head as he left Patcham on the outskirts of the city trailing in his wake. He figured that thirty minutes would give him ample time in which to do the short trip, with time in hand to gather himself. Following an uneventful journey he arrived at his destination. For a Sunday night, the car park, he duly noted, appeared at first glance to be crowded. Leaving him momentarily into doubting Brezznov's choice of venue.

On entering the main bar, he paused and took stock to seek out any form of recognition. In spite of his diminutive bearing and the presence of other punters, he managed to hone in on Brezznov who'd by all accounts, made one end of the bar his own. Shadowing him as if joined at the hip, he could also make out ex-cop Tommy Brandon. Although he noted, Aubrey Thorpe Millington was nowhere to be seen. Swallowing hard, Eastern inhaled deeply and made his way toward the two figures. Brezznov himself was eager to make the first move by extending his hand as Eastern approached. "Alex! Glad that you made it. I was beginning to forget what you look like." Averting his gaze he indicated towards his side-kick. "You remember Tommy Brandon of course?". Declining a forced handshake on personal grounds, Eastern glanced around and suggested that they find a less conspicuous location to further their business. They had barely made themselves comfortable at an adjacent corner table, when Millington made himself known.

With the introductions over and the benefit of a large Scotch to lean on, Brezznov indicated his intention to open up. "We all know why we are here, so I suggest a toast before we proceed to the success of universal crime gentlemen, so join me and raise your glasses to 'World Accounts Inc.'"

Given his dominance he proceeded to lord over the meeting, which included certain drip-fed lurid details, on a need-to-know basis of the pre-planned heist. From the SP, he'd managed to ascertain Eastern gathered that the operation itself would take place the following evening. Some two hours later the meeting was dissolved on the pretext that to any inquisitive onlooker, their association had been no more than a trivial 'boy's night out'. On a personal level, Eastern had ended the evening on a high. And now found himself struggling to contain his illicit luck. For the first time in weeks, after experiencing a run of grief, he was now in possession of vital SP and the bonus of being a participant in a suspected masterminded criminal coup.

Ten minutes or so after vacating the pub, a convenient lay-by offered him the security in which to contact Rogon at HQ, and subsequently off-load the verbal importance he'd managed to glean. Under normal circumstances, any contact using a specific security number that he retained, would officially be classed as being a 'CODE RED', privy only to Rogon himself. On this particular occasion the system wasn't without it's faults. And not before an exasperated Eastern finally made the desired breakthrough he craved.

"You took your poxy time before answering Rogon, so what is it this time? And don't bother giving me that old chestnut, 'I'm currently in talks with the PM at present'. Right now, I'm on the

A23 at Pyecombe, just north of Brighton, and I can hear loud and clear. So now I'm beginning to think to myself that the fucking agency is on a work to rule basis, and bollocks to the 'soldiers'. Let me remind you that I'm working on the front line, endeavoring to save your bleedin' neck and your pension. And that's besides my own!" If for one minute Rogon felt intimidated by his outburst, the he manfully kept it to himself by relying on his robotism persona to see himself through.

"My apologies for not giving you a 'green light' earlier on, Mike. Unfortunately, this is without problems. As director of the agency, my affiliations, as you're aware, extend and terminate at Whitehall and..." He wasn't allowed to complete his diplomatic monologue, as an irate Eastern steamrolled him into submission.

"Crap! Do yourself a favour and tear up the bloody script you're reading. And if you can spare me the time, we need to discuss a major breakthrough on the Brezznov file. Seriously though, where are you at this moment in time?"

"Good question. Earlier on this evening I was summoned to No.10 for a meeting 'extraordinaire' along with the PM. In fact I'm in a lobby now as we speak, having made my apologies." All things considered, Eastern wasn't totally convinced and pressed for some firm assurance.

"Meeting, what on a Sunday? Sounds like a bleedin' private members dinner to me, on the Government."

"Not a chance, Mike. In fact top of the agenda list is the alleged Brezznov affair itself, so any fresh substance you can throw at me, the better I like it." Eastern then went on to relate his evening's experience by setting out what details that were made available to him. As a result, it was now Rogon's turn to exact his own brand of consternation. "I can't believe you're telling me this. I'm actually struggling to take it on board, Mike. As lucrative as it is, Brezznov has caught the agency with it's pants down. The mere thought that he intends to carry out the 'heist' in the next twenty-four hours or so, is one thing. Attempting to police the situation at such short notice is incomprehensible. And that's without knowing where and what financial establishment he intends to infiltrate. At best, the current situation as it stands has the makings of my worst nightmare. Spooks will become the laughing stock of every Government agency resource from MI6 downwards. The facts when confronted, you have to agree, are beginning to read like a 'What happens next' comic strip! It wouldn't surprise me, for one minute, if the mission itself makes top of the bill on the Prime Ministers Question time." Although somewhat disconsolate, Eastern nevertheless, still managed to salvage his own thoughts as an epitaph. "

"Knowing the problem facing us makes me wonder, now, if 'B' had got it right in the first place."

"Meaning!?"

"Simply, that we wouldn't be having this bloody conversation. And that arsole Brezznov by default, would, by now, have full rights to a bleedin' body bag in the morgue!" It was always going to be a throwaway line and almost immediately become rejected out of sight, as Rogon decided to take the higher ground.

"With only the one positive to come out of this farce, namely the 'heist' tomorrow night, I suggest we review the negatives and see exactly what wer'e up against."

"You're not going to like what you hear, but seeing as you brought it up, here's a review of what we don't know. Firstly, the source of the 'hit'. Purely as an educated guess, I recommend that we throw a blanket cordon , say a half mile radius, around the City centre by pin-pointing Threadneedle Street as an integral map reference. From what I can ascertain, his choice of location would have to be a large sustainable and predominate financial banking establishment. And, with vital links of global proportion to be able to receive and carry out his intended 'scam'." At this juncture, Rogon appeared to be verbally drained, as the crux of the matter began to sink in.

"I suppose it's too much to ask what sort of time factor that Brezznov has put in place."

"Hazard a guess, I'd have to say late evening and taking in the early hours of Tuesday morning."

"God! What a crock of shit he's handed us. I won't know where to start once the PM gets involved, let alone Scotland Yard. Knowing their role in all of this, I suspect an impromptu retirement is the best I could hope for under the circumstances." Stalwart as ever, Eastern was quick to express his own version surrounding any personality doubts, by dismissing Rogon's abysmal show of defeatism out of sight.

"To my mind, your pathetic attitude is nothing short of bollocks. Just remember, it's how you finish that counts Rogon. The emphasis is on Brezznov from here on if you're talking success. Remember, the most vital aspect in this charade happens to be me. And as far as I'm concerned, I'm part of the 'firm' (gang) and able to monitor his every move. So let's have some solidarity feeling from now on. I'm not here to take on any prisoners. From where I'm standing, Brezznov is just another unwanted package of shit that needs to be eradicated, so trust me when I say I will endeavour to bring him down when the moment is right." If his extreme confession made Rogon feel any better, then he kept his thoughts on the subject closely under wraps. Instead, he fast-forwarded their conversation into focusing on what might become a reality on the Monday night.

"I can presume, at that rate Mike that the second he decides to make his move tomorrow night, you will be in a position to give me a 'code red' to act upon? As far as the PM is concerned I will assure him that contingency plans are in operation to counteract whatever route he chooses to take." Inwardly, Eastern now felt more relaxed within himself in knowing that Rogon had grasped the situation head-on, with confidence.

"You're right on both counts Rogon, so I'll let you get back to your party and lie your way out of any grief . As promised, I'll be in touch one way or another."

Twenty minutes or so later, found him in his apartment taking advantage of a spontaneous night cap, deriving from a personal touch by Joan via a bottle of his favourite tipple. From then on, he always knew that he was facing a long night ahead of him. As pre-arranged, Rogon received a 'code red' the following day, much earlier than he'd anticipated. In fact it was logged at 17.oo hours that evening.

The message that transpired, came across as brief and conclusive in it's very nature, leaving a somewhat shell-shocked and disorientated Rogon to confront his Whitehall demons on a disorganized scale. The information itself, for good or bad, read as follows.................

ROGON....take note that Brezznov has aborted the mission... and I repeat...mission aborted forthwith....Mike...over and out.

CHAPTER 10
THE FLIP SIDE OF SANITY

Following in the wake of Brezznov's unprecedented u-turn, the inevitable debate, two days later and chaired by the irrepressible Rogon, was always going to be a heated affair. Besides Eastern and agent 'B', those present at the meeting included an observer representing Scotland Yard, an official from the Bank of England, plus the Prime Minister's Private Secretary, and a certain Mr J.P. Stryker, (whom Eastern took an instant dislike to). His immediate self indictment being, 'The man appears to be out of his depth within the company'. For progression reasons, Eastern elected to get the proceedings underway, all due to his personal links with the file on the table. For his part, he was under no illusions as to Brezznov's erratic strategy by issuing his reasons why.

"For all present, I strongly suggest that his alleged operation to carry out what I believe to be a 'Cyber' heist', became derailed owing to the inclusion of a third-party breakdown." The Prime Minister's secretary at this stage, looked keen to open up his account by getting involved with the proceedings.

"Can you elaborate on that theory, Mr Eastern, and define your use of the word 'breakdown'?" Acting on instinct, Eastern dismissed what would have been his normal action without hesitation, in sympathy with the man's naivety, when associated with criminal jargon.

"Just my poxy luck to get shackled with a dumb pin-striped gopher. He needs to get in the real world, he told himself. Glancing across at Rogon, he attempted to rustle up a form of verbal support. In the end, it resulted in a feeble effort that was going nowhere. Meanwhile, his inquisitor was getting impatient.

"Mr Eastern...when you're ready?" As an articulate onlooker himself, Rogon was now forced to wince at the obvious cold hostility between the two men, which now began to ice up.

"Let the man down gently, Mike, for Christ's sake." muttered Rogon under his breath. He needn't have worried. Diplomatic as ever, Eastern had read the situation but, at the same time, wasn't prepared to let Stryker off the hook without making him wriggle first.

"For those of you who aren't familiar with the term 'breakdown', like yourself of course, Mr Stryker," he emphasized, "We constantly use an expression in our business to compensate for it. And I quote. 'A falling out between thieves'. Alternatively, if you bat for the other side and you're on the receiving end...." Hesitating, he averted his attention directly toward Rogon to cement his position, before returning to Stryker, "Then the expression 'Well and truly 'stitched-up' would apply. But I feel sure that you're well aware it is a colloquialism used frequently by the criminal fraternity.... isn't that so Stryker?"

If Rogon, at that point, had even the slightest irritation of being locked away in his person, he would have been compelled to share his dilemma with Stryker, who, by now, found himself reduced to virtual embarrassment and wishing he hadn't opened his mouth. True to form, and due to his exclusive persona, any sentiment was completely lost on Rogon's behalf, making it clear that he was eager to press on with the enquiry. "At what point did you suspect that Brezznov had a change of heart, Mike? Would it have been something he said that alerted you, or was it just a spontaneous move on his part?" Eastern then went on to explain his own movements up until four-thirty that day, prior to the alleged 'heist' being carried out, which included the call from Brezznov and quoted the man as stating "You are about to be disappointed and no more than myself. Unfortunately, as we speak I've been confronted with an unhealthy and unexpected glitch. Needless to say, the operation has been aborted until I tell you different. The problem itself happens to be an in internal one so I will be dealing with it personally. In the meantime, sit tight until I contact you.".... end of quote. A brief sustained silence ensued, allowing his words to be digested. It was then left to 'B' to endorse his own take on Eastern's disclosure.

"On the SP you've put forward Mike, I'm fully prepared to back your 'third-party' theory one hundred per cent. I suspect that you picked up on Brezznov's internal issue claim, by putting two-and-two together, by highlighting an unknown accomplice. Probably a 'face' within the 'firm', having a dispute of some kind, consequently leading to a fall-out." A relieved Eastern nodded in appreciation.

"I'm glad that you see it my way 'B' and, as you so rightly mentioned, I couldn't even begin to elaborate on an alleged co-conspirator at this stage."

Rogon appeared to be sceptical. "Assuming that one did exist, Mike, what role would he have played in the 'heist'?"

"I'd be clutching at straws if I knew the answer to that one, but I suspect it would involve somebody internally placed, therefore enabling him to give covert access when called upon. Thus handing Brezznov the key to 'Aladdin's Cave'. That's my immediate assumption."

"Okay, so wer'e probably looking for a 'bent' security guard or similar?" 'B' asserted.

"Precisely!" Eastern echoed, "Without him on board as an investment, the 'heist' would never get off the ground, as you well know and......."

"......knowing that you've got that monopoly over somebody, puts them in a prime bargaining position. Especially if they should decide to up their share of the ante involved." interjected Rogon.

"Now you're talking. I suspect Brezznov was being leaned on from that quarter."

"Christ's sake!" 'B' exploded, "If somebody is responsible for that, they must have some sort of a death wish. It's not exactly the

Gary Tulley

call of the month...is it?"

"At least it gave Brezznov the incentive when making the decision to call the operation off," Stryker bleated.

"Yeah, and for how long,?" demanded Eastern. "Once he has 'dealt with the business' as he stated, I can't see him sitting on the fence. People like him usually get what they want. Power is a form of bloody religion within the circles he moves in, so rest assured he will be back. The glitch he refers to, and I think we are unanimous on this, implicates person or persons unknown. And knowing how he works, the problem as he sees it will be eradicated, thus leaving him the window in which to progress. In the meantime gentlemen we need to take a step backwards and wait for his next move."

Following an hour addled with conjecture, the meeting was finally abandoned sine die. In contrast to Brezznov's windfall of grief, Eastern's solid intuition just happened to be on a roll, although having said that, there was no way he could have envisaged what was to follow. A few hours later, the badly mutilated torso belonging to a man, was fished out of the Thames by the river police at Rotherhithe docks. Adding to the trauma of the grizzly find, was the fact that the head and the hands of the victim had been forcibly removed.

News travels fast and Spooks hotline was no exception to the rule. "Good morning, Rogon, I was wondering how long it would take you to get back in touch? I presume your call has got something to do with the headlines in this mornings 'CLARION'."

"Well, Mike, putting coincidences to one side for a moment, and based on the supporting SP that we have, the grim circumstances don't leave an awful lot to the imagination...wouldn't you say?"

"I hear what your implying, Rogon, but first and foremost I don't do coincidences as you well know. I only deal in facts, so in my humble opinion this particular murder had got all the trappings of a gangland fall-out. Probably presided over by an aggrieved Brezznov! It now gives you a realistic insight into the kind of people we are up against. As I have said before, and make no mistake, the man is one mean bastard. Whether or not he was culpable in committing this latest crime, doesn't alter my opinion one way or the other."

The fact that the two were at opposite ends of the line, betrayed Eastern's rare moment of emotion, as Rogon exercised his bland opinion. "You worry me sometimes, Mike. Unlike myself you seem to have this unerring gift of being able to put things into perspective, especially when it matters most."

"Gift!? That's an over-reaction on your part, Rogon. I'd rather settle for common sense backed up with the bleedin' truth. It's never let me down yet."

"I'll make sure that I keep you up to that. Now, then, business. I strongly feel that we need to delve more into this latest killing, even if it does mean ruling out a connection with the crime committed and, indeed, Brezznov himself."

"I don't have a problem with that, except to say I suspect that the Met boys are far better equipped to deal with this one. To my mind, whoever sanctioned the 'contract' on the victim has to be a pro, and a wealthy one at that. Those responsible for the murder itself had to be well-paid and under no bloody illusions as to the extent of depravation they were paid to inflict on the victim. As far as forensics are concerned, I can foresee us being in for a long wait before any concrete evidence, if it all emerges. I should imagine those poor over-worked bleeders at the pathology lab, are climbing up the wall right now, trying to make some sense of the 'stiff'' (torso)."

"Yeah, I guess you're right, Mike. I'll just keep a need-to-know line open in the event something might turn up. In the meantime we are back to the waiting game, while, Brezznov decides on his next move." Whether or not, Rogon knew something that nobody else did, and kept it to himself, then only time would be the best judge of that.

Three trying weeks had now almost elapsed since the discovery of the gruesome 'Torso in the Thames' revelation. With Brezznov seemingly content to wage a war of nerves campaign, the only remaining chance of a possible breakthrough came via an auspicious phone call from regional forensics, logged to Spooks HQ. This, in turn, was backed up by a detailed up-to-date transcript containing their findings. As follows........The victim being of Caucasian Male missing dismembered head & hands.

Heavily built in stature and retaining a muscular definition. All organs were found to have no abnormalities and were functional up until time of death. Total body weight prior to death would be approximately some 100 kg's and would be aged between 30-40 years. He has of yet to be identified. The timing of the victims demise prior to being discharged into the water, would only have amounted to a couple of hours. The torso itself on examination was found to have been in the water not longer than 24 hours. Cause of death is unknown partly due to lack of skin impediments EG Needle punctures and abrasions to back up any additional theories, although the possibility exists that one could assume the victim to have been bludgeoned to death or shot in the head prior to decapitation. Asphyxia was also ruled out. the embodiment of distinguishing marks, namely, a series of some 7 exclusive Tattoos were present on the torso, 4 on the left upper arm & 2 on the opposing arm. The single 1 on the lower right leg in particular, still retained partial scab tissue. Most likely the result of having been a recent addition. Probably carried out in the last 7-10 days & depicted a venomous snake embracing a stiletto type dagger. Also apparent were 2 inscribed letters E&S, presumably one would assume to be the victims initials. (see enclosed photo). end of transcript.

With that in mind, the SP came as no great surprise to Eastern, even allowing for the fact that the crime was allegedly committed some three weeks previous. At least, it was something to dwell on, and the fact that he had been given the report first-hand, was pleasing. The dilemma now facing Rogon would entail the importance of Eastern's reaction to the transcript and as to whether it would differ from his own. Leaning back in his chair, he gave him a long searching look before speaking.

"So, what do you make of our mystery man thus far Mike? Would you say that we are nearer to maintaining a connection with Brezznov in mind?" Slowly lowering the forensic report, Eastern asserted a disdainful look that could have spoken for him as he levelled with Rogon.

"You're already aware of my take on the 'stiff', and this report you will find, in time, accelerates justice to my claim. I'll be frank with you and say that Brezznov himself could have written this, and included the name of the victim's tailor, amongst other things!" Sighing deeply, Rogon took on the appearance of a crushed man, before replying.

"I should have known better than to have asked, although you didn't pass any comment regarding the initials linked to the tattoo that came to light...any specific reason why?" "No, no reason at all. To my reckoning, it's origin will prove to be a formality. Even allowing for the fact that the torso had been immersed in water for a period. And phasing the tattoo to a degree, shouldn't have affected it's history. I can tell now, it is a custom-design job fused with military overtones. In short, the victim's credentials will be on file with the tattooist responsible for the work involved. Once the E.S aspect is clarified , this will give you the victim's I.D which can be checked out against any 'previous' he may have on record, if any. Personally, I'd let the 'plod' deal with it. That way they can furnish us with their findings.

"Uhm, sounds reasonable enough. That being the case, I'll make that official, Mike, asp."

"Fine, as long as you realize that even knowing the victim's I.D, you're still left with the grief of connecting, who ever he is, to Brezznov. Surely that's the crux of the matter, which leads me to ask, is 'B' still employed on surveillance cover since we spoke last? It's vital that we will still be able to monitor Brezznov's movements. Having said that, the man can yield the type of power he commands, merely by sitting in his own front room. Quite honestly, a poxy fly on the wall would be out of business in no time, working in Brezznov's bolthole, mainly through utter boredom."

Nodding in agreement, Rogon raised his shoulders in a gesture of sympathy. "Patience they say, is a virtue, Mike, and that's the only one redeeming aspect we have got going for us at present."

"Yeah right. That, and an unknown headless 'stiff'. Not much reward for months of graft is it? I'm beginning to feel synonymous with collateral damage. As of now, the idea of booking myself into a bloody health farm for a week or two, had crossed my mind." Even taking into account Rogon's unemotional standards, his unprecedented conclusion in reply, could nevertheless be found to be tainted with sympathy.

"Luckily, you're a born survivor, Mike, and that's why you do the damned job. If it's any consolation, I'm pretty sure that the lab boys will come up with something substantial in the next forty eight hours. Meanwhile, I can only advise you to get some well-earned rest while you can. They tell me that Brighton is in the throes of a mini heat-wave right now. And who knows? Brezznov might have a change of direction."

CHAPTER 11
A SUCCESSFUL NIGHT OUT

As 'eateries' go, the Dolce Vita could be found to be a restaurant apart. Especially to the majority of food buffs that patronized the venue. The fact that it epitomized Italian cuisine (and just happened to be Eastern's idea of fulfilment) only endorsed Joan's intention to make a belated reservation, intended to breathe some extra new life into a dejected Eastern, who could be found reeling of late from a bout of non- progression. "You'll need to hurry, Mike. The cab will be arriving at any minute now."

"I'm doing the best that I can, Joan, although I could have done with you giving me a bit more notice," he retaliated in a brusque manner. Although, deep down he was mindful of the fact that she only had his best interests at heart. "By the way, you never mentioned where....."

"There wouldn't be any point, darling," she hastily interrupted. Her well-timed intervention then coincided with the door bell sounding off. "Besides which," she continued, "our evening, as far I'm concerned is intended to be a surprise." Having said all that, there was no way possible that she could have known, at the time, that her heart felt prediction would be only one form of aspect, deriving from their spontaneous dinner date.

The 'Lanes', traditionally the heartbeat of the city was, by it's very nature, a Mecca for gourmet revellers. It could now be found to be alive with bodies, all intent on creating that certain 'buzz'. Vacating their cab in East street, the two made their way towards the 'Pump House' tavern, anticipating a liquid livener to kick-start their evening. Minutes after entering, Eastern downed the remnants of his favourite Scotch and gestured his empty glass toward the barmen for a refill. With Joan shadowing him, he turned to express his immediate thoughts. "God! I needed that. You should get me out more often. I've just got this feeling that were in for a good night."

A knowing smile briefly made an appearance, allowing his inner thoughts to go walk-about. "It's just occurred to me Joan."

"Go on."

"Rogon! I'd love to know what his idea of a good time is. I wouldn't even know where to start if prompted." Joan smiled broadly.

"Hazard a guess, Mike. I have to say that putting Intelligence papers and files in order comes to mind." This time the smile he evoked belonged to him, and just as quickly broke into a chuckle as, once again, he released his thoughts.

 It's just occurred to me, Joan. I reckon that you know Rogon better than I do. You have to say he's such a sad bastard. He really does need to get out more."

Checking the time, Eastern turned and cast a sweeping glance around the bar and beyond. Over the years it had become a habit that went with the job. His definition being 'Better you know the devil behind you, rather than the one facing you'. At one point his body stiffened, almost as if something had infiltrated his vision, causing him to attempt a double-take. This time he went with his gut, knowing it wouldn't take a steward's inquiry to confirm that the alien 'face', whom he'd witnessed amongst the crowd punters, was no stranger to him. In fact it belonged to none other than Tommy Brandon himself.

Moreover, it became even clearer to him that Brandon was heavily engrossed in conversation while in the company of two other unrecognisable figures, mainly due to the many misplaced punters haunting the bar. In a split second his vision evaporated as the returning barman eased him back into his own comfort zone.

"Your Scotch as ordered Sir....will there be anything else?" instinctively, Eastern averted his gaze and turned to confront him. The strained look he was wearing suggested that retrieving his drink amounted to the least of his registered problems.

"Sorry? Uhm...no, no thanks...that's fine." His distinct variation in his body language caused Joan to query his temperament.

"Are you feeling okay, Mike? You appear to be somewhat edgy. What's on your mind? Maybe we can talk about it." With a show of reluctance, Eastern concurred with a meaningful nod. Where to start would be the problem, knowing that business and pleasure in his chosen line of work, would normally be classed a 'no brainer'.

"That noticeable eh, Joan? Tell you what, let's grab a corner table while we can. It's paramount to me that I need to level with you." From the very word go, Eastern was under no illusions as to the fatal consequences arising from an unrehearsed outcome, should his cover come under scrutiny. Any confrontation could well be perceived as being highly volatile and dangerous. Not least at all of Joan herself who's present welfare needed to be considered. As if by clockwork, his brain had now fast- forwarded three hundred and sixty per cent, allowing a fresh set of rules to emerge. And, in the process, leaving his bewildered partner floundering in no-man's-land. "Forget what I said about the talk, Joan, we need to take a rain check on that. Right now I don't have the time to explain, but trust me when I say that right now this 'gaff' isn't a healthy place to be in. The sooner wer'e out of here, the better I like it." Downing his Scotch in one, he gripped her arm tightly and guided her through a side exit out of the bar and into the heat of the night.

Manfully removed from the scene of inexplicable confusion one minute, then being gently suffocated by the Latin ambience offered up by the Dolce Vita the next, shouldn't, under the circumstances have been such a hard act to follow. Unless of course your name just happens to be Joan Travers. Minutes after making themselves comfortable in a dining booth, she made it quite clear that there was more than a table d'hote menu to consider. "What the hell is going on, Mike? You still owe me an explanation for acting out of character earlier on in the pub. I'm beginning to think the evening isn't working out the way, that I intended it should be."

Like it or not, Eastern now found himself under orders once again. Only this time he was having to generate a suitable form of explanation. Without elaborating too deeply on the incident, he managed to 'air brush' the Brezznov connection into seclusion, for obvious reasons, and passed of the Tommy Brandon experience off as, "Some nasty people from my past who only get better if viewed from a distance. So you can see why, now, Joan, that I had to make the decision I did, at the time." Fortunately, the menu made better reading than her mind, in allowing her to shrug off further thoughts on the matter. As for Eastern, he should have known better, or maybe he was losing his touch with reality.

Good food and drink, laced with desirable company, doesn't include a rampant mobile sounding-off at ten o'clock on a Saturday night by playing 'gooseberry'. The look of consternation featured on Eastern's face as the caller's identity became apparent, sent a direct message to Joan. Slowly, and with deliberation, she lowered her glass away from her mouth. Pausing briefly, she momentarily allowed the moment to dictate her thoughts, prior to speaking in a hard-felt manner. "Before you say anything, Mike, you need to know, that I have your full interest at heart, based on how our evening is shaping up, only makes my reasoning that much more plausible....It's Rogon isn't it?" Nodding sheepishly, Eastern confirmed what he already knew to be the case and made a bad job of quelling his anger.

"I can't believe the arrogance of that guy. His timing is way off base. He seriously needs to get a life....trouble is" he faltered in speech, "the 'nuisance' isn't going to go away that easily, Joan I can only assume he needs to offload some vital information onto me. There's no way this is a social call. I'll give him two minutes of glory and then he can go back to playing ruddy solitaire, or whatever he does for entertainment." Grim faced, Eastern then made the prolonged connection. "This had better be good, Rogon, so don't feed me any of your bureaucratic shit, because right now it doesn't figure on my menu, if you get my point?"

Intrusion linked with regret took a back seat as an unmoved

Rogon proceeded to reply in a hollow manner. "Your choice of words are duly noted, Mike, so I feel I'm beginning to get the point, that is. You're obviously out socializing as we speak?"

"At least you got that part right!" exacted Eastern. "Just say what's on your mind and then I can get back to enjoying it."

"The MIU (Murder investigation unit) have been in touch. I thought that you might like to know that the Rotherhithe murder victim has now been formally identified at last." On the one hand, the news was good. On the other, the half-finished steak on his plate seemed to have lost it's appeal as the conversation sucked him in.

"Yeah, in that case, we know who to look for should he decide to go walkabout." He replied sarcastically, and added, "Talk to me in the morning." He then pocketed his mobile but not before switching it off completely.

"Was it worth it, the message, I mean?" enquired Joan, loosely. Eastern shrugged his shoulders before responding in a double-edged fashion.

"It all depends what your take on bullshit is, darling. There's certainly nothing in the content to suggest that I could lose my head over it." Grinning broadly, he signalled a nearby waiter, who was hovering, to fetch another bottle of wine.

CHAPTER 12
GAME ON

"Christ almighty! This one is better than the last one I had. Frankly, it was bloody awful." Eastern sounded off.

"I presume you're referring to the coffee, Mike? If so, then you have my full sympathy. I keep meaning to send a memo to the catering department." As yet, Eastern hadn't finished firing and still had an alternative can to empty.

Yeah? Well while you're at it, you might consider consulting your Whitehall gremlins for a decrease in your working life. I still haven't forgiven you for high jacking me last Saturday night." It was on the Monday morning following his disastrous dinner date. He now found himself seconded into a debrief of his own making, albeit 'circumstances beyond my control'. (The reference being the Tommy Brandon link). Now under scrutiny while seated in Rogon's office at HQ.

From the outset, the latter could be found to be at the peak of dogmatism in his approach. "I suggest that we deal with your fortuitous or not, situation, surrounding Brandon, first. It's fair to say the emphasis lies with the murder report on the 'stiff', which I find to be most compelling." Forced to bite his tongue, Eastern took solace, or what was left of it. It had been a long and trying weekend and 'brownie points' had long gone out of fashion. In his own time, he went on to explain, in temperate terms, his chance of sighting Brandon conspiring with two other close associates.

"It became clear, by their body language, that their presence formed an intentional business 'meet'. On assumption, I would have to say that either a deal had been executed recently, or at least that one was being discussed." At this, Rogon's interest instantly flared at the mention of the two accomplices.

"I find their participation highly interesting, Mike. On his own, Brandon wouldn't rate a second glance as such. He's just a paid gopher, but three 'faces' together could be classed as a conspiracy. So, based on the evidence to hand, I've got a hunch that Brandon and his pals are highly integral to a possible link to our Thames victim. What are your thoughts on that?"

"Touche Rogon, I couldn't agree more at this stage. And that's without knowing what you intend throwing at me next."

"For that, I need you to cast your mind back to last Saturday night, and I'll reiterate our brief, but, to my mind, warranted conversation."

"Huh!" snorted Eastern, "That's your bleedin' opinion, but you've got my attention anyway. Just make sure you make it stick." Rogon blatantly dismissed his final parting shot aimed at a personality war, and opened up, where he had previously left off, by highlighting his account of the facts arising from the ID report, appertaining to the Rotherhithe murder victim.

"It would seem that the unfortunate victim, whom we know now as being a Polish nationalist, has been officially identified under the name of Ernst Stowlowski. His name was also found to be consistent with the abbreviated initials ES. And contusive with a symbolic tattoo on his left leg."

"That's interesting. I can recall the initial forensic transcript having listed that observation." Eastern confirmed confidently. "Go on."

"The actual ID itself," emphasized Rogon, apparently created an impasse from the word go. Missing persons become a non-runner and our own vetting resources come up against a brick wall. The victim, it turns out, had no police record and was deemed to be an honest citizen."

"Poor bastard, you don't get many like him to the pound...do you?" He continued, "So! At last we have a name. Do we also have an address or, even better, an occupation?" Rogon confirmed his question with a ready-made nod of the head. And continued where he'd left off in a relaxed manner.

"That's a yes on both counts, Mike. The answers, in fact, emerging from the same source. While acting on your advice, the Met boys managed to track down a local tattooist responsible for Stowlowski's recent acquisition inscribed on his leg." If it was possible, Eastern smirked inwardly at Rogon's revelation as certain past suggestions came home to roost.

"It's good to know that you take in what I say at times, Rogon," he confided to himself, and strived to keep their conversation on track. "I presume the tattooist kept a register of his punters? Being as it's par for the course if the subject takes two or three sittings to complete. I bet the 'plod' couldn't believe their luck. It proves it can work for you."

"So it would appear, but to continue. On investigation, the shop-owner himself offered the team a wealth of SP, once the victim's initials were made available. The breakthrough then became a reality. It seems that prior to his murder, he was living in rented accommodation in Bermondsey. This was borne out after further enquiries, which, amongst additional SP that came to light, also included his passport. It soon became clear that he was working as a freelance security guard in the City. Mainly as an operative in overseas banking establishments. That's according to the agency who controlled his schedules."

Almost immediately, a wry smile enveloped Eastern's face as Stowlowski's working pattern collided with a raw nerve. "Without delving any further, Rogon, you'd have to say that the link inciting Brezznov into play, is staring at you in the face....wouldn't you say?"

"Exactly! You would have to be very naive to think otherwise, Mike, meaning that there's light at the end of the tunnel after all. Without sounding presumptuous, and knowing how your mind works as I do, I'm sure you could elaborate on that logic." Taking his reference as an olive branch, Eastern pursued his former line of reasoning.

"I honestly think that Stowlowski's murder is your classic 'nice guy, wrong place wrong time' scenario. I would go as far as to say I wouldn't mind betting that he was working at Brezznov's intended 'hit' at the time of his death. And, through circumstances, caused Brezznov to abort his plans...if you remember?"

"Yes, unfortunately. So, what to your mind, was his motive for silencing Stowlowski?"

"That's the easy part. The poor sucker obviously had access to privy SP that could indirectly put Brezznov in the frame by blowing his plans apart. And then he made the fatal mistake of sharing his knowledge with someone. From then on............."

"....................once Brezznov found out." Rogon interjected. "Stowlowski was a dead man walking. I was also informed that a covert call was made to West End Central, approximately twenty four hours before the murder, stating that an alleged 'heist' was imminent in the City. The origin and timing of the call was never disclosed. And the caller, a male, then hung up without revealing their identity."

"Huh! No prizes for guessing who that might have been." Eastern exacted with confidence. "Not that it's going to do us any good of course." Looking a trifle confused at his response, Rogon opted to digress.

"On that basis, where do you suppose Stowlowski obtained his alleged SP from in the first place Mike?"

"Presumably, a third party connection, without question."

"Could you be more precise; I feel I'm missing something here." Inhaling deeply, Eastern replied more in frustration than prolonged tedium.

"That will entail chasing bloody shadows, as I've mentioned before, in this line of enquiry if you recall? I explained some time ago that without the use of person or persons unknown, working on the inside, and familiar with the in-house security system, then you can forget the whole deal. The days of coming through the back door are a thing of the past, Rogon. These days it's all about complexity, plus sophistication and a suitably placed large 'wedge' (wad of money)."

I see, so in this case, once Stowlowski realized that he had stumbled upon an internal conspiracy, became the time that he decided to take some action."

"Exactly! hence the phone call to Central. Although, by then, I reckon his card had already been marked, and within hours the rest, as they say, is history. Not much of an epitaph is it; to wind up labelled as just another murder statistic?" Having set the scene, it was now left to Rogon to mop up any outstanding loose ends.

"Oh, one other thing, Mike. Just bear with me for a second. Working on the assumption that Brezznov is behind the murder, would I be right in thinking that the two 'faces' you witnessed last Saturday, along with Brandon, could well have been the killers and were being paid off?"

"Yeah, it certainly gives credence to support our overall consensus thus far. Given the circumstances, you're right to consider their role as conspirators. I could kick myself now for not getting a better visual look at them. But that's the high and the lows of the business I'm afraid."

Before adjourning the debrief, Rogon brought Eastern up-to-date with a day by day account of Brezznov's movements. Which were still under covert scrutiny, ably supported by agent 'B'. As was to be expected, the report gave no indication to suppose that Brezznov's past or present situation could implicate him in any way the Rotherhithe murder, or indeed to whoever was responsible. Meanwhile, at the other end of the spectrum, the MIU based at Rotherhithe, contacted Rogon via a fax outlining an updated document on the murder case thus far. In part, it confirmed that Stowlowski's missing body parts had been discovered. The grizzly remains of the security guard were found by a local 'wino' in a disused lock-up, close to where the victim had previously been living. It further went on to say, that a ballistics report carried out by forensic, had officially confirmed that the cause of death came from a gunshot wound to the head, at close range. Death, it appears, would have been instantaneous, the lab concluded. Further investigation had also revealed that a DNA sample, extracted from the remains, was adjudged as being compatible with the victim's torso. In conclusion, it was stated that the bullet which killed the victim, was fired from a .38 COBRA Colt or 'Snubbie', as it is known in the business. The 'round' in question, itself was located and retrieved, having been found lodged in bone structure behind the right ear. Any ongoing SP pending, would be available as directed....end of Fax.

For Eastern, the ongoing two weeks would now become a learning curve akin to patience. Not that he required a refresher course as such. He was well aware that when you're dealing with someone of Brezznov's indifference to timing, what could be adjudged as being finalized one minute, could also be rendered totally obsolete the next. As for Joan, she readily confessed to being, 'decidedly positive' when Eastern confirmed to her that Brezznov had finally made contact with him at last. And indeed Rogon himself, who when confronted with the news, actually allowed the beginnings of what Eastern described later as being, 'The premature birth of a token smile emerging from his face.' Business as usual, now took on a whole new meaning from Eastern's perspective, as he wilfully kicked deja vu into touch.

"This has to be the big one," he informed Rogon, "Brezznov is as hungry for this as I am. He's done his homework. All he has to do now, is to prove himself. And me? I'd willingly settle for a ringside seat and watch the egotistic bastard take a premeditated dive!"

"Amen to that!" declared Rogon in a defiant manner. "He's been a thorn in our side for far too long now, so I feel sure that favourable consequences will have a lasting effect with Whitehall in mind, besides creating a coup for the agency. As of yet, although equipped with the knowledge that the proposed 'heist' was indeed a reality, Eastern could still be found languishing in no-man's-land. Meanwhile, as was expected, Brezznov could be found exercising his control-freak syndrome, by withholding critical operation details, namely timing and destination plans. All this, prior to forming the 'firm' for at least a further twenty four hours.

"Forced into walking on bleedin' broken glass would be less of an ordeal than this enforced waiting game, Joan. I swear to God that the guy is more concerned with his poxy image that carrying out the job."

"As I recall, Mike, you have always maintained that he 'gets off ', as it were, by employing the little Caesar routine.. It wouldn't surprise me one bit if the creep has it in his mind to contact you tonight." The attributes deriving from ESP (extra sensitive perception), is recognised as containing no guide lines. So, therefore, any likely outcome arising from the adage 'be mindful of what you might wish for, just might come true', appeared to be in the ascendancy that same evening as Eastern endeavoured to relax for a while.

"Mike! are you going to answer that or not?" an impatient Joan pleaded.

"Say what?"

"Your mobile, can't you hear it? or maybe you just don't want to." His initial thoughts were reserved for Rogon, familiar as he was with the latter's habitual bad timing. Stirring himself, he tentatively reached out for the 'nuisance' and eyeballed the screen. Instantly his body jerked upright spasmodically, as the caller's name came home to roost. Instinctively, he averted his gaze toward Joan, who was looking on with terminal interest. "You don't have to explain anything, Mike," she stated calmly, "It's Brezznov.... isn't it?" Nodding briskly, Eastern concurred and gave his nemesis a green light with a stage thrown in.

"Is that you Alex?" Brezznov could be heard to inquire sharply.

"Speaking Victor." Came back the reply. "Glad you made contact at last. I could use some serious motivation right now. What have you got lined up for me? Or maybe I shouldn't ask."

"On the contrary my friend. Although your patience is only secondary to what is now in place. And what I have to offer you as promised. In a few hours from now Alex, the world's financial system will have been unconditionally raped of it's power to function in terms of rigid legitimacy."

"Shit! what planet is this guy on?" The moment of truth had finally come home to roost. Dealing with the velocity of it was something else. "A 'heist' is a heist' is a heist', but this?" Brezznov's prophecy ranked incomprehensible in terms of arrogance, leaving Eastern to question the man's sanity. Divided to the extreme, he was found himself locked in to Brezznov's commitment.

"I am now in a position to level with you, Alex. At the same time, confident that I can count on your input and approval." Just for once, Eastern found himself floundering as the impact of the call took a stranglehold on his senses. He could now be found nodding in robot fashion to an audience of one, while his dry throat took a vacation.

"Alex! Are you still there? Queried Brezznov. Pulling himself together, he retained his cool and pursued their conversation in a business-like manner.

"Yeah. Just getting my head around it. I gotta tell you, that's one hell of a call, Victor. Saying that, I wouldn't want to be a long term investor when you pull it off." What then resembled a primeval laugh saddled to ongoing success, could be heard as his nemesis continued to self-tighten his power-mad grip to consecrate quote.....'A fraud to surpass all frauds.' Eastern was forced to listen as he took pains to mock selected aspects of authority encased by doctrine within the operation. Ten, or so, tension-fuelled minutes later, Eastern finally locked his mobile and slumped back into the refuge of his chair. His immediate reaction entailed pouring himself a large whisky with no conditions as to it's quantity.

First you see it, and then you don't, applied, as a copious measure sought his gut. It was then left to Joan to ease him back to reality. "So, where do you go from here, Mike? I presume that was the call you were dependent on?" She was keen to know. In spite of his Scotch content, he was still partially at odds with what had transpired, and took his time before replying.

"Shit! I still can't believe it; It's actually on at last the 'heist', I mean."

"Am I allowed to know when?" Joan asked sheepishly.

"Yeah! Every damned right but, would you believe, in three or four hours from now?"

"I presume that you will inform Rogon shortly, knowing what you now know?"

"I wouldn't hold your breath, Joan. Knowing Brezznov's past commitments, I've got more chance of getting any kosher SP from out of a Xmas cracker." What had evolved in the time it takes to make a phone call, had now reduced the force of 'karma' into feeling nothing short of a stroll around a cup of tea! Not that he was decrying the situation confronting him, or indeed the time gap left in which to savour the moment. Months of strategic planning had now culminated into such a short space of time, leaving Eastern facing a full reality check as he consulted his watch.

"According to Brezznov, I've got an hour to get myself organized before the 'meet' at his flat in Hove. The time now is just approaching eight-o'-clock, so I'd............."

"........what! As apposed to Ruby's cottage? The meeting, I mean?" Joan interjected.

"Good thinking. That's certainly a valid point, Joan, although Rogon and I agreed that once 'B' became aware that Brezznov was on the move, he would have to back off. The last thing we need at this juncture is to allow the agency to screw up. There's far too much at risk."

"God! So, basically, you're out there on your own darling?" she demanded. "That's typical bloody Spooks legislation. Next time Rogon has a birthday, remind me to send him a damned condolence card." At least her dry sarcasm broke the tension.

"Good try, darling. Unfortunately, it would be money wasted on his plastic humour. Now, I really must get myself organized. In the meantime, can you order me a cab, please, for, say, eight-forty-five destination Wilbury Road Hove. Dealing with Rogon would be his next prime move, via a 'code red' initiative, to refresh his contact details aligned to progress and his own personal safety. At no time would Rogon contact him as pre-arranged, in the event it could blow his cover.

Some ten minutes later and hyping on apprehension, Eastern paid-off the cabbie off and entered the block of flats, sometime residence of career criminal one Victor Brezznov. The exclusive aura which the latter personified, was still in situ, Eastern noted from the moment he put his foot in the door. Thereby giving the impression that he'd never really been away. In a matter of seconds, he felt consumed by a dark, almost threatening, atmosphere which carried it's own health warning. Brezznov then pulled him back from the brink with an offer he couldn't refuse. "Whisky? If my memory serves me correctly, Alex. I have a bottle specially blended to mark the occasion. Personally, I don't touch the stuff myself." Their brief and unproductive greeting then ground to a halt as the internal intercom made itself heard. Moments later, Cyber mechanic, Aubrey Thorpe Millington, closely followed by gopher Tommy Brandon, made their way into the lounge. Millington, he observed, was in possession of a laptop.

"That's going to take a good hiding later on tonight," he mused, and decided to put himself about. Securing his glass while hiding behind a screen of double identity, he made his way towards them. For Eastern, the moment became totally surreal as they acknowledged his presence. Brandon making more impact than his companion by attempting to draw Eastern into conversation.

"Well, all 'firmed up' and nowhere to go," ventured Brandon. "What do you suppose is on the cards tonight then?" Shrugging his shoulders, Eastern discounted his offer for small talk in exchange for a session of what he would class as 'verbal diarrhoea'. And to make matters worse, issuing from the mouth of a 'bent' copper. Fortunately, Brezznov stepped in to bale him out as he clamoured for attention.

"Gentlemen, please. Listen up. You're obviously all wondering why I've summoned you here tonight? To put it mildly, we are going to rob a bank....so what's so special about that, you may ask? Well, now is the time to learn. The 'gaff' we are going to 'hit' is reputed to be the largest Banking Corporation outlet in the City. For want of further interest, Eastern's eyes focused on Millington as Brezznov delivered his coup de grace. Something instinctively told him that the man, in some form or another, had sampled previous connections to the bank in question. His thoughts were then rapidly lost in transit as Brezznov continued to hold centre stage.

"This operation has been a long time coming into existence, and for that reason alone I promise you will not fail. For my part, it's fucking personal. For you it will be a guaranteed payout that follows. But be warned gentlemen, do not compromise the planning and the time that I have invested in this 'heist'. Remember this. Reward is payable and transgression is only payable by death!" With the rules of play now firmly instigated, he went on to outline specific details, that up until now, had remained privy only to himself. Taking a step back, Eastern's sub-conscious suddenly kicked in. "I'd give anything to know what Rogon would make of all this, especially if he was a fly on the wall. At worst, our next conversation will give him something to dwell on, and.........," he stopped short in order to stifle a dormant chuckle before continuing, "who knows? It might even put a smile on his face." Any ongoing thoughts on that conception were allayed as Brezznov began to wind down.

"In twenty minutes time, gentlemen, we will be heading for London, so I suggest you top up your glasses now." Breaking off, he threw a set of car keys at Brandon, swiftly followed by a verbal nail in the coffin. "That is, except you, of course, Tommy. We wouldn't want any grief from the 'Old Bill', would we? Oh, one other thing I failed to mention....mobiles!"

Eastern gave a start, "Where the hell is he going with this one?" He was left pondering. And was swiftly left to find out, much to his utter frustration.

"As from now, all mobiles will be deactivated and left here until we return. This is merely a temporary security blanket measure, to counteract the highly sensitive atmosphere we will be working under."

"Total bollocks!" Immediately came to mind as Brezznov continued to exploit a one-man attack. "I'm willing to bet he's already got that aspect covered. This is all about bleedin' trust with him., he questioned. And reminded himself that under the circumstances, Rogon would now have to settle for a belated early morning 'code red', long after the 'heist was accomplished. Shortly within the hour, Gatwick IA just became another earth-bound satellite in their wake, as they sped past on the M23.

Within the confine of the Jaguar, a disgruntled Brezznov was still calling the tune. "For Christ's sake, do something with that poxy radio will you!? Fucking music. Find me something with a bit of class, Tommy. I need to relax." An hour later, with the distinctive sounds of Bizet and Wagner still lodged in his brain, the 'heist; became a reality. Eastern, alongside the other three members of the 'firm', entered the premises, completely unchallenged.

Belonging to the European headquarters of Hong Kong's Hirito Mitzitomo Banking Corporation, situated in central London. The time was now logged at approximately ten forty five. All existing internal CCTV cameras had earlier been doctored, and rendered useless by the same person responsible for the 'firms' illicit entry. That same person had also installed specialist key-logging software onto a whole range of Mitzitomo's PC's, some three weeks previous. The planted discs, in turn, would now prove compatible by enabling them to record strategic passwords. And, use account details of the banks customers, thus enabling them to complete the 'sting' (fraud).

Brezznov now dominated as Millington was given the nod to set the 'heist' in motion. Demoted to a spectator, Eastern could only look on and watch in awe as Millington went to work. Firstly, by entering the website of SWIFT, a highlighted reference to the (Society for Worldwide Interbank Financial Telecommunications) used in excess by some 6-8,000 organizations to transfer cash around the globe. By utilizing the relevant stolen passwords, Millington was now in a position to access the accounts, of four Chinese management company's. Plus various other major banking facilities.

These accounts, in turn, would be systematically raped of their money, and then allocated to banks of Brezznov's choice. Furthermore, bogus accounts and companies were installed purporting to trade in any commodity from steel to textiles. Heavily engrossed as he was by Millington's performance, Eastern had failed to notice Brezznov sidling up beside him. The cocky air that he exalted, complimented a well- rehearsed appraisal in terms of performance. "Education, isn't it, Alex? Unlike the old days when you needed a 'shooter' (pistol) to do the talking for you. As for the amounts of money involved here, we are not talking 'grand's' here, my friend, but millions of pounds. And that's without having to break into a sweat. Tomorrow morning, the financial world, as we know it, will be on it's knees. In the meantime, watch and learn."

Reluctantly, Eastern now found himself having to accede to Brezznov's take on Cyber crime, as Millington continued to exploit the fraud, simply by putting into place further transactions in France, India, Singapore and Israel. As a starting point, £13 million could be found earmarked for an account in Mumbai, followed by the sum of £25 million allocated for banks in Italy. £63 million is then made transferable to designated accounts in America, while a further £12 million to a pharmaceutical company in Sweden. In all, a total sum of some £231 million is put into place.

Finally, Millington checked the relevant transaction forms and gave Brezznov the overriding satisfaction of pressing the appropriate 'send' tab.

Seconds later, he glanced up from the monitor screen. The expression on his face morphed into one of pure evil, laced with overwhelming triumph, as he spoke. "Gentlemen, as I predicted earlier, that by working as a 'firm' we have successfully committed the biggest 'heist' in British banking history." Five minutes later, their night's work completed, the four men, Eastern included, exited the banking facility as quietly as they had entered, having amassed a monetory fortune on paper, without having extracted a single coin of the realm per se.

CHAPTER 13
WIN SOME, LOSE SOME

The unforgettable trip to London and the anti climax of the return journey now seemed light years away. But the explicit memory of the 'heist', now barely 24 hours old, freely monopolized Eastern's thoughts to saturation point. As expected, it was finally left to Rogon to take the brunt of his verbal indulgence as they conspired together, bent on seeking out any positives from a situation, which was looking about as rare as an Icelandic four leaf clover! "Do you realize, Mike, you haven't stopped talking for nearly an hour, and yet you're telling me that the 'heist' itself only took barely thirty minutes?"

Eastern remained unrepentant while on a verbal role, and wasn't about to stall. "Without repeating myself, I just can't believe it was that easy for Brezznov to carry it out, especially when you consider the amount of money that was involved. Frankly, he made climbing Everest look like a walk in the bleedin' park!" Screwing up his eyes in obvious anger, Rogon made a feeble attempt to hide behind them before replying.

"Without question, Mike, the buck stops with me, I'll be the first to hold my hands up on this one. Wrongly or rightly, the agency gravely underestimated the man's capabilities and, as such, I take full responsibility for the outcome." Eastern readily dismissed Rogon's voluntary sentiments with a wave of his hand, and focused on another line of thought.

"Do you know what really gets to me from my angle?"

"Go on."

"The irony of it all."

"In what regard?"

"The fact that I was there, witnessing the whole fucking charade, yet powerless to do anything about it."

"Don't beat yourself up over it, Mike, you were only acting out your brief, remember."

"That's as maybe, but you're missing the point. What sticks in my craw is the fact that he's manipulated the bloody system by milking it of millions of pounds. And the actual money he'd purloined hadn't even been registered as stolen. To make matters worse, he was in a position to exit the bank without taking a damned penny of the with him! I mean, how bloody galling is that?"

"I can only say, Mike, that by Brezznov removing your mobile from out of the equation at the eleventh hour, it made the 'heist' possible."

"Maybe who knows? One thing is certain, even if you decide to pull Brezznov in at this stage on 'suss' (suspicion), the best you could press for would be illegal entry and stalking a fucking computer!"

"Believe me, Mike, when I say I'm living your frustration, but we're still only talking early days as yet. And, as you once reminded me, 'It's not how you start but how you finish that counts'." At worst, it would have been one positive to extract from their meeting, and an added plus of further action to come over the next forty eight hours when, 'the shit begins to hit the fan at the Mitzitomo bank'. As an alternative reminder quoted by Eastern. The fact that he had been present at the 'heist' itself, had given him the full rights to prophesy what was about to happen.

Any attempt at proving Eastern wrong, would have been classed as a disaster, especially when seeking a title for the total mayhem that bank officials now found themselves knee-deep in, on the Monday morning post 'heist'. Blank monitor screens could be seen to be prominent everywhere. And network cables either severed or misplaced. Without question, Millington, as 'key master,' had undoubtedly earned his night's money by doing the business to full effect. On his reckoning alone, he had estimated that the utter chaos he had incurred, would take approximately between two-to-three hours to reorganize the system back to it's full potential. In which time the two hundred and thirty one million pounds he had procured would now be sitting in pre-allotted banks, ready to be milked off into smaller sums and subsequently placed into secondary accounts.

The monies would then be ripe for being 'laundered' at Brezznov's convenience. Shortly after one-o'-clock that same day, the IT staff had managed to regain a form of control of the system. From then on, their screens were literally blitzed with incoming messages. One in particular came via SWIFT referring to the £231 million. 'We have reason to believe that a coding error has occurred, please clarify" and went on to state, 'Could HIRITO MITZITOMO confirm that earlier transactions carried out were officially authorized?'

Elsewhere, in a rented and secluded private residence somewhere in Surrey, officially authorized?"

Elsewhere, in a rented and secluded bolthole somewhere in Surrey, Brezznov could be found 'lording it up' in his elected guise as self-styled 'public enemy number one'. Although, even money, it seems, can't buy perfection. What he hadn't reckoned on to gate-crash his party, would be the intimidation stemming from human error emerging from his own ranks. Unbeknownst to Brezznov at the time, whilst the 'heist' was in progress. Millington, in his egotistical quest for glory, had inadvertently made a trivial, but hugely significant faux pas, in terms of success, when dealing with a particular and crucial IT programme, his drastic actions, in turn, would now have far- reaching consequences attached to Brezznov's game plan. The overall effect being, the monies which they so desperately sought after, still remained intact in the accounts of the MITZITOMO'S investors.

In no time at all, the bank made a clear-cut decision to contact SOCA (Britain's serious organized crime squad) who, in turn, and by arrangement, confided in Rogon at Spooks HQ the following morning. Subsequently, they then detailed agent 'B', accompanied by various other operatives, along with Eastern, to convene at MITZITOMO'S for a thorough investigation. This, in turn, was fronted by the latter who lost no time in getting back to basics.

"Firstly, I suggest that we examine the CCTV footage available to us, Benny, especially the coverage that takes in the whole weekend, It might produce something of interest."

"That won't be a five-minute job, Mike. You're looking at upwards of fifty hours or more to sift through. Presuming it's available of course, and that's only internally."

Eastern wasn't about to take any prisoners in knowing that the following few days may or may not offer up any fresh evidence.

"Nobody suggested that it was going to be easy, Benny, but then again, Brezznov isn't your usual run-of-the mill villain either. I feel sure that there's more to this 'heist' in spite of what I know already."

"I'll take your word for that, Mike. All I need to be aware of, is where you're coming from."

"Faces! in a word. The unknown conspirators lurking in the background, know what I mean? Take the in-house security guard for instance, or whoever it was that sanctioned the necessary access on the night of the 'heist'. To my reckoning, he's only one amongst many that we need to bring down, if wer'e going to crack this case in it's entirety."

"Huh, no pressure there then," replied Simmons in a jocular fashion. "By the way, what do we know of Brezznov's movements since you last had contact with him?"

"We don't! in a word," an exasperated Eastern countered regretfully, "as far as the agency is concerned, he's gone completely off the radar since the 'heist'. In fact, I'm still waiting for a call from him myself for further direction. What we do know from our resources, is that his apartment in Hove has been vacated per se. Plus, there's been no movement at Ruby's cottage either. Putting it mildly, the assole has done everybody up like a kipper, and......" He left off abruptly as a hidden scenario then invaded his thoughts. "Call me stupid if you like, but I'm beginning to wonder if Brezznov knows more about me than I give him credit for."

Outwardly, an astonished Simmons appeared to be fazed by Eastern's sudden revelation. "Surely you're not suggesting that he's known all about your true identity all along...I mean, what could he hope to gain from it? No, I just don't buy it, Mike."

"I fully respect your views, Benny, but then answer me this. What would fulfil Brezznov's status more than money, and even power, come to that? Well, I'll tell you.

It's all quite simple really, when you work it out. To me, the guy, to my mind, is totally motivated into bolstering his own precious fucking ego...full stop! By sucking me in to the 'heist', he figured I was easy prey to nurture along as a guest on his egotistic bandwagon. Think about it, In a sense he's created a double whammy. Not only has he pulled off the impossible, but he's also fucked the establishment."

"Okay, so just for the moment, let's assume that you're right, Mike. It still begs the question you need to ask yourself. How the hell did he manage to find out that you were indeed a Government plant. And even more so...when!?" There comes a time for uncertainty, and then there's just being plain open-minded realism. Eastern rode with the latter like a fish to water in reply.

"How much time have we got, Benny?" he requested, knowing full well that it was a loaded question. Given a platform to work on, he went about explaining that he'd had his suspicions for some time. 'In that my role in the 'heist' had been a calculated 'set up' from day one. And manufactured by person or persons unknown, either by monetory arrangement or had his suspicions for some time. 'In that my role in the 'heist' had been a calculated set-up from day one, and manufactured by person or persons unknown, either by monetory arrangement or a form of conspiracy. I'm also fully convinced that it's origin stemmed from the time that I spent 'banged up' in Foredown, whilst endeavouring to get Brezznov on side."

This latest outburst had now left Simmons struggling with a consequential situation, knowing that his own input in the case could now be in jeopardy. "You certainly kept that bloody quiet for long enough, Mike. I'm beginning to think that my own cover has been blown apart. I just wish you had mentioned it beforehand." There was no doubting that Simmons, as a result of this latest information, now felt slightly vulnerable. And insisted on knowing the full extent of what relevant SP Eastern could be holding back. "You damned well owe me, Mike. Wer'e supposed to be in this shit together. So if you're in a position to implicate certain people and by that, I mean names then you had better come across with something a bit special. Like yourself, I intend to see this crock of shit through to the end." And added, "Not only that, Brezznov needs to know who he's damned well messing with..... right?"

The habitual grin that he had now provoked from Eastern's face, sanctioned any negative doubts that Simmons might have held regarding their joint relationship. He listened intently as Eastern opened up. "In that case, 'B', cast your mind back to Foredown and think Donavon. What comes to mind?"

"The closest thing to hell on legs will do for a start, although I could improve on that," retaliated Simmons, and continued his one-man assassination, "that man was one mean bastard as I recall. In fact, he always got what he wanted one way or the other....yeah, as 'screws' go he was one lousy assole to mess with." Smiling was beginning to become an epidemic as Eastern nodded his approval.

"I have to say, Benny, that's a far better reference than I would have given him, but seriously, to my mind he is the crux of the matter. I strongly suspect that he overheard a conversation between Rogon and Governor Whiting regarding our covert internment. Then, armed with that crucial knowledge and the chance to get his 'holiday money'........"

"...............he then approached Brezznov with his nest egg at the first opportunity, and the rest, as they say, is poxy grief on grief!" he interrupted. "On reflection," concluded Eastern, "when you stop to analyse it, it all begins to make sense now as to why the late Steadman was taken out the equation. It's bloody obvious to me now that the man knew more of what was going down, than what he was accredited for."

"And, as result, the poor bastard paid for that with his life," echoed Simmons. A sustained silence ensued as they both drew on the past facts, leaving simmons to ask the sixty four dollar question. "So , with that in mind, where the hell do we go from here? And, more importantly, what would you advise as to our approach, based on the fact that Brezznov owes you a strategic call?" Briefly, he allowed a renegade hint of doubt to surface before adding, "assuming, of course, that you've read the current situation right?" Beyond that, any door that might have been left open to pursue further uncertainty to creep in, had now been slammed shut as far as Eastern was concerned. Indeed, his present thoughts were now jumping and clearing three hurdles in front of the game.

"I've never been so sure of anything in my life as I feel right now, Benny. I'm convinced that there won't be any call in the immediate future, if at all. I can promise you that much. Brezznov, to my mind, has achieved what he set out to do, which includes 'fitting' me up. The writing was on the wall from the moment I handed my mobile over prior to the 'heist', but that's another story so I don't intend dwelling on that. As far as luck goes, and God knows we can use some. That much, I suspect, rests with the CCTV cameras."

They say, and I quote...'there's luck and there's bad luck'. Unfortunately, the latter of the two could be found at a premium. After sifting meticulously through hours of footage, most of which had been obscured intentionally or completely blocked out, had left their exhaustive attempts to unravel any evidence, with nothing to show for it. Consoling the team didn't come easily, and led Eastern to remind them that the external footage had yet to be examined.

From the moment that they started their investigation, it became abundantly clear that certain cameras, for want of a reason, hadn't been tampered with. After extensive scrutiny, one in particular actually highlighted the breakthrough that Eastern and the team had craved for. It was then left to a jubilant Simmons to break the news to Eastern, at his newly rented 'safe-house' a stone's throw away from the bank. "Mike? Yeah, you probably guessed. Listen, I'll make it short. You need to get your arse over to the bank a bit lively, but what I can tell you now is that it's all good news." He then hung up. Twenty or so minutes later, the pair could be found examining screen 'stills' depicting Brezznov, accompanied by Millington and Brandon, with yours truly taking up the rear. "Now this is the all-important one, Mike," stressed Simmons. "I want you to focus in on the security guard who's giving you access. Does the face mean anything to you?" he urged. Engrossed as he was, Eastern was left in doubt as to the figure's identity.

"Absolutely, without question, Benny. In fact his name came out in conversation one time. The guy is called Peter Carroll and he happens to be the manager in charge of security at MITZITOMO. Tell me if I'm wrong, but haven't we already had the man in for questioning? Prior to him going missing that is." Simmons acknowledged his interest with an enthusiastic nod.

"Yeah. Bang in order, and then for some unknown reason he gave himself up. And do you know what? The wanker promptly denied all knowledge that he was on the premises during the night of the 'heist'. The only other SP we have on him is purely basic. Apparently he's aged 41, married, and had been employed at the bank for three or four months. Incidentally," he added, "Carroll's references, when examined, all held water, would you believe?" Taking nothing for granted and bearing in mind the severity of the case, Carroll was brought back in for questioning once again. When confronted with the explicit external video evidence, he quickly reneged on his original statement by stating.

"While under extreme pressure I found myself forced into a powerless situation from two 'faces', who made it quite clear that my wife would be hospitalised, or worse, if I didn't co-operate with them. And if I still refused to take their threat seriously I would be missing my knee caps." End of statement.

Shortly after that, a member of the investigation squad came across another internal camera that had somehow been overlooked. As luck would have it, the footage it contained was found to be intact, and showed Carroll, along with Brandon and Brezznov, looking on as Millington worked on the keyboards. Insistent to the end,

Carroll still refused to ID the 'firm' at work, when challenged. But finally relented under extreme pressure by stating, 'I think that one of the gang might have been French or Belgian.' He then refused to answer any more questions. Digging even deeper, the team discovered that Carroll's telephone records revealed that he had made a number of calls to Belgium. Investigating the alleged calls, they were told, could take some time to verify their content. So it was left to Rogon who decided, there and then, to contact INTERPOL with the exhibit video, in the event that Carroll's alleged 'foreigner' might show up on their records.

The result, when it came back, proved to be invaluable in terms of enabling them to construct a profile consistent with the agency's case. Heading INTERPOLS findings also included a dossier relating to Millington which, amongst other things, gave his age as being thirty four, last known address, (in Paris), and claiming to be a respectable business man at that particular time. This evidence was later upturned by an update on their data base, showing that he was wanted in connection with fraud and handling fake ID documents. Beside Millington, a dated file included a reference to Brezznov's involvement, when dealing in black market diamonds, besides three conspiracy-to-murder charges. All of which were alleged to have been carried out in Holland. The file itself, was dated as being some six months prior to him being sent down for his role in the Hatton Garden diamond murder.

Now, seated around a table at Spooks HQ, Eastern and Simmons had been summoned to air their views, thus far, in conjunction with Rogon's own enquiries. Meanwhile, prominent banking institutions around the world, held their breath in anticipation alluding to a monetory tsunami flooding their accounts. Head bowed and deep in thought, Eastern dismissed Rogon's invite for a drink, for the second time in as many minutes, with a controlled shake of his head. He recalled having had bad encounters with the Government issue coffee on previous occasions.

As an outsider looking in, it would be fair to say that he was portraying a man suffering from collateral damage, mainly due to extreme frustration bordering on a non-negotiable impasse, regarding factual progress to the case.

"Mike!" Recalling his own name didn't present am immediate problem, knowing what galaxy it stemmed from. It concerned another matter. "Mike! Wake up man,"

Once again his name rang true. Only this time with added conviction attached, allowing his inquisitor to gain entry into his sub-conscious thoughts. Momentarily startled, Eastern glance upward in realizing that there was no escapism from reality. "Shit! I'm sorry guys, I was somewhere else for a minute." For his sake, it was left to Rogon to bring him back down to earth.

"If I didn't know you any better, Mike, I'd have to confess that you're letting our man Brezznov take you over." In the end, he could have saved his breath as Eastern responded.

"In a sense you're completely right, Rogon. Right now, he's so bleedin' close to me I can almost reach out and touch the bastard. And the irony of it all, is that he could well be a thousand miles away for all we know, seated around a swimming pool and giving it large." As a committed spectator, his views hadn't gone without notice, leaving Simmons to eagerly express his own singular views.

"I hear what you say, Mike, but rest assured that every commercial airport in the country in on red alert as we speak. Trust me when I say that Brezznov is going nowhere!" Eastern gave out a token sigh of relief, but struggled to hide a lining of conjecture in his reply.

"That's one consolation, Benny, although, knowing how he operates, I suggest that we check out private air strips as well. Remember, Brezznov has got a licence to print money at any given time, which gives him carte blanch to every availability open to him" Retaining his air of positivism, Rogon blissfully reminded the pair that the present state of play wasn't all one-way traffic, and dwelt on the agency's attributes to date.

"Whatever happens, we mustn't lose sight of the fact that we can place the 'firm' entering and actually carrying out the 'heist' in the bank. Coupled, of course, with a threatening to cause GBH' charge where the security guard is concerned. And that is without a few other offences I could name."

Let's not forget the Stowlowski murder, of course," Eastern hastened to add. "Which reminds me. Is there any connection between the victim and Carroll. Apart from the fact they were both employees. I'm thinking along the lines of co-conspirator here, or maybe I'm just clutching at straws."

"I think that's wishful thinking, Mike, although Carroll certainly knows more than we give him credit for. With that in mind. I think we need to broaden our investigation into the case, as far as that is concerned. Incidentally, the Rotherhithe MIU haven't unearthed anything that's workable as yet. To my mind, I honestly feel that Brandon holds the key to the solution when searching for a murder-related link to Brezznov. Let's see if we can't get a trace on him...last known address...drinking habits...clubs pubs etc, even it means punting a 'mugshot' (photo) around. Somebody out there must know of him, and not necessarily for all the right reasons. They would be only to pleased to shop him. You can bet he's 'stitched up' enough underworld 'faces' in the past, being as he's an ex 'bent' cop. I'm rather hoping that this in turn, could well mean that those other two 'gorillas' (villains) I saw him doing business with in the pub that night, might, just find themselves a victim of circumstances by entering the equation."

Shortly after the meeting, while participating in a kosher cup of coffee of his own making, Eastern made the decision to forego his 'safe house' electing, instead, to return to Hove. And the chance of a relaxing break for a couple of days, allowing the case to materialize, or not. Or, at least, that was the idea. On reflection he should have known better, and to have realized that the perpetual chain of office slung around his neck, was also attached to Rogon, who, for his part, had no intention of severing the link which, in this case, stretched all the way to the M23 at Godstone in Surrey, via his mobile.

"You can go to hell!" seemed an appropriate answer at short notice, as Eastern identified the origin of the call. He ended by stating, "even a bleeden' Spook needs time out." Booting the accelerator, he cruised into the fast lane, intent on heading for Brighton.

CHAPTER 14
YOU'RE NICKED!

"Depending on how important the call was, you have to say the man's got a damned nerve, Mike. Just because he's married to Whitehall, he must assume that we enjoy a prehistoric-style relationship. Personally, I wouldn't rush to call him back." An indignant Joan was voicing her opinion in no uncertain terms at Rogon's latest impromptu call , in spite of him being in possession of the facts regarding Eastern's uncharacteristic arrangements.

"I wouldn't stress yourself out on that score darling. I don't intend to." He paused to reflect on a sudden notion. "Do you know what, Joan?" The expression on her face belied the content in her reply.

"Before I answer that, Mike, I'm beginning to get this feeling that we have had this type of conversation before." Joan replied suspiciously.

"I realize it might sound crazy, but in a strange way I actually feel sorry for the guy in a funny sort of way. Sometimes, I honestly think that all he wants is somebody to talk to, know what I mean?" His implication somehow got lost in translation as Joan summed up.

"Oh! And here's little old me thinking he's been having an affair with a computer all these months, what do I know?" joked

Joan. Little could she have known at the time, just how much her insensitive observation had a ring of truth attached to it. If she had stated 'fax machine' in lieu of 'computer', she would have been right all along, in a literal sense that is. What she couldn't have known, was that since Eastern's absence from HQ now reaching some forty-eight hours ago, Rogon's only source of comfort could be found to be lavished on a fax machine. Report after report had eked it's way through, each singular one revealing nothing of consequence relating to the 'heist'.

Then things became interesting, as a fax, sent directly from a leading Singapore bank, stated that two men armed with a faxed letter of authority on MITZITOMO'S stationary, requested that the sum of eleven million pounds to be transferred from the account of a specific steel company to an account at another bank. Immediately, bank officials became suspicious of the deal involved, due to the amount of money that was involved. On investigation, the said money requested for the transfer, didn't appear to exist in the alleged steel company's account. Rogon's next move involved him collating information stemming from the fax sent to Singapore. On scrutiny, it transpired that the source of the document originated from copier printers outlet based in Eastleigh Hampshire. It was also revealed that the recipient of the fax at the time of presentation, came via two men. Armed with the information at hand. Rogon instructed Simmons to liaise with the local 'plod' at the copier shop, in an attempt to discover if any of the staff were in a position to possibly ID the perpetrators from selected 'mugshots'.

From that moment on, fortune shone on Simmons side in the form of a young sales assistant. The youth was adamant in his choice of selection; that two photo's in particular matched the two former customers, associated with the alleged ownership and presentation of the fax. In no time at all, Simmons swiftly verified them as belonging to Aubrey Thorpe Millington and his side-kick, Tommy Brandon. Rogon, it would seem, was now on a roll. His bizarre love affair with his fax machine had now soared to new heights. Banking facilities from around the world having contacted SWIFT, could now be found seeking urgent advice from

SOCA, as a knock-on effect came into force from the 'heist'.

Subsequently, Rogon became inundated with documents laden with SP. One account that could not be ignored was found to be lodged with the BANCO SAN PEDESTA in Spain It came as no surprise to him, to find that the sum of twenty-six million pounds, had been allocated for transfer from the MITZITOMO Corporation to Spain. Thereafter, placed in an investment account with a company listed under the name of GLOBAL Associates inc. The initial investment itself, could also be utilized for various other financial deposits. The idea being, that the monies lying in situ, could then be milked-off at stages, and from then on, placed into other selected lucrative deposit accounts.

Other details which came to light, included the fact that one of GLOBAL Associates directors, was a man calling himself Reginald Stockfield. The latter's name also cropped up on various other major accounts, benefiting from MITZITOMO. Stockfield himself, SOCA went on, although unknown to them at this juncture, was obviously a key player in the fraud. As a result, SOCA consequently advocated a full-blown investigation into the man's background. Bogged down with solid information, but jubilant with the present situation, in knowing that Spooks had at last secured a springboard in which to work on, Rogon detailed Simmon's to collect Eastern from Hove and return to HQ, where he could bring him up to speed on the fresh reports now circulating regarding the 'heist'.

Needless to say, their journey back to HQ proved to be an eventful one, as Simmon's summed up his personal take on the matter in hand. "It would take far too long to explain the current situation, Mike, but you can take it from me there isn't a pit deep enough to contain the shit that's flying out of this proverbial fan! As things stand, and bearing in mind the logistics involved, I still reckon that wer'e only looking at the tip of the iceberg. You can rest assured that, without question, Brezznov has achieved what he set out to do, and," he hesitated, "that's without knowing the full extent of what is going down. Even SOCA are having to draft in extra operatives to try and contain the monetary chaos."

From his own standpoint, Eastern now found himself reeling

from the effects alluding to a verbal hammering, although a fully justified and inevitable one. Once back at HQ, it was left to Rogon to take the brunt of his pent-up misgivings. "Frankly, the situation is becoming worse by the bloody minute. God! What an unholy mess we've got to contend with, and here's me thinking I don't want to be the guy who says "I told you so."

"I think we all get your point, Mike, and I'm forced to agree that, on reflection, different steps could have been taken to eradicate the disaster that Brezznov has landed us with." A wistful smile captured Simmon's face, as a hidden thought emerged.

"No prizes for guessing what that could have been, then?" he reflected, as an image of himself pulling a trigger of convenience flashed to mind. Meanwhile, Eastern could be found wrestling with the idea of putting together a revised game plan. In the space of a short time, a lot of water had gone under the bridge. Stemming the flow was going to take a lot of thought. "Like it or not, I suggest that we get back to good old- fashioned policing, rather than hang about waiting for something to happen."

Just for the record, and I'm talking earlier on now, you did stipulate Stockfield didn't you? demanded Eastern, and came across as being overbearing in his approach, almost enticing words into Rogon's mouth, as his attitude took Rogon completely by surprise.

"Steady on, Mike, it's only one name listed amongst others. Besides which, from what little we know about the man, we would be hard-pressed to fill the back of a postage stamp." For reasons that he intended to make clear, Eastern felt the need to pursue his enquiry.

"No offence, Rogon, its just that the name itself seems a trifle unusual. And for that reason alone it bothers me; in fact it's not as inclusive as you might imagine."

"Is that merely an assumption, Mike, or do you have a hidden agenda?"

"In answer to your first question, on the contrary, the name seems to have struck a chord somehow. If my memory serves me correctly and I am going back five or six years ago. I happened to be working in conjunction with the Met at the time, on a highly charged drug case concerning the activities of a local 'Baron' (supplier). The guy himself traded in the home counties under the name, would you believe, as one Reginald Stockfield! Then, following a successful 'bust' (raid' at his business address, It soon became evident that certain documents which came to light, clearly indicated the name Stockfield was merely a pseudonym he used, when, in fact, his true passport revealed him as being a S/E business man listed under the name of William Gauntly."

The ghost of a smile that reflected on Rogon's face, almost made him appear to be briefly humanized as he expressed his satisfaction. "Taking everything into account, Mike, you would have to say that your fortuitous expose rates with Karma at it's very best. The sooner we can get a trace on our Mr Stockfield, the better. There shouldn't be too much grief attached when bringing him in. Even if he's back in the UK he's obviously travelling under a false passport, but at least we now know what he looks like."

"Yeah, as if that's only all we had to bloody worry about. The way this case is panning out, it makes you wonder what else Brezznov intends to throw back at us in the wake of this of this Stockfield development? There's 'faces' coming out of the woodwork now that we could never have envisaged. Although this is Brezznov we are dealing with here. And as we all know, he's had a PDH in grief. Period!" Briefly, a pall of silence hung over the proceedings as Rogon and Simmons mentally absorbed the extreme dilemma facing them, as forwarded by Eastern. Not for the first time, it was left to Eastern to claw back a form of positivism in the shape of basic policing. "Of course!" he sounded off, "Why the Hell didn't I think of that before? 'Ruby cottage', it's just occurred to me. Have the local 'plod' carried out a follow-up investigation on the place?" At first glance, Rogon, appeared to be reluctant to answer.

"For what purpose, Mike? I can only assume you mean for detailed forensics? No, I haven't been informed, as yet, of any such undertaking or movement carried out on the property. So what is your line of thought?"

"Right now the bloody obvious comes to mind. I suggest that Benny and myself make our way over there first thing in the morning, with an open mind. On the chance that we might unravel something. In the meantime, I'll get you to contact Division at Crawley and get SOCCO involved, plus some back-up to meet us there. I seriously intend to take the bleeden' place apart."

"That'll be my pleasure, Mike. At least we are in a position to do something constructive," retaliated Simmons, "We seem to be going nowhere fast at present."

"Precisely! And the sooner Brezznov gets to know that he's the bait, the better I'll like it. I'm hoping that our actions will cut down his confidence of freedom down a few degrees. Personally, from my experience of him, I honestly don't think that he's too clever at handling pressure. The minute he feels the heat is on, will be the moment he needs to start looking over his shoulder and........."

"..............that's when he's liable to start making mistakes," echoed Rogon.

Yeah, right. And lets forget that the biggest one, to date, is for him to think that he's got one over me!" From then on, what should have ended the night on a high note, unashamedly disintegrated as Rogon, with a complete lack of consideration, suggested that they wind-up with a Government-issue coffee before leaving. Apparently, he was still struggling to down his first cup, long before Eastern and Simmons both arrived back at their respective digs.

Foremost on Simmons mind the following morning, included the usage of the unadopted lane leading up to Brezznov's bolt hole which, from his point of view, resembled, 'the nearest thing to a bloody assault course'. On arrival, ten or so daunting minutes later, a much relieved Simmons, along with Eastern, parked up.

"We're a little bit earlier than I thought, Benny." Remarked Eastern after consulting his watch. "Although that's not a bad thing. SOCCO won't be around for a while, so while we're waiting I suggest that we take a look around the back of the 'Gaff'."

"Any particular reason why, Mike." Simmons enquired.

"Well, whoever was here previously had obviously decided to pull out in a hurry. I've just had a glimpse through the window and the only thing standing upright is the bleeden' wallpaper!"

"Huh, so why doesn't that surprise me? He's got more to hide than most people. Trashing the place would come as a mere formality to a devious bastard like him.".

"And that's exactly what I'm counting on, Benny. Destroying any incriminating evidence would be a priority to Brezznov. I figure he might have had the use of a fire as a cop-out. Let's go take a look." As hunches go, Eastern's reasoning couldn't be faulted. Within minutes, the remains of what was once an open fire greeted them both. More interestingly enough, it soon became clear that the remnants had more to answer for than they could have envisaged. On close inspection, the half-charred remains of personal stationary along with files littered the surrounding undergrowth. "Presumably blown there by the wind," suggested Eastern, "And to our distinct advantage, I can see SOCCO having a field day sifting through this bleedin' lot, let alone the cottage itself."

The two then lingered long enough to exchange their views with the DS fronting the raid, before heading back to Spooks HQ. "I couldn't see the point in us remaining there any longer." Eastern advised Simmons later, "We're better suited elsewhere. If anything substantial does turn up that will prove to be kosher, then I'm sure the team will do the business." At least their spontaneous trip hadn't been a waste of time, as Eastern later explained to Rogon. "The signs themselves were clearly visible. The way I read it, Brezznov is beginning to panic. You can almost sense the cracks appearing in his manic ego. Nobody with his sense would have left an intended fire, of that importance, burn, without seeing it through to the end.

Right now, my guess is that he's kicking himself for not finishing what he started out to do."

Nodding approvingly in a robotic manner, before replying, gave out the impression that Rogon's mind was undoubtedly lodged elsewhere, "yes." He concurred vaguely, "Sounds to me like that could be costly for him should anything happen to surface." He replied in a matter-of-fact fashion. It immediately occurred to Eastern that Rogon's manufactured reply had started and finished as a throwaway line. Causing him to believe that maybe Rogon was seeking a change in direction. His ready-made intuition wasn't about to let him down as the latter took on a fresh approach.

"Now then listen up. I'm pleased to tell you, gentlemen, that due to a fortuitous report released by the Sussex police HQ, And in conjunction with Brighton Central, less than an hour ago, has of now created a whole new scenario revolving around the ongoing 'heist' enquiries. This latest fax I've received, contains high profile SP, including solid forensic back up, enabling Central to be in a position to obtain and give us a positive ID on the two suspects linked to Tommy Brandon." From A-Z in seconds didn't come easily and Eastern needed to think on his feet.

"The two 'heavies' I witnessed in the pub you mean?" Eastern blurted out.

"Or rather the two that you didn't see, Mike! But yes, you're right, of course," Rogon was quick to add, and continued. "This breakthrough couldn't have come at a better time. There's satisfaction in knowing that there's light at the end of the tunnel at last." By now, Eastern was verging on an in-built confidence-booster.

"Shit! Now that's what you call progress. My day just got better and better. You have to say that is one hell of a coup? So what's the full facts behind it?"

From what I can gather, Mike, it all kicked off less than twenty four hours ago. It seems that the police were called to intervene in a what appeared to be a fracas of some kind, involving two men at a night club in West Street, Brighton. Before the 'plod' arrived, what had started out as an altercation, now spiralled out of control and, in the process, leaving one man seriously wounded as the result of a shooting."

"Strange. I don't recall having read about that in the Stop Press." countered Eastern.

"No, you wouldn't have been in a position to, Mike. Following an intense interrogation of the two assailants, it rapidly became clear that what was emerging meant more to their case than they could have imagined. Consequently, their Press Officer issued an immediate ban on reporting limits and thereafter contacted us."

"Hazard a guess Rogon. I'd be inclined to say that besides SOCCA, Ballistics appear to be the key players here if we're talking results?" Rogon was nothing short of emphatic as he meticulously detailed the report.

"That's an under-statement, Mike. Not only have Forensics proved that the weapon used in the affray was identical to the one used to murder Stowlowski, but a logging scan on a retrieved mobile, revealed listed calls were made to a William Gauntly. And, would you believe, Brezznov himself? The calls themselves, incidentally, were made over a three-month period prior to the Rotherhithe murder."

"Gauntly eh? He's like a bleeden' bad penny the assole. I'd like a two-minute session alone with him in a cell. I'd make him sing like a double-breasted canary." The sweet smell of success that Eastern afforded himself was nothing short of textbook, as once again he plagued Rogon for more details. "Tell me, the two 'gorillas' (Heavies) in custody. What do we know about them at this stage?"

"That's the easy part, Mike. Both individuals were known 'faces' by the police from having substantial 'previous'. In reality, they were both small-time crooks working as a double act, mainly in Protection rackets as collectors. Anything to do with 'muscle'. You know the routine."

"Yeah. You bet I do! And you can now add murder to their portfolio as well. Not only that, if I didn't know any better, you'd have to say that the Crown has got themselves a bloody watertight case even before a hearing." Content as he was to sit back and absorb their conversation, Simmons suddenly felt the urge to digress.

"Hold up a minute the altercation in the club do we know how or why it kicked off?" Rogon lowered him down gently and continued.

"With respect, it's difficult to say, Benny, but the fact that Regan, one of the accused responsible for the shooting, was found to be in possession of a large 'wedge' at the time of his arrest. This leads us to assume that money is the key factor in this case." Simmon's brain was now perspiring on overtime.

"Is there any reason not to think that the 'wedge' could have been a blood settlement for Stowlowski's murder?" Shaking his head vigorously, Rogon put Simmon's mind to rest.

"Categorically none whatsoever." Never sounded better as Rogon continued to compound his own views. "Even though it's only early days yet, the feedback from the MIU at Rotherhithe, combined with certain disclosures from Brighton Central, Leads us, now. to believe that there is a distinct possibility that the origin of the money derived from Brezznov's quarter. In fact, Regan's Defence Counsel are currently proposing a 'super grass' deal for their man as being the best way forward in terms of confirmation."

"Say what!?" exploded Eastern, It was quite plain that Rogon's analysis had left Eastern far from impressed, and eager to voice an opinion himself on a personal level. "Deal! A poxy deal. What bleeden' planet are Counsel on? From where I'm sitting, that assole Regan, and his sidekick, are clearly 'bang to rights'. Full stop! Me! I wouldn't give them the satisfaction of negotiation, given the chance. Beside's, Regan's not even in a position to tell us the whereabouts of Brezznov per se, let alone Millington and Gauntly. No, as far as I'm concerned, we require a shift on emphasis, and by that I mean ploughing our resources into bringing the main contenders down. That, surely, is our prime target.?"

It was finally left to Rogon to rubber-stamp Eastern's philosophy. "As things stand, Mike, and having heard the flip side of the coin, I tend to agree with you. It's fair to say that the 'plod', from their perspective, have got the majority of the groundwork to their case, covered. So until we know any different, I vote we isolate ourselves from the situation and concentrate solely on Brezznov's movements. As a precautionary measure," he went on, "it might pay me to contact certain colleagues of mine based around Europe, on the off-chance that a sighting could become a probability."

On that understanding, their meeting was then dissolved perse.

CHAPTER 15
AN OPEN 'CANVAS'

If any sympathy at the present time happened to be the only outlet available that Eastern could rely on, then his entrusted partner, Joan, would have been the last person to allow him to go on suffering in silence, while, ever cautious, that time, as an aspect, can be unrepentant.

It had now been almost two weeks since his last meeting with Rogon, in which time any reference appertaining to Brezznov, and the likes of Gauntly seemingly appeared to have died a death. And, in the process, leaving Eastern constantly reminding himself of that cessation and, to quote Rogon, 'we need to isolate ourselves from the situation'. In this particular case, the well-established adage 'be mindful of what you wish for', would have served as a grim reminder that the latter is always on hand to come back and haunt you.

Fortunately for Eastern, he was afforded a welcome compromise to his enforced sabbatical, in the form of Joan herself. To her way of thinking, good conversation complimented therapy to the extent that the commitment she endorsed, especially coming from a woman, seemed to carry more weight. "Why beat yourself up over somebody else's problem, Mike?" she was quick to enforce, "You're not the one on the loose. Not only that. No news is good news surely? I strongly suspect that, sooner or later, Brezznov will feel the need to surface, even if it only means that he has to show the world that his over-played ego hasn't been dented as yet."

The valid expression, 'follow that', wouldn't have gone amiss, although it would have taken a good man to overshadow her frankness. Instead, it was left to Eastern to state the obvious. "And here's me thinking that I knew it all, Joan. Next time I'm feeling despondent, I'll exercise some lateral thinking...right?"

Meanwhile, in the West End of London, an imposing and dapper well-dressed figure of a man, could be seen entering a highly renowned international art dealers. An hour or so later, he exited the gallery and drove off in a private hire car, after having purchased four exclusive works at a total cost of £275K. For exclusive reasons, known only to himself, the signature on the credit that he used for the transactions, were clearly visible as being registered to one Reginald Stockfield.

During the hours that followed, three other notable galleries in the surrounding vicinity of Mayfair, were unwittingly subjected to sales misrepresentation as Stockfield continued to flaunt the same credit card. All in all, he had collectively amassed by fraud, the total sum of four hundred and thirty five thousand pounds in illicit purchases and then retreated into obscurity. Shortly after his alleged client Reginald Stockfield had departed the premises, the proprietor of the first art gallery that he had visited, found himself facing an unwanted quandary, attributed to Stockfield's actions when verifying his fraudulent pin number. Without further ado, he decided to share his dilemma with the local police.

It didn't take him too long to realize that you can't choose just whom you want to converse with. Unfortunately, and just to add to his pain, the Desk Sergeant at West End Central was nearing the end of a hectic shift, when the call came through. And his long-suffering patience was about as rare as the proverbial Dodo. "Hello Sgt Drake speaking how can I help?"

"I'm sorry. The receptions not that good. Who did you say you were?" came back the reply. There and then, Drake decided to dump the etiquette and join the club of one.

"You're talking to the police, Sir. What seems to be the problem?"

he demanded in an over-patronising manner. A minute or so after relating his ID details, the gallery owner, Rupert Helligan, as he was known, endeavoured to outline the circumstances that instigated him into placing the call. Having salvaged enough SP to warrant Helligan's problem, the Sgt hastily played his 'get out of goal card'. "Stay right where you are Sir. In the meantime, I'll organize a DC to drop in and interview you say in twenty minutes. Bye now." Slamming his receiver down, he consulted his watch.

Unbeknownst to the Sgt at the time, a certain DI Warring, purely by chance, had found himself party to their conversation, just as he was about to use the security exit button granting him access to the public lobby. In an instant, his digit froze, as did his intentions. Slowly he lowered his hand and averted his attention toward the Sgt. Assuming that a reprimand could be on the cards , Drake then took the initiative. "I'm sorry, Sir if it was about ..." By allowing a brief moment of guilt to creep in the equation, then he had completely misread the situation. Moving swiftly, the DI dismissed the apology out of sight and insisted that they focus on his last phone conversation. "This is more important, Sergeant, so think hard. Do you recall the name Stockfield during your call just now? Or maybe I completely misheard you. In which case, just forget that I asked." Apart from the fact that Sgt Drake was now holding an all-important redemption card, in remembering the content of the call, gave him the impetus to use it to good effect.

"On the contrary, Sir, you heard right the first time. The person behind the call was indeed a Mr Stockfield; a member of the public. He was part and parcel of the report that I was dealing with. In fact, I left it with him that as he'd be shortly getting a visit, I thought it was the best way round it, as he was beginning to get agitated." The Sgt's confirmation that his enquiry was in the same ball-park as his own gut-feeling, now convinced DI Warring that the name Stockfield, coincidental or otherwise, had struck a synonymous chord, alluding to an ongoing enquiry, previously circulated by HQ. This one, in particular, could be found related amongst other interlinked crimes associated with a major international cyber fraud. Without further ado, Warring pursued his hunch.

"In that case Sgt, you'd better give me the log details and

I'll take over from here. I strongly suspect that there's more to your call than meets the eye." Fifteen minutes later, DI Warring, accompanied by plain clothes DC Collins, identified themselves to the gallery owner, Rupert Helligan. "What led you to make the initial call, Sir?" enquired Collins, in a subjective manner.

"Well, it was like I explained to the officer on the phone, there was a considerable amount of money involved in the sale. Not that that's unusual, you understand," he hastened to add, "but to make the point, I do have a reputation in the business for our quality of stock."

"I've no reason to think otherwise, Sir, but I need more than self-appraisal. If it wasn't a money issue that brought us here, then maybe you had better have a re-think. I'm a busy man." As he finished speaking, Collins threw Warring a sideways glance in an effort to relay his own thoughts.

"Another damned goose-chase. I wish he'd get to the bloody point!" he told himself. At this point, Helligan appeared to be intimidated by the look on Collin's face and decided on switching to a fresh approach as a distraction.

"Oh, but it was about money....well, plastic that is, Constable."

"Plastic? Would you mind elaborating on that, Sir. I'm not sure where you're coming from."

"Putting it another way, you would expect that somebody parting with £275K wouldn't have a problem with their pin number... would you now?" Subjected into being a bystander, an impatient Warring decided to pull rank.

"Could you endeavour to be more explicit, Sir? We need to confirm exactly what caused you to be suspicious of your Mr Stockfield in the first place. Helligan acknowledged the request in a positive manner and continued where he'd left off.

"As I was saying, I was first drawn to the fact that he somehow seemed to have a problem remembering his Pin number. As a result, when he finally succeeded in entering it, he apologised and aborted the attempt by stating something like, 'I misplaced the last digit', or words to that effect. I reminded him that he needed to enter 'clear', and start again. As a result, I was able to verify that the new sequence had been validated and that the transaction had indeed gone through. If the truth was known, I felt more out of sync than he was. His actions appeared highly irrational at the time."

"Uhm, I can see now why you contacted us. Your Mr Stockfield's actions appear to be unconventional to say the least," a grim-looking Warring implied.

"So what happens now, Inspector?" Helligan enquired tentatively. It was now Collin's turn to jump the queue, and went for the jugular.

"Tell me, would you recognise the man again, Sir?" he demanded.

"Absolutely!" Helligan expounded. "That, and his arrogant attitude toward art, he wouldn't have known a Picasso from a Constable. No pun intended of course, but all-in-all, a horrible little man to deal with."

"No doubt, Sir, but right now we need you to accompany us back to the station to look at some 'mug shots'......"

"Mug shots!?" interrupted a wary Helligan.

"Nothing to get alarmed about, Sir, criminal profiles to you." Warring assured him, "we're hoping you can assist us in a specific enquiry that we're following."

Twenty minutes later, a disgruntled Helligan found himself ushered into an interview room at West End Central. Putting Helligan at ease, DS Collin's lost no time in producing an album containing listed known felons, as a warm-up process. Having drawn a blank, he then followed that up with his 'no brainer', namely a 'mugshot' of the alleged Reginald Stockfield, and sat back to acknowledge a result. It was never going to happen today or any other day. Helligan simply shook his head and handed back the 'mugshot' without a trace of emotion. "I'm sorry, Sergeant, I can honestly state that I have never seen or met this person before in my life. Why should I have done!?"

No comment would have sufficed as a reply in Collin's case, as he struggled with the outcome. "In which case just forget that I asked, Sir," confirmed Collin's, dryly. Apart from the fact that Sgt Drake was holding the all-important redemption card, consistent with the conversation, gave him the impetus to use it to good effect. What Helligan hadn't bargained for, effectively became a verbal slap in the face. "I must ask you, once again, to take a much closer look at the face, Sir. I can't emphasise the importance of your judgement in knowing what's at stake here." As before, a somewhat confused Helligan turned his attention, albeit a brief glance, to the photo in question. Only this time, oozing confidence when replying.

"In danger of repeating myself, I can categorically state that I have never, at any time, seen this man before....ever!" Rattled as he was, Collin's wasn't about to throw in the towel that easily.

"In that case, Sir, let's move on. Here, I need you to check out another profile for me and see if this does anything for you?" Within seconds of studying what was now on offer, Helligan's body language could have been guilty of an adrenalin boost, superseded by a look swamped with recognition.

"That face...that...that man! He's the one I sold the paintings to at the gallery. I swear to God that's him alright." Collin's immediate reaction was to sit bolt upright and throw an intense look of utter disbelief at DS Warring, who, by now, was looking completely stunned at Helligan's frank omission. The short hiatus that ensued, served as the time allotted for Collin's attempting to find his voice. When he finally got round to it, the name he uttered with deliberation meant nothing to Helligan. But to the other officers present, their reaction was received like 'manna' from heaven.

"Brezznov! Sir. Would you believe he's identified Brezznov?" Some fifteen or so minutes later, shortly after Helligan had departed, DI Warring sent a detailed Fax, to Rogon at Spooks HQ. Being privileged apart, even a fly on the wall wouldn't have had a problem spotting it. But then we are talking a rare occurrence here, except to say that the perpetrator could be found on his own at the time in question. It was long, and it was drawn out, and the event was capped by a rare smile exuding from Rogon's face, no less. Gloating over the Fax for the third time, as he did, still felt good to him and only then did he decide that the time was now ripe to share it's contents.

While ignoring the fact that he himself was a confirmed 24/7 man, as opposed to other people sharing normality, meant little consequence to him. In no time at all, he shelved consideration and hastily contacted Eastern, who, in return, took the full brunt of a verbal onslaught. "For Christ's sake, slow down, Rogon, and start again. I realize what you're saying has to be important, but, frankly, your not making any bleeden' sense....besides which, your flaming timing is way out of line, as usual." Having stated his case, he turned and threw a knowing glance at, Joan, who could be found hovering in the background. Judging by the exchange look on her face, she was now fully aware of the situation.

"I know, you don't have to say anything, Mike." she proffered in a habitual manner. "I'll phone the company and put the cab on hold...okay?" Obliterated by reluctance, Eastern nodded and contemplated on a twenty ounce 'rib eye' steak, swiftly disappearing from sight. And just as quickly he returned to their conversation in hand. Five minutes on and with the gist of the call firmly implanted on his mind, Eastern let Rogon go. Joan was the first to break silence. "Judging by that look on your face, Mike, I suspect that our date is still, hopefully, on. Could it be that Rogon has found himself a woman?"

Her impersonal comment on the latter's much-maligned sexual prowess was a topic too hard to ignore, leaving Eastern, to reply in a facetious manner. "That's a stupid question to ask me, Joan. When was the last time you saw a white traffic light!?" At least, Eastern, managed to catch up on his steak later on that evening. This, in turn, gave him some added time, as a bonus, to reflect on at a later date.

CHAPTER 16
SUPPOSITION & POETIC JUSTICE

From the very moment that he'd woken up that following morning, Eastern, for the first time, felt a real sense of being. This, in turn, enabled the usual mundane trip to HQ seem like a walk in the park, in comparison. Unlike his nemesis, Brezznov, who, in another world, was set squarely on the road to perdition. Dismissing out of sight the offer from Rogon, aligned to a Government-issue coffee on his arrival, would also prove to be invaluable in terms of decision making, during the sensitive hours that followed. Having tasted the starters via a code red call 24 hours earlier, from Rogon himself, Eastern was still hungry to get to grips with certain secreted SP. And maintain the 'high' that he'd inherited.

Within minutes of entering the briefing room at HQ, it became clearly visible, that a certain something was going around, and that Rogon was plainly full of it. "Hi Mike, good to see you... coffee? Oh no, you don't, do you. I keep forgetting. Well, they say absence makes the person fonder..." And that's when Eastern realized that Rogon hadn't really gone away at all.

"You forget to mention the all-important 'heart' ,Rogon," he volunteered as a reminder, knowing that the latter's heart and soul could be found logged as a statistic, if required, embalmed on a 'chip' in a Whitehall vault. 'So why should anybody else have one'? he told himself, as an afterthought. Rogon fidgeted in his chair. Although blissfully unaware of his 'gaff', he was impatient to proceed.

"Do you realize, it's been a couple of days now, since you were here last, isn't, it Mike?" For someone who appeared to be on a high one minute, the ground suddenly manifested itself as being perilously close to the next. Leaving the only available remedy in an upsurge of answers to quell his curiosity. Eastern then felt contracted to make the point.

"Tell you what, Rogon, I've got a better idea. Let's both cut to the chase, forget the crap, and give me one good reason, stemming from our conversation last night, for making this meeting worthwhile," he demanded.

"Just for once, Mike, I don't envisage a problem with that, so try this one for openers. What would your reaction be, if I was to tell you, that our man, Brezznov has finally surfaced at last?"

"Two things immediately come to mind. One, I don't do thoughts, Rogon, as you've been aware of lately. And predominantly, I only deal in facts dependent on how kosher your contact is. Although, having said that, I have to say that you seem to be pretty damned sure of yourself. Frankly, that's quite a statement to throw at me, considering the time of the day."

"And your second being?" enquired Rogon hesitantly. A quizzical look shadowed Eastern's face, and in doing so, caused him to deliberate before replying.

"Are you suggesting to me, that you have a 'mole' (spy) secreted within MI6?" For a brief second, Rogon allowed the hint of a smirk to emerge from behind a blanket of officialdom, before replying.

"You're obviously out of touch where ethics are concerned, Mike. When it comes to internal Government issues, Spooks will always remain an independent force unless special circumstances dictate otherwise. Although you must be aware that we have been collaborating with the Met of late, deriving of course from a Whitehall mandate. I'm sure that when you have read this Fax I have here, you'll be the first to agree and accept that third-party interest can prove ethical at times." He then handed it over for

Eastern to peruse. It soon became evident to him, that, from the outset, this was no ordinary Fax, purely by origin alone.

"Uhm, that's interesting. I can see it's been sent via West End Central. Lets hope that they know something we don't." He wasn't about to be disappointed. The contents contained in the opening paragraph alone were enough to convince Eastern that 'lady luck' had returned from leave, and could now be found in the ascendancy, As follows: Can now officially confirm that one, Victor Brezznov, wanted for international fraud, money-Laundering & conspiracy to murder, has been formally identified as such, through the judicial process, while posing and operating a monetory theft under the pseudonym of one, Reginald Stockfield, aka William Gauntly. The latter is also currently wanted for questioning regarding a joint international Cyber fraud. At this point, no further sightings of Brezznov have been reported since he was last active. In the meantime, all ferry and airport controls have been issued with an ongoing security update. etc..........etc........

Secluded in his own private bubble, Eastern allowed his body language to do the talking for him as he absorbed the SP. Moments later; it was left to a highly charged Rogon to furnish Eastern with a revised breakdown of the established facts, leading up to, and beyond, the initial sighting of Brezznov, prior to his audacious theft.

"....so in conclusion, Mike, you have to say that his movements after parking the getaway vehicle, and bearing in mind his personal security from then on, beggars belief."

"Security! In what sense? I'm sorry, Rogon, but I think I'm missing something here."

"I'm simply talking about his complete and utter disregard for it. It would appear that just before he entered the art gallery, his profile was captured on a convenient CCTV camera. And get this, he was actually posing into it as if to say, 'take a good look, I'm back'. Not that it really mattered of course," he continued, "because fortunately, as we now know, the gallery proprietor was in a position to ID him later, anyway. So, whatever you're feelings are Mike, you have to admit that the man has got some bloody nerve."

A contemptuous look then clouded Eastern's face, before he replied in a forceful manner. "Nerve you say? As cliches go Rogon, I'm forced to say that your insipid observations amount to nothing short of bollocks. Your confusing one man's stupidity with textbook ego and, in the final analysis, it will cost Brezznov dearly. For example, if you recall Helligan's statement when questioned and I quote that he, being Brezznov, 'wouldn't have known a Picasso from a Constable.' this tells me that he know more wanted those paintings than the 4th of July being in December! No, I'm afraid that whatever way you design it, he's letting us know that he deliberately set out to fuck the system, once again. And, as before, he's done it in style."

"Now that I've heard the flip side, I feel bound to agree with you, Mike," sighed Rogon, "but, at the same time, let's remind ourselves that. Brezznov, purely by default, has virtually put it in writing hat he is still operating in the UK. At least that narrows down his choices of freedom....wouldn't you say?" Momentarily, Eastern, for reasons of his own, declined the offer of an opinion, knowing that his present thoughts lay elsewhere. Finally, convinced that his initial motive held water, he opened up by expounding a dual format, "William Gauntly, aka, Reginald Stockfield presumed self-styled silent partner of Brezznov. Do we have any additional SP over and above what we already know about his movements?" Looking somewhat flummoxed over Eastern's sudden change in direction, had now left Rogon briefly searching for an answer himself.

"Sorry, Mike, you've rather jumped ship on me as far as that goes. Saying that, a follow-up enquiry wouldn't go amiss, although it could possibly entail the Met boys coming on board. Mind you, what wouldn't the agency give to have Gauntly in custody? And not forgetting yourself of course, Mike, In the past, you've always maintained he's the key master to a host of defining boxes. So, all things being equal, where are you going with this one? I ask myself."

"Two things come to mind, Rogon, the first being your initial interest in Brezznov's chances of survival. You're right, of course, to assume that the odds are now in our favour regarding his termination. And secondly, if my gut feeling remains in situ then our enigma, William Gauntly, could hold the link into realizing Brezznov's reign, sooner than later." What now had started out as an informative meeting, in Rogon's view, had now morphed into a need-to-know prelude on his part.

"Seeing as though you appear to be in the chair on this one, Mike, I'm eager to establish what your theory is behind the emphasis being laid on Gauntly? As usual, I'm beginning to fear that, once again, I could be missing out on something." Eastern allowed himself a fleeting smile at Rogon's omission. And just as swiftly dismissed it out of sight in favour of one of his own.

"Now then, I want you to cast your mind back to the art gallery fraud scenario and, more importantly, to the credit card that Brezznov used, if you will."

"Simple enough. Made out to Stockfield...right?" confirmed Rogon.

"Yeah. Exactly, only that. that's what's bugging me. Okay, so we know the name is an alias and that it's history lies with Gauntly, long before we found out of his alleged association with Brezznov. So, putting Stockfield to one side for a minute, it makes sense that Gauntly recognizes the card as being his property, so......"

".......what is Brezznov doing with it in his possession?" intervened Rogon, and continued to pursue a further line. "What if there is an underlying purpose behind the use of the card in the fraud, that we're in the dark about?" This time it became Eastern's turn to overlap Rogon's assumption again.

"Precisely! And I make the point that it couldn't have been for the intention of framing Gauntly," he insisted, "because Brezznov, as we know, by bringing his singular ego into play, made it quite clear, via the CCTV, that he alone was responsible for the 'scam'. Which leads me to think, and I stress, that Gauntly himself isn't even aware that Brezznov is in possession of the damned credit card. Full stop!"

"If that is the case," responded Rogon, "it could well mean that to obtain the card illegally or otherwise, Gauntly would have had to have been in the country at the same time as Brezznov, thus enabling him to lay his hands on it."

"Absolutely, and that in itself could be a blessing in disguise."

"As you say, and amen to that. Although, judging by his recent performance, and by that I refer to Brezznov, of course, for reasons of his own, he has never given us any clear indication that he's in a hurry to leave the country, as yet." Acknowledging Rogon's theory with a sustained nod of agreement, Eastern went on to express his own views on their conversation so far.

"So, just to digress far a brief moment, and bearing in mind the emphasis that you've placed on Gauntly. You would have to say that unless there is a conspiracy of sorts going on between the two alluding to the credit card. I for one wouldn't be a happy man if I was Gauntly, in knowing that Brezznov has been using it for his own means."

"And there you have it, Mike." Exacted Rogon. "When putting the problem in layman's terms, not only has Brezznov shafted his alleged partner in crime, but he's also telling the world that, as from now, I've become a solo act." Eastern's eyes then lit up, as he absorbed his colleague's in-depth theory.

"Uhm, now that I can see where you're coming from. Is there a possibility that we could capitalize from his ego trip, and gain an advantage in the broader sense?" he queried hopefully. Nodding briskly in a decisive manner, Rogon was swift to retaliate.

"Unreservedly, I would have to say, Mike, as things stand, we've been gifted some bullets so let's start by firing them. By the way," he added, "I presume that the tabloids aren't, as yet, aware of the details surrounding the robbery up West?"

"Heavens, no. Not at this stage. It's clear to me that we need to process what we're looking at here, before we even consider a release of any kind."

"Excellent. Now this is what I suggest we do, Mike." He then went on to advise Eastern to contact West End Central, with a view to authorising their Press Officer to release a media statement regarding the robbery, the contents of which, would be to emphasis, the fact that the theft, from start to finish, involved a pre meditated collusion between Brezznov and Gauntly. But, more importantly, that Gauntly himself was the major instigator. "If that doesn't cause a 'turf war' (pecking rights) between the pair of them," he concluded, "then I'm one hell of a lousy judge."

Quietly confident, within himself, that Rogon's 'poisoned scheme could trigger a worthy result, Eastern, nevertheless, still retained a degree of scepticism. And was quick to relay it. "Gauntly isn't going to like the idea that he's been 'fingered' (held responsible) for the theft, one bit. I only hope it says enough to coax the assole out of hiding. And, furthermore, that he takes his grief out on Brezznov." Rogon wasn't for turning. As far as he was concerned his motive was etched in granite.

"Like!?" he retorted, "I couldn't give a cuss what the man thinks. So what's he going to do if it all goes belly up....sue me for bloody slander!? Besides, you're forgetting that the Press release is out of our hands, as such. The crux of the matter is that we rile Gauntly enough to make him want to show his hand. And do you know what, Mike? I feel safe in knowing that he will. I just happen to have this feeling about it, so trust me."

"I've no reason not to, Rogon," Eastern was swift to add, "and I have to say that playing one off against the other also appeals to me. Good old-fashioned policing works for me too. Know what I mean?" He continued to support his theory in the same vein. "Seeing as though you're a past master at that type of situation , I can't see how, working as a team, we can fail. And as far as those two assole's get off, pride and ego in their case is delicately poised on a parallel with insanity, and reasoning can so easily become distorted........."

"............and that's when stupid mistakes creep into the equation." Exacted Rogon.

Momentarily, their joint thoughts were put on hold by the sound of a knock on the office door, and, in turn, followed by a diminutive figure entering the room clasping a document of sorts. "Apologies for disturbing you Sir, but this fax came through via Central a few minutes ago, marked urgent, It requires your immediate attention." A short hiatus ensued as Rogon randomly scanned the fax before replying.

"That will be all for now, Milton. I'll let you know, sooner than later, should there be a reply. " Nodding robotically, the courier swiftly exited the room. The moment then became a cue for an evergreen Eastern to open up.

"More bureaucratic shit to get your head around I presume?" he remarked dryly, and motioned toward the fax on Rogon's desk top. He might as well have saved his breath, as the cutting innuendo went directly over his head, as he blissfully focused his full attention toward the fax. In his own time, he then broke off, before picking up with Eastern.

"Three words, Mike. On the contrary, what we have here is a hugely significant development concerning our operation. Or, as you might refer to it, as being 'bloody Karma'". For a second, Eastern found himself lost and bewildered for an answer to Rogon's spontaneous reference, by allowing a vent of intrigue to get the better of him.

"In that case, I suggest, that you'd better share with me, what you obviously consider to be so important, and not before you eclipse yourself by becoming over- humanized." His derisive remark was typically lost in transit, by allowing the implication to die a death, as, once again, Rogon contemplated the contents of the fax.

"Ah...yes, I thought I was right the first time," he proclaimed. "I see there's a reference enclosed here regarding a certain HMP official'"

"Sounds interesting...go on."

"The memo is listed under the name of Donavon. Does the name ring any bells?" he quizzed, and gave a self-assured look, before continuing. "I have reason to suspect that the man was a one-time acquaintance of yours, Mike." His choice of words, when summing up his findings, had now set a precedent in terms of setting up a collision course with Eastern's now enflamed hostile temperament.

"Poxy acquaintance!" He retorted, "A sewer rat has got more going for it than that mean bastard. Yeah, of course I knew him, as you well know, and certainly not by bleeden' choice. As far as I'm concerned, that chapter of my life, when I was at Foredown, is now dead and buried. So why the hell would you want to remind of it?"

"Lets just say it's another way of endorsing your closure on the issue, Mike." admitted Rogon, "and by the way, our Mr Donavon," he strongly emphasised, "Is no longer with us."

"What, thankfully pensioned-off you mean?" Eastern replied solidly.

"That's one way of putting it, Mike, but in official terms I would have to say permanently! As of three hours ago he's been lying in a morgue pending a token post mortem."

"No shit!" Exclaimed Eastern, who was now clearly taken aback, "bloody dead eh? Mind you, I'm not exactly broken-hearted. So what's the story behind it all?"

"Without the full facts I'd be hard-pressed to say, although everything points to him being targeted, and in the process, mowed down by an unmarked vehicle, minutes after coming off a shift."

"So it goes, without saying, that we're talking murder here then?"

"Without question, Mike. The local 'plod' are calling it a vengeance killing. This theory was verified later by two of his associates who were both present at the time the 'hit' occurred."

"That being the case, were they able to obtain a make on the vehicle itself?" implored Eastern.

"Not a single shred of evidence, would you believe. Unless a white van counts for anything, and to quote one report, 'the number plates had been removed and the van stolen to suit. All in all a highly professional job you have to say. So even if the 'plod' were fortunate enough to locate the van," Rogon went on, "they're only going to find a burnt-out carcass."

"End of story, as they say, and well fucked!" Concluded Eastern, and pursued the same line of thought. "apart from knowing who was responsible, it's needless to say that I'll go along with my gut on that one."

To understand Rogon, one would need to delve beyond a facade of bureaucratic doctrine, addled with political correctness. And nobody knew, not even Eastern, as to how his thoughts translated at any given time. It soon became apparent, that he wasn't about to let Eastern's theory on Karma slip into oblivion. "I find it strange but also fascinating," he tendered, "that alternative expression you so often use,

"What goes around comes around. I can see a distinct link there, with Donavon's pre-meditated murder, and yourself, Mike. As I recall, you always maintained that he was the one responsible for blowing your cover, while you were operating in Foredown, by collaborating with Brezznov, no less."

"Yeah. And what a price he paid for it, although I'm not surprised. The obnoxious bastard upset a lot of people on the inside, but outside, in the real world, you have to say that he was a dead man walking. I can't say I'm sorry the guy was 'mullered' (killed). To be honest, the guy was living on borrowed time. Whoever was responsible for driving the vehicle that did the business on him, must have taken part in a bloody raffle to get the job. Personally, I'd like to have shaken the driver's hand."

Also prominent on his mind at the time, led him to question his former suspicions surrounding a further victim's activities, 'In that he had access to damning evidence via his role as prison 'gopher', now bore out a margin of substance. His theory being, that prior to his murder, Steadman was possibly on the verge of going public by disclosing certain covert SP he'd been privy to. 'I also suspect,' he went on, 'that Donavon managed to acquire first-hand knowledge of Steadman's intentions. From then on, he decided to utilize the damning SP to target his victim with blackmail'. Rogon threw him a concerted look, and nodded.

"Lumping all the evidence together, Mike, I can see the reasoning behind your logic. Unfortunately for Donavon, whoever his killer may have been, and Steadman's come to that, must have been privy to the same SP."

"Exactly! And on that basis it's all too bloody convenient, as murders go," he assured himself, "And that just about sums up the whole rotten mess, although," he concluded, "the question still remains. Which person, or persons, stood to gain the most from Donavon's timely murder?"

Their meeting then shuddered to a halt, as Rogon's fax machine once again kicked off. "Anything relevant to the case in hand?" enquired Eastern dubiously.

"Uhm, could be interesting," advised Rogon, "It's a follow-up from West End Central. "Apparently, they're now saying that they have clear confirmation regarding the Rotherhithe murder suspect, namely Charles Regan....."

"And?" an impatient Eastern cut in.

"It appears that, reading between the lines, Regan has finally accepted a plea bargain in exchange for crucial evidence. And, damning Brezznov for his role as co- conspirator in the Stowlowski murder."

Anticipating an immediate reaction, Eastern nevertheless appeared subjective in his reply. "At the risk of repeating myself, I have to say it makes my blood boil, knowing that the system is railroaded into having to corroborate with scum like that!"

"Looking on the plus side though, Mike, ventured Rogon, "If wer'e talking assets, then I feel that the deal in question, irrespective of it's origin, at least counts for another nail in Brezznov's coffin." A somewhat ambushed nod of agreement from Eastern, then sealed their incommodious conversation. But not before Rogon reminded him to take full use of his strategic flat in London, as opposed to his Brighton residence.

CHAPTER 17
A PROVIDENCE CALL

Placing his proverbial grief to one side for a spell, an unwarranted seventy-two hour respite, cleansed of contact, and via the clutches of Rogon, would, under normal circumstances, be considered as a reprieve to savour. Now, with so much enforced time on his hands, the logic attached to the theory somehow appeared to have back-fired on him.

"I'm beginning to suspect that the current situation is fast becoming bloody personal," he related to Joan that particular morning, in a phone conversation following another mood-swing, and as such, continued to vent his frustration in a well- rehearsed vein. "I'm sick and tired of sitting around waiting for some thing to happen...know what I mean? It's almost as if the criminal fraternity, as a whole, has decided to take a damned sabbatical!"

Some time later, resigned to adjusting to the untimely habit of catnapping as a means of killing boredom, meant that re-entry into the real world (should a reprieve arise), would be less of a chore. When the impasse to his problem was finally broken by the melodic tones emerging from his mobile, he instinctively awoke with a jolt and snatched an intrusive glance at a conveniently-placed clock, for mental guidance. If he'd have been a gambling man, the self-nominated odds of six-to-four on and four-to-six against, as the caller being either Rogon or Joan, in that order, would have registered as a good bet. He then averted his full attention toward his mobile.

The moment then became a first for Eastern, as his in-built 'gut' instantly nosedived out of contention, and, in the process, forced his assumption to be dragged down with it. At least he had the token compensation of resurrecting a clear head, in spite of a sudden adrenalin rush which consumed his body, as the truth of the matter hit home- base. But then he was going to need every human faculty available to him, knowing that it wouldn't warrant a second glance, to ascertain that the caller belonged to none other than his ongoing enigma...Victor Brezznov himself.

So, how does one deal with an inconceivable situation arising such as that? Especially when the circumstances are prominent and in your face. It's not every day, especially Eastern's, whereby the 'mountain' in this case Brezznov decides,

instead, on an unofficial pilgrimage to contact 'Mohammed'.

For Eastern, the God given art of thinking on one's feet had, in the past, become a necessary trait of his make-up, should an untoward situation present itself. Without any hesitation, he immediately decided to adopt a nonchalant attitude toward Brezznov, with a need to patronize his ego quality, should it arise. Or, In the event that the latter might inadvertently reveal something of substance, it could prove to be beneficial. Settling for his past trend, a clear-headed and relaxed Eastern then sat back and allowed his inquisitor to do all the talking.

As he fully expected, his nemesis had still managed to retain his unswerving egotistical charisma from word go. "Mike!? I presume that you're still using the name, or is there another pseudonym you needed to throw at me.? No! We both know, by now, that would be a fucking waste of time, especially with my prime influence. So for the moment I'll stick with what I know, that way we've got a shared understanding...right?"

"Yeah....yeah, what ever, you supercilious little bastard." Eastern consciously reminded himself. And left him to continue in the same disillusioned vein.

"So, now that the dust has settled for the moment, I feel inclined to talk about what's been going down, hence the call. You have to say that I'm a man of my word, Mike. I refer, of course, to the 'heist' and it's successful consequences. On reflection, you should have been a wealthy man now, coming from what was on offer. Although, thinking back, it's fair to say you had me fooled for a while. Unfortunately, you made the same mistake as a lot of other amateurs, by underestimating my supreme capabilities, which....."

"I imagine that the late Steadman and Donavon alone, would clarify that point, without too much trouble, assuming that they were here, of course." Eastern interjected, and went on. "Unless their combined murders were purely coincidental in bringing my true identity to bear? Having said that, you only knew the alleged Robert Ruark, and that, I strongly believe, is the one concern that's bothering you, above all else."

"Bollocks! Don't flatter yourself my friend. When it suits me, you too will become expendable. As far as Steadman is concerned, I like to think that I did the slime ball a fucking favour. Sooner or later somebody else would have leaned on him, and, me? I got lucky and just happened to jump the queue. Basically, you need to understand the situation from my viewpoint. The minute his acquired knowledge became personal, became the moment the creep signed his own death warrant. Plain and simple. Therefore, In the end, the outcome came to be a necessity."

"Necessity!? stormed Eastern, "Your in-vogue arrogance is bigger than your fucking ego. And Donavon. What category did he slot into, before you decided to have him 'blown' away?"

"Huh, your ambiguous observations do you credit, Mike. I wonder if the organization that controls you, respects your input? I have my doubts."

Unbeknown to him, Brezznov's throwaway implication and choice of words, had somehow struck a parallel chord in his sometime fragile association with Rogon, and Spooks as a whole. Furthermore, he was now left debating just how much knowledge Brezznov did have privy to. In the end, it became sink or swim time. If he were to pursue Brezznov's poisonous reference, It could well be misconstrued as being a moment of weakness and a possibility of game over, should he allow himself to get riled.

Biting his lip, he decided, instead, to bring the Stowlowski murder into play. "Seeing as death sticks to you like shit to a blanket, Victor, Let's talk about another 'contract' that appears to bear out your hallmark. I refer, of course, to the unfortunate security guard's demise, whilst operating at the Mitzitomo bank. Does that mean anything to you?"

"Should it?"

"Don't act dumb, Victor. Your ego's slipping."

"As it happens, I did hear a whisper. Foreigner I believe. Yeah, a Polish guy. Wrong time wrong place I guess. A hazard of the job I reckon. So how do you figure out my involvement in the guy's death? I wouldn't have known the 'stiff' if he was standing next to me," Eastern held himself back before replying, to savour an impromptu verbal error of judgment put forward by Brezznov. Although the icing on the cake became slightly soured, due the fact that he wouldn't be party to the look on Brezznov's face, when he delivered his coup de grace.

"Polish!? Correct me if I'm wrong, Victor, I don't recall mentioning the victims nationality.....but you did!. And that created your first mistake, the second being that it took forensic a month to ID the body remains. So, along with the Met and my organization, we are the only people" he left off, briefly' to take stock, "apart from who was responsible for the murder, of course, to have been aware that the victim was indeed of Polish origin." Brezznov appeared to be rattled and it showed in his response.

"You're full of crap d'ye know that?" he retorted. It had become obvious now that Eastern had touched a nerve alluding to a moment of weakness on his part. "Playing the mind game card doesn't wash with me." He went on. "You're way out of your league and clutching at straws. All you've got is rubbish hearsay, you couldn't make a statement like that to stick if it was written in fucking gold leaf, and you know it." Like it or not, Brezznov had made the point by leaving Eastern nursing a choice complex. As it turned out, his dilemma proved to be a no-brainer as he responded to his nemesis claim with a poignant and determined laugh.

"You do realize, of course," replied Eastern, with deliberation, "that I can categorically state, on record, that both suspects directly responsible for Stowlowski's murder, are at present held in custody. And have been for the past three weeks."

"Which more than backs up my claim then?" Brezznov snorted. More in desperation than factual content.

"No can do, sunshine. You are involved in a three-way conspiracy right up to your poxy neck. And that goes for you pal Tommy Brandon as well. For the record, the two suspects that we are holding have entered into a plea bargain which has been sanctioned at high level. Any day now, they'll be 'singing' so bleeden' loud, they'll make a boy scout seem like public enemy number one putting it mildly, you're not as flaming smart as you think you are. So you'd better get used to the idea that you're not premier league anymore."

"Yeah, well fuck you, Eastern. My day will come. You haven't even seen the best of me yet."

"Wise-up Victor you can't run for eve. Sooner or later you're going to trip up my friend, and when you do I'll ensure that I'm on hand to see that you stay down."

Brezznov, now found himself reeling from a verbal and factious assault, over which he had no control over. Inwardly, he was hurting badly along with his dented ego, having to pay the price for his inbred arrogance. For once, it would seem, he had finally met his match, albeit a confident thorn in his side. Seeking a verbal swipe to take the edge off Eastern's glory, was fast becoming rarer by the second. On hindsight, he needn't have bothered, and was forced to allow what thoughts he held to evaporate, as his enigma came back to haunt his private space yet again.

"Paintings!...works of art....old masterpieces. That sort of thing. What do they do for you Victor? Or is that too personal a question?" As before, Brezznov found himself trapped on the ropes, as the planted implication hit him squarely between the eyes.

Almost immediately, a random criminal buying spree, fraudulently procured from selected art galleries in the City sprang to mind. There was no question that Eastern now found himself on a roll as he remembered one particular acquisition that Brezznov had allegedly purchased, resulting in his deception becoming just another day in the office for West End Central. His nemesis reaction, when it surfaced, came as no surprise to Eastern, knowing that the fuelled bullets that he'd fired, had found their objective target.

"Where the hell are you going with that crap?" snarled Brezznov.

"Going? You ask." The implication in his reply opened the floodgates as to what was about to follow. "That depends solely on third-party interest, Victor. By that , I'm thinking William Gauntly. If not, then I suggest his elusive shadow, Mr Stockfield, no less. Ring any bells?" The resounding silence that ensued came as no surprise to Eastern. His only regret lay in the distance between them, as he sub consciously manufactured his own image of a demoralized Brezznov.

"Talk and more fucking talk." His desperate reply, when it finally emerged, was about as predictable as the 'talking clock. He continued to rant in the same vein. "You don't know shit from shit Eastern. Gauntly isn't even in the country. You know nothing mug. As it happens he's well off the 'manor' and giving it large in Spain, as we speak." His arrogance had now overtaken his common sense by releasing a veritable one to many omissions, leaving Eastern to verbally punish him.

"Thanks for the Press release ,Victor and the confirmation of your association with the guy. Unfortunately, your newspaper only ranks as fish and chips fodder."

"That's bollocks!" He asserted vehemently. It's common knowledge he did a runner some weeks ago." Putting an earlier joint proposal with Rogon to one side for the moment, Eastern elected to play his mind games card.

"I think I need to mark your card, Victor. The word on the street is saying otherwise, my friend. In fact, right now you're not exactly the flavour of the month, by all accounts. ....know what I mean?"

"Gauntly and I," he spluttered, unable to finish what he started.

"Are what exactly?" gave Eastern the signal to countermand.

"....mean nothing to each other. I don't run with poxy losers. I'm at the top of my game. You seem to forget that I've fucked the world's banking system. what else is out there?"

"Somebody in your position right now, I would have to say, financially, not a lot." Eastern conceded, "Although, having said that, I can't see Gauntly agreeing with you on that score."

"What is it with you and that assole?" retorted Brezznov.

"Basically, Victor, you've been away far too long, so let me educate you. Your ongoing problem concerns street lore so I'll spell it out for you. Firstly you don't fuck your own up. Using Gauntly's plastic to obtain those paintings wasn't a clever move, In fact very amateurish, to say the least. Your blind show of arrogance has rebounded on you by making you a much-sought-after commodity, and subsequently placing a price on your head. Where the hell are you going to run to? I ask myself. No, as of now, my friend, you've inherited more grief than a poxy Harley Street psychologist."

"Grief! Is that so? Does the 'street' also mention the word respect? What I've achieved makes me untouchable. Money wise, I can buy my way out of any grief coming my way. Talk is cheap and unproductive, whereas money controls actions and speaks for itself, so I don't intend losing any sleep over any lousy threats." Bearing in mind Brezznov's financial status, his bargaining ability, should it ever come into play, could mean the difference between life and death. Between gritted teeth, Eastern was forced to accede on that point.

"I know it and he knows it, indirectly, the asshole is worth more alive than he is dead!" he muttered to himself. Unless...? A dormant key of supposition, suddenly rotated full circle and, in doing so, opened up an opportune door of expectation. "Of course! How could I be that dumb?" he rebuked himself. "This situation isn't all about emphasizing Brezznov at all." His regenerated sub-conscious was now working on overtime. Extreme verbal scenarios whirled around in his head. One being more prominent than the rest, alluding to a belated statement made by Rogon, 'that Gauntly is the one person holding the key to 'Pandora's box'. Digressing was one thing, Brezznov, on the other hand, had conclusions of his own in force, none of which were about to include Eastern.

"If you're looking for answers, you sucker, then forget it. The ball stay's squarely in my court. I'm done talking. Oh, one last thing mug, this number, not unlike myself, is non-traceable." And then he hung up, leaving Eastern to reflect on what might have been. Prevalent on his mind revolved around his enigma, William Gauntly. For somebody who had only entered the equation a few weeks after the 'heist', the present onus on his importance now transported to being manifold regarding Brezznov's future.

Assumption on assumption amounted to a shit load of frustration for Eastern. His take on the 'odd couple' was fast losing ground. Question! "By using Gauntly's plastic in the art robbery, the latter would surely have had to have been in the country at the time. And not as Brezznov maintained, 'giving it large in Spain'". He questioned himself. "Unless, of course, there was a hidden motive behind it's use, as Rogon suggested meaning there could have been a collusion between the two. When coming from an alternative angle, he revised the fact that, "Any proceeds from the robbery, as such, based on the CCTV evidence, would be cancelled out when it was known that money was never the motive." Putting all that to one side, Eastern also considered the fact that just maybe, Gauntly hadn't been aware that his plastic had been used. In which case a major fallout would be on the cards, and Gauntly would be in a prime position to straighten Brezznov out. "He'd certainly have the know-how and the funds to see it through."

Lurking in the background and central to his unforeseen existence, Eastern held a nagging doubt as to Gauntly's persona as a whole. "There's more to the man than meets the eye. It's almost as if he's appeared from out of nowhere. The next available minute, he's catapulted into contention as being the main 'running man'.

With so much supposition to dwell on, sleep didn't come easy that same night. Even the maturity contained in his tried and tested 'poison' appeared to have gone on a sponsored walkabout. At least Joan was on hand the following morning, attempting to revive his flagging spirits.

"You look completely bushed, darling. So much for sleeping. I hope you're not allowing that ignoramus, Rogon, to get to you? Without stating the obvious, is there anything that I can do to ease the situation?" Her frank naivety acted like an adrenalin boost by accelerating his flagging thought process.

"Believe it or not, Joan, he's the least of my current problems at this moment in time."

"I see. Look, why don't we grab some leisure time and eat out tonight? It'll do us both good. I wouldn't mind going Italian for a change, what do you say?"

"Say? That's the best offer I've had all week. Yeah, go for it, Joan. Let's get off this crazy world for a couple of hours."

Suffice to say, their spontaneous evening started well and terminated even better. As before, he didn't get much sleep afterwards, but then, by the same token, he wasn't complaining either!

CHAPTER 18
A LIFELINE

A remedy for escapement: Take two people soaking up the ambiance of a renowned Italian restaurant, relishing a Spaghetti alla carbonara, washed down with a three year old Calabretta Gaio Gaio Rosso wine, would, in the majority of cases, constitute a table in heaven. Alternatively, two minutes into an investigative conversation with Rogon, could well trigger off an illegitimate recipe for disaster. And It then became reality time, as Eastern entered into a probing conversation, along with Rogon, at Spooks HQ the following morning.

"William Gauntly, nee Reginald Stockfield. Two pseudonyms, one person! I don't know what your thoughts are on the matter, Rogon, but, personally, I have reservations as to the genuine article."

"I see." His reply came across as being highly disconcerted, Eastern noted. "So how long have you held this omission? Only I get the impression that there's more to your implication than meets the eye. And how, pray, does what I think fit into the frame of things?"

"Not being bloody evasive for a start, would be a help. "

"Well, that's as maybe, although I think you're placing too much emphasis on the guy."

"But that is my point. You're talking singular and I'm thinking the complete opposite. At the moment we're only assuming that his twin ID is what's stated on his records. Okay, so we know now that he relies on a 'bent' Passport to move around for convenience, but what if it should turn out to be a genuine one? And I strongly believe this to be the case, then we're literally looking for three bloody suspects as opposed to one!"

"Uhm, I take your point. At least we have a 'mugshot' to work with."

"Bollocks! You need to take a refresher course, Rogon. If his passport is 'bent' then the ID photo is worthless. Think about it."

"You're right, of course, and I'll give it some thought, Mike." On that note, Eastern bit his tongue and centred their addled conversation by reactivating a past hypothesis.

"Something I've been meaning to ask you. When do you intend going public with that contrived Press report concerning Brezznov and Gauntly, AKA Stockfield? As I recall it's been almost two weeks since we both discussed the idea and, so far nothing has been forthcoming."

"Ah, I was wondering when you were going to throw that one at me. At least I'm now in a position to put your mind at rest. Apparently, when I first offered up the scheme. The powers-to-be rejected our idea on the grounds that our conspired representation of the facts, would appear to be detrimental toward any specifically named suspects. And, indeed, any subsequent trial that could possibly follow"

"Damn the bureaucrats," responded Eastern, "It's results that count, and not the amount of bullshit they can throw at you. So where do we go from here?"

"Bear with me, Mike. I've kept the best till last. Thankfully, our strategy is still ongoing....."

"....but you just said."

"Give me a chance to finish." Rogon asserted. "I wasn't prepared to take no for an answer and dutifully arranged an extraordinary meeting, with the PM. As a result of that meeting and due to the high-profile circumstances surrounding the case. I can now confirm that Whitehall have sanctioned our original conspiratorial

Press release."

"No shit! Eastern exploded. "Now we're in business at last, it doesn't get any better than that, does it? I take it you'll be dealing with the Press directly? If that is the case, then we need to hit every damned tabloid available. And make a meal of it" What could have been misconstrued as resembling a knowing smile, overshadowed Rogon's face as he confirmed his actions.

"I can categorically state, that the media process is operational as we speak, Mike. It's up to the Press now to exploit our logic......" A clinical knock on the office door momentarily put a restraining order on their conversation. "That'd better be important, I gave orders that I wasn't to be disturbed," Rogon expressed indignantly. Pressing a security button, the door opened to reveal a po-faced looking courier clasping a document which he duly handed over. "Thank you, Milton, that'll be all for now."

The expression littered on Rogon's face as he methodically surfed the Fax, gave no indication as to the importance of the content it held. His body suddenly stiffened as he digested the enclosed information, giving Eastern cause to jump the verbal queue.

"You look like the bleedin' cat who got the cream, Rogon. So, when do I get to know what's in the fax, or is it a State secret?" A direct question warranted a direct reply, and Rogon wasn't about to hold back on State etiquette.

"A secret? No! A fact? Yes! When you stated, that we were now back in business, earlier, I'm in a position to rubber-stamp that for you. Now get this. A report has been issued, via the Sussex police, that Brezznov, of all people, has been sighted on the outskirts of Brighton. Would you believe?"

"No kidding! Details.....can you be more specific?" spluttered Eastern.

"It appears that he was spotted less than an hour ago, when checking out of a petrol station off the A23 adjacent to Clayton Hill."

"Yeah, I'm familiar with the locale, although I'm slightly confused about the actual sighting itself."

"Confused you say?"

"Yeah. The fact that there's no 'mugshot' of him, as yet, in the public domain, throws a doubt on the claim."

"I can put your mind at rest on that account, Mike. As luck would have it, the person who verified the sighting, happened to be an off duty-prison warder from HMP Foredown who was visiting family in Brighton at the time."

"That's conclusive enough for me. What about vehicle ID...plate number etc? Any joy there?"

"I'm afraid not, Mike. To quote the warder ' It all happened too quickly....a fleeting glance, except to say that Brezznov wasn't alone, inasmuch as he had a driver as a companion'"

"Really!? Now that in itself is food for thought. Anyway, apart from stating the obvious, why did the warder report the incident? Seeing as though he wouldn't have been aware of Brezznov's role in the 'heist'."

"Namely, because he was aware that he'd violated his parole licence weeks ago."

"Of course, I'm not thinking straight. To be honest, I'm still struggling with the idea that the arrogant bastard is back on the 'manor' again. If he's looking to do some unfinished business, then he needs to be at the top of his game. As things stand, he's rode his luck once too often, you have to say."

"And some," concluded Rogon, "Incidentally: the driver of the vehicle himself. Have you given any thought as to his ID?" Off the cuff, positivism could be reputed as being a form of arrogance in itself. In Eastern's case, surmising wasn't even an option when he replied.

"Even given half the facts to mess with Rogon, I'd wager that it was the elusive William Gauntly behind the wheel."

Winding up their briefing, and mindful of the sighting alluding to Brighton, Eastern proposed that he would continue the investigation at street level, in collaboration with his 'snout'. "The fact that gainful information at street level, is classed as first hand," he emphasized, "equates as being word-priceless." An hour later, found Eastern rapt in deep conversation with evergreen 'snout', Ray 'news' Carter. "So, like I say, just do what you're bloody good at. I badly need a result on this one. So I don't give a shit who you upset to make it possible. The quicker you get it sorted, the sooner you get your dough. And remember, the minute something breaks, I need to know about it through the usual channels. Irrespective if the SP is trivial or otherwise, it's that bleedin' important to me. And, before I forget, you just had a raise in pay on this one....this time its fucking personal."

CHAPTER 19
DAY OF RECKONING PART 1

Patience, they say, is a virtue (providing of course you've got the patience that is to sustain it) forcing a philosophical and somewhat disillusioned, Eastern into rewriting the script. A week had now gone into retirement since his business arrangement with Carter and, as yet, he had nothing to show for it. "I reckon the bloody 'underworld' in Brighton has gone on a sabbatical," he bemoaned to Joan at the breakfast table. "Unless Carter has lost his touch." Sympathy is a great crutch, and coming from a woman, tends to make a problem that much more accessible, especially where Joan was concerned.

"No news is good news, Mike, think about it. I can't see Brezznov walking up and down West Street waving a banner with 'I'M BACK' written all over it! Carter has never let you down in the past and the 'CLARION', remember, have kept to their part of the bargain. Everything is in place, you can't do any more. For what it's worth, the image that they've created of him, literally screams out that he's public enemy no1. If it makes you feel any better, Mike, the biggest mistake Brezznov has made so far is taking you for a fool."

"I love you too darling," echoed Eastern, pausing before replying confidently, "Yeah, you're right, Joan. Sooner or later something will give and when it does, I'll be on hand to pick up the pieces. That's a guarantee. By the way who's the letter from?"

"Letter? Oh, it's from Toni...my journalist friend from London, if you recall."

"Of course I remember her. Has she still got that flat in Hove?"

"Yes, in fact she's written to say that she is travelling down the day after tomorrow, and that she intends staying over for a couple of days."

"A 'girlie' weekend eh? The break will do you both good. I presume you'll stay at the flat with her. Cram in as much as you can...yeah?"

"Great idea, Mike. I'm sure you'll cope on your own without me around?"

"Don't worry. I won't be alone, Joan, I'll give DS Johnnie Curtis a bell (a serving police officer and acquaintance attached to Brighton CID). I can't see him turning down a night out, strange, when I think back."

"Uhm, sounds ominous, Mike. Do I get to know what is bothering you?"

"The police corruption case of course!" (a former ordeal involving Joan's ex husband some months previous). Without thinking, he unwittingly perpetuated her question. "I'm sorry darling. I didn't mean to bring up the past. It just came out."

"That's fine, Mike. I've resigned myself to moving on. There's no point in dwelling on the bad times. Anyway, I'm sure that Johnnie will make ideal company for you."

Forty eight hours later, satisfied that Joan was safely lodged at Wilbury Road Hove, he decided to contact DS Johnnie Curtis for a proposed 'meet'. "Hi mate...yeah...it's Mike. Who else. What are you up to these days?"

"Nothing exciting, same old shit different day...know what I mean? So what's occurring I ask myself. If I didn't know you any better, Mike, I reckon you could well be involved in this current Brezznov case?" A sustained silence prevailed as Eastern gathered his thoughts. Curtis had inadvertently put him on the spot and he needed to deal with it. Going public on a phone line could prove to be dangerous. The less said about the case the better.

"I reckon State security would beg to differ on that score, Johnnie," he remarked Jokingly, and hoped it would suffice. "Besides," he continued, "I don't need the grief these days.... know what I mean. I'll be honest. I've got some time on my hands right now. Maybe we could possibly meet up for a drink tomorrow night. What do you say?"

As responses go, Curtis didn't need asking twice and supplied Eastern with the appropriate arrangements and left it at that.

Briefly, his thinking slipped from one scenario to another as he disengaged the receiver. Somebody, he noted, had been trying to get through to him while in conversation with Curtis. Within seconds of checking the number out, a much relieved and apprehensive Eastern made the desirable connection. "Carter! Where the bleedin' hell have you been all my life? It's been almost a fortnight since our arrangement and fuck all! So whatever you've got in the way of SP had better be kosher."

"Mr Eastern...guv, you know me," whined Carter, "It aint been easy I promise yer. This Brezznov geezer is a major player and bloody exclusive with it. The guy is obviously corrupted with dough so he's in a position to buy his own silence.

You know how it works. If the word on the street isn't there, then it's not anywhere. As it happens, I got lucky. I've got another client in the CID who I deal with now and again. He's a bit 'sussy' (dubious). One phone call from me to the right people and his pension winds up in the 'karzy' (toilet). Know what I mean? Anyway, I've had a word, and your man Brezznov is definitely back on the 'manor'."

"So, is that it? retorted Eastern. "I could have worked that one out for myself, you cretin, I need more than that, Carter. For what I'm paying you I want the dog's bollocks in return. Like I said before, this time around it's bleedin' well personal."

"I hear what you say, Mr Eastern, but I can't give you what ain't there. Although, for what it's worth, my client made it clear that he was 'under orders' from above to keep shtum (quiet)where Brezznov is concerned. And that's why I'm short on the SP."

"Uhm, even with what you've got on him? Shit! Why do I get this feeling that something is going down that I don't know about?" Eastern mused.

"Yeah, same as, I thought, it sounded iffy at the time. I'm sorry guv but I can't give you what ain't out there. I only hope that you manage to nail the bastard."

"That is one certainty you wouldn't want to bet against, Carter. Trust me I will. I'll give you another forty eight hours from now in the event something breaks. Meanwhile, if I don't hear from you, the usual arrangement applies...be lucky." He then hung up.

The following day became a lesson in patience and cold comfort thrown in. Not having Joan around made him realize the importance of their relationship. At least the anticipation of meeting up with DS Curtis once again, had given him something to relish.

That same evening, while seated in a secluded bar off West Street, Eastern opened up to Curtis and emphasized his frustration over the Brezznov case. "I'm beginning to feel like I'm the last person who knows what the hell is going on. What little information I have managed to obtain via my, 'snout', appears to be public knowledge. And as for that bunch of plastic puppets at HQ, I'd get more feedback from a tailor's dummy...know what I mean?"

"Yeah, I know where you're coming from, Mike, believe me, you're not alone on this one. Not that I know any more than you do, I hasten to add. In fact, apart from a very selected few. By that, I'm talking the CS (chief superintendent) upwards. You can't help but get the distinct feeling that Brezznov, in name alone, is synonymous with taboo."

"So it's not only me who's out in the cold then, Johnnie?"

"Far from it, mate' this manufactured silence that's in operation, is leading up to something big. Trust me, you heard it here first."

"It's all so bleedin' unnecessary. It's fair to say that Brezznov, has got the establishment by the bollocks. When I think back, a colleague of mine had the right idea some months ago. When you're presented with a mad dog, you put it down!" (The reference being to agent 'B' and his philosophy toward enduring grief)

"Legal termination eh, Mike?"

"That's one way of putting it I suppose. Sometimes you have to bend the rules to suit...know what I mean?" Having exhausted their intense conversation, their time was spent in genial banter until closing time, and a firm resolution to keep in touch.

Twenty or so minute later, after dropping Curtis off via a taxi, he arrived safely back in the 'village'. Once inside his flat, Eastern lost no time in pouring himself a nightcap, and duly headed for the comfort of an armchair in which to mull over the evening as a whole. Foremost on his mind, centered on Curtis's startling revelation towards an internal police security blanket. "At least my gut instinct hasn't lost its touch where that's concerned." He confided in himself, ' I can only hope that it surmounts to being for all the right reasons'.

Downing the last of his 'poison', he decided to check his landline for any possible messages, having previously disconnected his mobile for sanity reasons. In total, there were two messages for him to conjure with. The first extolled simplicity, while the second call, left him reaching out for his trusted bottle of Scotch. Not that he needed an excuse for a drink, but trading with the likes of Rogon at twelve midnight in full verbal flight demanding an explanation for living, fully epitomized the expression 'piss off' in anybody's language.

Purely on the grounds of inhuman blackmail, Eastern felt loath to continue listening to Rogon's impassioned plea akin to Queen and Country. Whereby, he would be plucked for safety at 5pm the following morning from Mother Earth as we know it, and then transported by car to a secure installation located within a stone's throw of Downing Street. Needless to say, sleep that night came at a premium, as a mixture of apprehension and high expectancy took control of his senses. And then it became early morning and time to leave. The process involving his departure, he noted, even down to the vehicle he was bundled into, including his habitual blindfold, had an exclusive take of its own. Unlike his normal routine, Rogon's scripted message, and the erratic timing of the event, had seen to that. "There has to be a climax to all of this," he firmly convinced himself.

With so much anxiety baggage going on inside his head, it subsequently drained the duration of the journey by cutting time. The same could be said regarding the sequence of events that followed, as he unceremoniously exited the limousine. Still blindfolded and flanked by two burly bodyguards, he traversed a five-minute assault course consisting of stairs, lifts and corridors, before eventually coming to a sustained halt. His blindfold was then removed by a bodyguard, who then ushered him into a plush seat which he gratefully accepted.

Instinctively, he stretched his eyes to gain some form of recognition as to his surroundings. Focusing in on Rogon was the easy part, although he did have an immediate problem in distinguishing the two dignitaries seated next to him. Habitual as ever, Rogon was the first to break the silence with the use of a double-edged introduction.

"Good morning, Mike, I trust your calling wasn't too much of an ordeal? Please, take your time to get adjusted. I'm forced to pre-warn you, that the content of what we're about to discuss in the next hour or so is highly sensitive, and embodies State security at the highest level. With that in mind, any decisions that you arrive at throughout the proceedings, will I stress, require extreme consideration on your part."

"Yeah, I get the picture, Rogon. Nothing changes...does it? Except of course, the added bullshit. Although I'm beginning to sense that this meeting hasn't got the makings of a vicar's tea-party. Having said that, you can rest assured, that you have my full attention."

"Thank you, Mike. If we are to reach a satisfactory conclusion as to what's on the table this morning, it's imperative that we remain in unison."

Slowly and surely, the relevance of the meeting began to bite, and Eastern wanted more in the way of introduction.

"Before the briefing gets underway, I want to know who I'm dealing with, Rogon. If things get personal I'll be looking for assurances that sort of thing. You understand?"

"Absolutely! And you have my word on that, Mike, but first things first. I'd like you to meet the P.M's private Secretary, David Goodridge, on my left, and representing the Metropolitan Police, seated to my right, Commander Grant Baxter. Feel free to express an opinion at any time, Mike, and question every proposal on offer. Your input, as always, will be paramount should a veto

Gary Tulley

situation arise."

"I don't have a problem with that, Rogon. The quicker we are done here the sooner I get home...right?"

"And so you shall, Mike. And, before I forget, you should also be aware that the proceedings are being taped." Having dealt with the standard protocol, Rogon declared the briefing in session and pivoted his opening gambit toward 'public enemy No.1'. "Brezznov!" he expounded, "Is, as you're all aware, fast becoming an embarrassment to say the least. The sooner he's back behind bars, the better. I think we all agree on that score. However, removing him from society is proving to be a problem, which in turn leads me onto you, Mike. And your role in the scheme of things.'

"Huh." Eastern muttered in a derisory manner. "'I was wondering how long it would take before you got me involved. Don't let me stop you now."

"With all due respect, Mike you're the one person who could bring about Brezznov's downfall. And that claim, is fully supported by Commander Baxter, along with Goodridge here."

"If I didn't know you any better, Rogon, I'd have to say that you're hiding something from me. Patronising doesn't work for me, as you know. Normally, you send for me...give me a brief... and I deal with it...end of.." Grim-faced, Rogon averted his attention toward team Government. For a few minutes the three men remained fully engrossed in a whispered huddle. Finally, Rogon broke ranks and issued Eastern with a firm directive.

"Tomorrow morning, Mike, should you wish to accept the proposed mission on offer, you will be required to front a State-engineered operation, code-named 'Cuckoo's Nest'."

"Uhm, sounds impressive, Rogon. All you've got to do now is convince me it's kosher. So, cards on the table, lets hear some straight talk." Without further ado, a much relieved-Rogon signalled his intention to continue.

"Before I elaborate on what we have in mind, you need to be aware of the risk factor involved, Mike. This operation, should you undertake it, and bearing in mind Brezznov's involvement, will be potentially dangerous, to say the least......"

"........I wasn't expecting it to be a flaming walk in the park Rogon," jolted Eastern, but I do accept your point. The way I see it, the guy has shot his bolt. In spite of his financial pull, he knows damned well that he can't get out of the country, and therein lies his problem. We have to assume now, that he's done running. And for reasons of his own, has decided that Brighton suits his destiny."

"You seem pretty sure of yourself, Mr Eastern," asserted Baxter, 'Maybe you know something we don't."

"If I did, Commander, we wouldn't be having this conversation. Lets just put my theory down to experience. I refer, of course, to my enforced time spent at HMP Foredown with Brezznov. A 24/7 internment, shackled to a guy like him, can reveal certain characteristics to emerge. Foremost in his case, as I recall, being one of sheer arrogance. And as we all know, that particular trait has been the downfall of lesser ambitious criminals than Brezznov in the past. With that in mind, I rest my case."

A sustained silence prevailed, allowing Eastern's analytic prognosis to sink in.

"Touche, Mr Eastern, I'm beginning to feel that I might have underestimated your underlying capabilities. Although I take no satisfaction where caution is concerned, you understand. On the face of it, I think we're going to get along just fine." Breaking off, he motioned to Goodridge who looked better suited holding a 'Bridge' hand for a form of redress. "Is there anything you'd like to add at this point?" Baxter enquired hotly.

Shaking his head, he readily declined his offer and reminded Baxter that he was merely a political observer," in that case I suggest that we push on. I'll leave you to put Eastern in the picture regarding the details of the operation, Rogon. I get the impression, that you two seem to share a common bond, as far as timing is concerned." For a split second, Eastern struggled to stifle a well-aimed outburst at Baxter's ingenuous remark, "Timing!.... you idiot. The word isn't even in Rogon's blasted vocabulary." Diplomatic as ever, he kept his thoughts to himself and gestured for Rogon to continue.

"Before we discuss the operation fully, Mike, you'll be pleased to know that Aubrey Millington is being held in custody, as we speak. It appears that he was apprehended a few hours ago by Passport Control officials at Gatwick, when attempting to flee the country."

"Now that's what you call a result. My day just gets better and better. One assole 'banged up' and another two to go!" he asserted, causing Goodridge to cringe at Eastern's bar room persona, and leaving him in no doubt as to what he could expect forthwith. For his part, Rogon appeared to be hedging somewhat in his approach before replying.

"Judging by that remark, I can only presume that you're taking our friend, Gauntly, into account?"

"Unquestionably. I'm surprised that you need to ask ." At this juncture, there was no way that a gob-smacked Eastern could have prepared himself for what was about to unfold. as Rogon took centre stand.

"I'm afraid there's no easy way of saying this, Mike. I can only say that, in my defence, what I'm about to tell you is only one part of a massive internal, but legitimate, cover-up, set in motion as a joint enterprise by the Government and Spooks. This, in turn, has now culminated, bringing operation 'Cuckoos Nest' into being. That being the case, and for the record, I can categorically state that for reasons that will become clear, William Gauntly, in name and body, has never, at any time, existed. And I humbly apologise on behalf of my colleagues for letting you think otherwise." Mouth agape, Eastern found himself reeling on the ropes yet again. This time coinciding from another formidable disclosure. For want of an escapism, the sudden urge to 'kick ass' figured highly as an option.

"What is it with you bleedin' people?" he demanded." Especially you, Rogon.

One minute you're feeding me buckets of diplomatic shit, and the next opportune minute, you conveniently renege on everything we've previously stood for. For two pins I...."

"Mike! listen to me," implored Rogon, "calm down and try to understand where I'm coming from, and by that I mean the system. Due to the complexity of the operation, a decision, taken at the highest level, prevented me from allowing you access to multi-privy information. Any disclosure on my part would have rendered the whole operation into becoming a no-brainer".

"Yeah, well fucking bully for you, Rogon. So tell me, how long has this 'cover up', as you choose to put it, been going on for? Or does that come under the Official Secrets Act as well?"

"I've no intention of going down that road, Mike, but don't think, for a minute, that I'm getting any satisfaction from what has now transpired. This meeting is all about transparency and as of now, you are integral into bringing about the success of operation 'Cuckoos Nest'."

"If I didn't know you any better, Rogon, I'd feel obliged to take that last statement as a compliment. So, putting that to one side, for how long has the operation itself been in existence?"

"Would it surprise you, Mike, if I said approximately a year before you came on board?"

"Shit! What do I know?"

"Believe me, months of meticulous planning has gone into developing this project, hence the enforced security blanket surrounding it in the past."

"Hell, Rogon, you don't do things by halves, do you? So, looking back, my internment was only a small part of the operation?"

"Precisely! Although in real terms, your time spent inside Foredown helped to institute a major over-all contribution."

"Uhm, right now I find myself struggling with that prognosis."

"You do, in what regard?"

"Simply by knowing what we know now. Just to digress for a minute. Brezznov, by his own admission, figured out that I was a 'plant' (incognito) and subsequently played me along like a wet fish."

"Well, if it's any consolation, you can blame the late Steadman, for that, Mike. Having said that, the flipside evolving from one man's fatal mistake, has now left the agency with an unexpected legacy."

"Uhm, something positive at last to dwell on, so, convince me. Right now, the only legacy I've got, Rogon, is a bleedin' headache, whilst trying to make some sense out of operation 'Cuckoo's Nest'. Which reminds me, I've still got an ongoing problem with our man

Gauntly. According to you, and I quote, 'the man never existed', is fast becoming my problem, Rogon. That being the case, how the hell did Brezznov manage to obtain and use a bank card belonging to Gauntly, or even Stockfield, come to that?" When responding, Rogon, afforded a rare smile, as a bolster, before continuing.

"I was wondering when you were going to play that card, Mike, and I bow to your tenacity. Briefly, when I stated earlier, that Gauntly never existed, I agree, that on hindsight, I should have given you the benefit of time, to digest the fact of the matter."

"I accept that. So, now that you do have my full interest at heart, I feel that a good reason to justify the fact, wouldn't go amiss. The sooner I know what the hell is going on at this stage, the better. All I require are some facts."

"You have my full attention, Mike. So, on the assumption that you have already done your homework, I can categorically state that the two names, Gauntly and Stockfield, were alias's, used by an agency, Spook, working in conjunction with operation 'Cuckoo's Nest."

"Now why doesn't that surprise me. And the bank card itself?"

"Forwarded to Brezznov, via the same undercover agent, the intention being that it would hopefully encourage Brezznov to surface."

"Well, you certainly succeeded in doing that, Rogon, almost to the tune of four hundred and fifty thousand pounds in art-work, and he still evaded capture. By the way, the alternate covert agent that you're using on the case. Would we have met before?" Rogon steeled himself before replying, as if in anticipation, stemming from what could amount to, as being a verbal hiding.

"Once again I....." "a simple yes or no will suffice, Rogon." Eastern cut in.

"In that case, you will have to cast your mind back to HMP Foredown."

"Huh, I'm not likely to forget that episode in a hurry."

"No, quite. Putting that to one side, I'd like you to dwell on the inmates you mixed with, if you will, especially within the domain of the prison kitchens. Does the name, Fuller, mean anything to you?" Almost immediately, Eastern's body language spoke volumes, as a link to his past internment flooded his subconscious.

"Indeed I do. In fact, if I didn't know any better, I'd have to say that the man in question, including Brezznov, could well have been joined at the hip. I soon became aware that their relationship stank of an uneasy conspiracy. So, why Fuller, and where does he fit into the scheme of things, if at all?" Nodding graciously, in a benevolent manner, Rogon replied in a patronising manner.

"As before, Mike, you're explicit observations have, once again, done you credit. This in turn, makes what I have to state, that much easier. Fuller, in fact, is a covert Spook agent....."

"..........what! he interrupted, "you certainly took your time going public with that. Presumably, you had a good reason for not divulging it earlier? Just give me the facts of the matter, Rogon, and be done with it. I only hope that Fuller, is in a position to throw some light on Brezznov's whereabouts."

A pregnant pause followed, allowing Rogon time to gather his thoughts. In one sense, he'd managed to 'get-out-of-goal'. His eleventh-hour decision to expose Fuller, had received a far better response from Eastern than he'd anticipated. Outwardly, his body language, personified 'game-on'. "As I stated earlier, Fuller has been working under the same directive as yourself, Mike."

"Fine, I don't have a problem with that. Obviously, he was interned at a much earlier date than myself, from what I can gather from his relationship with Brezznov?"

"Once again, your prognosis precedes you, Mike. In fact, Fuller was interned, alongside Brezznov, some six months before you came on to the scene."

"With respect, Fuller certainly had me fooled. His alleged association with Brezznov, was almost believable in my eyes. Which is more than that asshole Brezznov can say. Yeah, I've got a good feeling about where this is all going."

For once in his life, Rogon found himself on a 'plastic' roll, and it showed in his body language. "Hopefully, with the intention of bringing the bastard down, and out of circulation for good!" he exacted, confidently. The vibes that he was now giving out, washed over Eastern's, body, goading him into an immediate reaction.

"Christ, Rogon, and here was I, thinking that your-robot-syndrome was impregnable. Attitude, that's what it's all about. Hang on to it. We have got a lot of talking to do....right?" Acknowledging Eastern's sound advice, became the easy part. conclusions, were always going to be the hardest nut to crack. In the end, it was left to Rogon to put Eastern's mind at rest.

"Trust me, Mike, things will improve. This particular case, frustrating as it is, has been a challenge from the beginning. Nevertheless, using our combined genre's, and by that, I'm talking about a game-plan alluding to a conclusion. What do you say?" Nodding vigorously, Eastern catapulted himself into the verbal arena.

"So, what is the position with Fuller, at this moment in time?"

"Interesting point, Mike. Since Brezznov's Banker's card spree-up West, Fuller has had nothing substantial to share, in the way of information."

"I'm not surprised. He always kept his plans close to his chest. Incidentally, is Fuller still on his payroll?" Rogon didn't hesitate when replying.

"Yes, thank God. Although any SP we do manage to get, is always going to be second-hand. As you're aware, Mike, Brezznov has gone to ground for reasons of his own. Subsequently, even Fuller doesn't know where he's holed-up"

"At least he can't leave the bleedin' country. Saying that, I don't think he gives a shit anyway. He's willing to sacrifice anything, rather than blunt his poxy ego."

Without prompting, a rare smile of recognition briefly crossed Rogon's, face.

"Was it something I said, Rogon?" questioned Eastern.

"Yes, as it happens. You mentioned his ego. That's got me thinking. Knowing his perversion to a challenge, lets..........."

"..........offer him one that he can't refuse." Eastern interjected.

"Only, this time, we'll be in a position to be in front of the game, dictating the rules to suit ourselves." For a second or two, a sustained mask of satisfaction carpeted Rogon's, face. Finally, he spoke with grim determination.

"I could kick myself. It was there all the time, staring us in the face. His egotistical trait holds the key to his destiny. Used in the right context, and by that, I mean as a retaliation force, you then expose the flip-side, thus creating a........."

".........fully-blown weakness, attached to a host of scenarios." countered Eastern, "which leads me to suggest that his biggest weakness, when all things considered........"

".........are diamonds!" This time, the moment became ripe for Rogon to intervene, and he lost no time in making a case for it, "If we play our cards right, by devising a scheme to suit his ego, I feel sure that we can nail him."

"Uhm, I like that, Rogon. Right now, a legal 'scam' comes to mind."

"And the bait being?"

"Why, diamonds of course. What else?"

"I couldn't agree more, in fact..."

"Go on."

"Our joint conclusions seem to tie in with a report sent in by Fuller, a few months back."

"And?"

"He stated, and I quote, 'Brezznov revealed to me at one stage, that taking ownership of a particular world-renowned diamond, would become the pinnacle of his career.'"

"Ironic isn't it? It's almost like 'karma' has come back to haunt him. Do we know the stats connected to this acclaimed diamond?" Disengaging himself from their conversation, Rogon referred his new-found interest toward a de-briefing file situated on his desk. After a minute or so, he looked up and spoke. There was no denying the tension attached to his voice.

"Ah, here we are, Mike. God, you're going to love this. You've got to admire the man's taste. No wonder he wants it that badly. The profile report alone will make you feel dizzy, and that's just reading it." Tentatively, he handed the file across for Eastern to peruse. Easing himself back in his chair, he blissfully awaited a foregone reaction.

"Fucksake!" expounded Eastern, "that's not a diamond, it's a bloody rock."

"If that's an assumption, then you're closer to the truth than what you think, Mike.

If that doesn't entice him out, and back into circulation, then nothing will."

"Yeah, exactly my sentiments. The worst way it'll give him something to think about. Going on from that, how does the diamonds potential rate, on a scale of one-too -ten, for example?" Rogon shook his head and shrugged his shoulders, as a mark of defeatism, before replying.

"Value-wise, I couldn't begin to scratch the surface, Mike. What I can say is that the 'Kimberley Legend', as its called, is still uncut to this day, and weighs in at 1,255.3 carats. It originates from South Africa, having been discovered there in the eighties. Arguably, any diamond expert would have no hesitation in ranking it alongside the 'Koh-i-Noor,' the 'Centenary', or even the 'Cullinan'. That gives you some idea of what we're looking at here, especially when you consider that the 'Cullinan' diamond itself, originally weighed in at 3,160 carats alone. It has since been broken down to eleven stones. But please, read on, you'll find the complete history in the file. Personally, I found the contents absolutely fascinating."

Some tension biting minutes later, Eastern glanced upwards, trance-like, mouth agape. Momentarily, he appeared to be lost for words. Finally, it was left to Rogon to extinguish what had virtually become an ordained hiatus. "This is a rare moment indeed, Mike. Certainly for me. I never thought I'd see the day when you'd be stuck for something to say."

"Yeah, well milk the moment, Rogon. A verbal glitch, as far as I'm concerned, is rarer than a 'penny black'. On a serious note, I feel as if I've been on a conducted educational tour, for the last five or so minutes. We are talking serious mind-boggling money here. I'm just worried that Brezznov might even struggle, in terms of finance, to make the 'Kimberley Legend' his own. What are your thoughts on that?" Should he have harboured any concerns, at this juncture, then Rogon, for reasons of his own, ineptly kept them to himself.

"In spite of frozen assets in operation, Mike. I feel quietly confident, that he's got the bollocks, and arrogance, to play along with whatever we propose. No, I'm not unduly worried. We'll cross the monetory bridge when we come to it."

"Is that a 'we' as in you and me, Rogon? Your memory seems to have gone into hibernation. I'm only here for Queen and country, under a bleedin' distress warrant.

In other words, don't give me any grief should the mission go belly-up. The buck stops with you, Rogon. When this is all over, I got plans....big plans, which doesn't include a life membership working for Spooks."

Rogon's jaded feeling, were lost in no-mans-land. Unperturbed, and emotionless, Eastern's sentiments, washed over his plastic persona and dissolved. Finally, he replied in a robotic manner. "In fear of repeating myself, Mike. I have always maintained that you have the right fibre to make a good agency man. Having said that, your affiliation toward the agency has always remained subjective, to say the least. This mode will, in time, cease to exist. You will always be one of us, Mike. Not necessarily in day-by-day performance, but merely in spirit, until such time your presence is required. Think of Operation 'Cuckoos Nest' as being a dress rehearsal, for want of an example. Thus far, this is your second mission with Spooks. I think I'd be right in saying that you probably thought that after the Police corruption case, which I hasten to add, you dealt with most admirably, you wouldn't be seeing me again. But there you have me, Mike. Fortunately, Spooks had other ideas. I therefore rest my case. You really are becoming a habit these days. Rest assured, you will get used to it in time. Right now, we, as a combined unit, have a job to do in bringing Brezznov down. I therefore suggest that we take time out to digress further on. As you so aptly put it, a 'legal scam'"

In Eastern's case, once in a lifetime would be countermand to a trivial lack of insensibility, but to find himself verbally grid-locked, twice in 24/7, was, to his way of thinking, far beyond reproach. They say, and I quote, 'the pen is mightier than the sword'. Not only had Rogon verbally infested Eastern's body, but had come through the back with a bloody great bow on it! Briefly, a sustained silence ensued. The only answer available, could be found coming from a small trickle of blood, resident on Eastern's chin. It's origin being from a gouge in his bottom lip via an irate tooth. Finally, he allowed a look of disbelief to fall away, before breaking their unearthly silence.

"Well, that fucking told me! Rogon. But hear this. The minute I get to see Brezznov 'banged-up', like it or not, I'm out of here... end of." True to form, an unrepentant Rogan legitimately, master-minded the last word.

"That's what I like about you, Mike. So indulge me, when I state you prefer to say it as you see it, it's a great attribute, and a requirement that the agency looks for in a Spook. Now then, down to business. The ball is in your court regarding a 'legal scam', and you have my full backing on it. Then again, owing to the intensity of such a scheme coming into being, I will, of course, need to consult Whitehall as to our intentions. Not that I have any concerns in that department, you understand. The PM will be glad to wash his hands of it. With an election on the horizon, a result could be a penultimate vote-winner. Going on from that, the security involved, as I see it, will be hugely immense, due to the many aspects that will need to be covered."

"We're obviously talking a 'code red' here?" Eastern remarked dryly.

"At the very least, Mike. And beyond that I venture to say."

"Guess you're right. Moving on from that, assuming that we're in a position to operate 'Cuckoos Nest', how does Brezznov fit into the scheme of things, should he suddenly decide to make a move, publicly of course?"

"Good thinking, Mike. The fact that we need to catch him 'bang-to-rights' in our 'scam', would mean that we could throw the key away, and mark him down as a has- been." At least his remark afforded a smile from Eastern before replying.

"Yeah, I like that. Porridge for life. Let him screw on that. So, I presume that in the meantime, you'll instigate a 'softly-softly' approach, by issuing a restraining order, on any unforeseen police action?"

"Precisely. I'll get, Milton involved. Admin is his territory. He'll make sure that the process is put into place straightaway." A few minutes later, following a brief phone call, a contented Rogon picked up where they had left off. "Coffee? I suggest that we adjourn for ten minutes before regrouping. Incidentally, Mike. On the strength of your long-term commitment to Spooks, I have had a word with the catering staff, and have been assured that certain measures have been put into place, thus ensuring your personal satisfaction."

"Nice try, Rogon but utter bullshit. I don't suppose, for a minute, that the Government-issue coffee I've been used to in the past, tastes any different than it did before. On the flipside of things, I'd like to run a proposed 'scam' past you. Hopefully, it might turn out to be something that we can both agree on, for a change."

"I'm open to offers, Mike. So, try me."

"Are you adverse toward auctions in any way?" Seemingly taken aback, Rogon looked completely out of sync with their conversation.

"Auctions, you say. I think I'm missing something here. Can you elaborate on that, Mike?"

"Indeed I can. Crazy as it may seem, my intentions involve, setting up a fake jewellery auction, to include lot number five, the 'Kimberley Legend', as the main attraction. What does that do for you?"

"This is a joke, right?" demanded Rogon. Unperturbed, Eastern continued to expand on his alleged 'joke'.

"I can categorically state, that I have never been more serious in my life. I realize, that, on the surface, the whole scenario appears bizarre, and basic to say the least. But basic works for me. You place a carrot in front of a bleedin' donkey, and you've got it's attention. Whether he likes it or not, Brezznov including his poxy alter ego, will be sucked into a web of intrigue, all for the want of a diamond. And that, I prophesy, will be his epitaph."

If ever a plastic agency man could do shell shock on demand. Then, Rogon was in the running for an 'Oscar'. "It's sheer madness, unbelievably stupid, but hell, I love the whole damned nerve attachment you've placed on it. The more I think about it, the more its growing on me. Reverse strategy, Mike. It speaks volumes. I can see where you're coming from at last. The 'Mountain going to Mohammed'."

"Exactly. All we have to do now is to create a plan of execution, which he will hopefully adhere to. To save time, it might pay you to set up an extraordinary meeting with the PM. Without his blessing, we can forget the whole damned charade. For what its worth, and it is only a technical point, you might make it clear to him that the 'Kimberley Legend' itself won't be seeing daylight, outside of the alleged auction house."

"Leave it with me, Mike. Getting through to me was the hard part. If anybody can convince the PM, then I'm your man. Actually, time I've finished putting our case across, and the benefits resulting from it, of course he'll be only too pleased to 'rubber stamp' our proposal."

"Tomorrow won't be soon enough for me. Going off the subject for a minute, I'm going missing for a couple of days. That is until we get written confirmation on where we're heading, there's nothing to keep me here for, besides which, after London, the sea air in Brighton, and Joan of course, will clear my head. Have you got a problem with that at all?"

"Good God, no. At best, I can only make preliminary enquiries at this stage. I suspect that Fuller will be back in touch any time now, if so, you'll be the first to know, should his report contain any viable information."

After 'God-knows-where', and as many days, Eastern's flat in Brunswick Square, verged on a parallel with Utopia. The minute he stepped through the door, Joan was all over him like a rash. "I'd almost forgotten what it was like to be human." He quietly told himself, in a benevolent manner, and toyed with his glass of scotch, before turning his attention toward, Joan. Relaxing in his favourite chair, earlier on that evening. Eastern found himself reflecting on his spontaneous decision, to abort the agency in lieu of Hove, "can't tell you how good it feels, Joan. Life after the agency, know what I mean." For her part, Joan had already written the script, by suitably bypassing any form of confirmation.

"Putting aside the hidden grief, and frustration for a minute, our indulgent relationship, Mike remains solid. What we don't need is baggage, and by that I mean....."

".....Rogon and the damned agency. He was quick to add. "For what its worth ,Joan. I've already made my future intentions clear, should it ever become an issue. The Brezznov case, depending on it being sanctioned, will be my last. Win or lose, Rogon and the agency can go to hell, I'm done. My life is here, this is where I belong."

"That was quite a speech darling, I applaud you for it, welcome to the real world. An admission like that, shouldn't go unnoticed, what say you, we eat out tonight?"

"I could say, you've talked me into it, but then again, I thought you were never going to ask." Eastern gushed, "so, what'll it be, English or Italian? it's entirely your call." Knowing Joan like he did, the enquiry as he perceived, became a 'no-brainer', as their conversation slipped into gear.

" That's gracious of you, Mike. But 'Jamie's' Italian restaurant seems to be the in place at the moment, I think we'll give that a try."

"Jamie's' , are we talking as in, Oliver? "

"There's only one. Apparently, he's got a place in Black Lion Street, it'll make a change from the Dolce Vita, don't you think darling?"

"Fine by me, I'll get a cab organized.." At least their evening had got off on the right foot. Just after eight o-clock that same evening, the pair were exchanging pleasantries, whilst absorbing the ambiance native to 'Jamie's,

"Well, what are your thoughts, Mike?"

"I have to admit that I was sceptical at first, but, no, I can see why its so popular. The menu reminds me of a 'Food Junkies' Utopia, I'm totally spoilt for selection."

"I'm told, and you are a steak person, that the Chuck flank steak with smoked cheese Mortadella, is the business. Me? I'll settle for the Prosciutto and shaved pear salad."

"The steak sounds great, but you know I'm not a cheese person." Joan allowed a knowing smile to take over her face.

"You should get out more often darling, the 'cheese' is a misnomer, in fact its a pork sausage cut into cubes."

"What do I know, Joan. One things for sure, I've a hell of a lot of making up to do, after this mission becomes a statistic."

Some thirty or so minutes later, Eastern had just finished

refreshing their glasses via a bottle of Dino Pinot Grigio, when their memorable evening came to a shuddering halt, care of Eastern's mobile. It became clear, that Joan was not amused.

"Who the hell would want to...." She faltered, "oh no, it couldn't be, could it? tell me I've got it wrong, Mike." Imagine yourself holding a live grenade with a five second detonator. with nowhere to run, and then you realize its only a mobile you're holding. And the difference is? none! Stony-faced, Eastern pocketed his mobile way out of sight, lost in thought, somewhere, "Mike!" Exasperated, Joan felt that she was on the outside looking in, "for God's sake, Mike. Was it something I said?

Whatever way, I don't find your attitude at all amusing." Seemingly oblivious to his whereabouts, She became aware, that Eastern was laughing to himself. Seconds later, an off switch, submerged inside his sub-conscious, depressed. He was back.

"Joan? Are, there you are, sorry, for a minute I was......"

"..........on another planet."

"The message, you know, the one on my mobile? Somehow, linked up to something you said earlier on. It was so bloody surreal. What was it you said? Ah, I remember know, you said something like, 'welcome to the real world'."

"Where is this all leading up to, Mike? I don't understand what's going on." Drawing on his breath, a controlled aura notably surrounding him, came into play.

"Basically, Joan. I could well become part of it, sooner, rather than later, on a permanent basis.'"

"This conversation has got Rogon written right through it, if I'm not mistaken." He smiled obliquely, in a manner that she was unaccustomed to, before finally speaking in a forthright manner.

"Regretfully, you won't have to worry anymore on that score, Joan."

"Regretfully?"

"I'm afraid so, there's no other way of putting it, unless, ever, fits the part." How does one define the word 'ever', when its handed to you in a throwaway line.

"I shouldn't have asked, It's Rogon isn't it." Eastern appeared to be fazed, as he took his time before replying.

"Regretfully, no, Joan. Although it was the agency, who were trying to contact me. I'm afraid that, Rogon won't be bothering us, you, me, anymore. I've just been informed by Milton and I'm sorry, but there's no easy way of saying this, Rogon is no longer with us, in fact he's dead.

A sustained silence followed, in which time Joan found herself struggling to absorb a political 'bombshell', literally handed too her on a plate. "I...I don't understand, Mike. How, when, why? Its all so sudden. I'm so sorry, In spite of......."

"..........don't beat yourself up over it, Joan." He interjected, "I'm as shocked as you are. The best thing we can do right now, if you don't mind of course? would be to get a cab home. I can't speak for you, but I've completely lost my appetite."

"That's understandable, darling. We can do all the necessary talking, once we're home." Twenty minutes later, a sombre looking, Eastern attempted to redress the situation.

"Milton has assured me he'll be back in touch shortly, Joan. Hopefully, through him, we can make some sense from out of all this. To be frank, I'd never have thought that somebody's death, let alone Rogon's, would effect me as much as it has. Love him, or hate him, he was flesh and bone after all. When I think back, the altercations, the poxy grief I hurled at him, and there's a man who once saved my life If you remember......"

"..........Including mine, Mike. Its so easy to forget. I think we both need a drink, gather what thoughts we have. God! What a damned mess."

Methodically, Eastern took the top off his scotch, savouring the content, before gulping it down. Slowly he raised his glass upward. Here's too you, Rogon I'm going to miss you, and your self-centred plastic image. I don't do promises as you know, but I won't rest until that bastard Brezznov, is out of circulation. I owe you that much."

Less than five minutes later, Milton phoned. The message portrayed, was brief and specific, 'drop everything, there will be a car available in fifteen minutes.' In no time, Eastern, was reluctantly saying goodbye to his belated 'real world'. "Once I know more, I'll be in touch, Joan." And then he was gone, foremost on his mind entailed a promise that he'd made too, Rogon. Unforeseen timing plus a sack full of unanswered questions, finally derailed any normality, existent in his body and brain. Tiredness gripped him, gracefully, he allowed his futile body, to slump back onto the leather clad seat. Within seconds, his 'real world' had become a distant memory.

"Ah, there you are, Mike. My apologies for plucking you out of obscurity, at such short notice. I just wish the situation could be reversed, but when needs must....."

".......then its time to act accordingly, Milton. So, without dwelling on sentiment, lets get some positivism ongoing. Rogon is dead, but we still have a job to do. As far as I'm concerned, nothing changes. Seated around a table, buried in the heart of Spooks agency Head Quarters. Eastern, along with Milton and Spooks second in command, Carl Levinson. Were conducting an extraordinary briefing. Also present, were a representative of a notable auction house, and a top ranking met officer.

CHAPTER 20
DAY OF RECKONING PART 2

Once all the formalities were out the way, It was left too Levinson to get the briefing under way. "This is a sad day gentleman, and I take no pleasure by sitting in Rogon's chair. Present today, are Anthony de Ville representing the auction world, followed by CI Rogers for the Met, and Spooks agent, Mr Mike Eastern. As his acting predecessor, I fully intend to carry on, where Rogon had left off. Make no mistake, operation 'Cuckoos Nest', is still ongoing, hence the briefing. We all know why we're here, and that is to devise a co-ordinated set up, revolving around the 'Kimberly Legend' , strong enough to induce Brezznov's interest. We all have a part to play in our own genre's, so for, Rogon's sake. Lets get our heads together, and thrash out, an intimidation plan."

Eastern sighed, and drained the last remnants of his sixth coffee. "Well at least, Rogon got that bit right." He told himself, "even, Joan would have liked that." Levinson then alerted him to the fact, that he was satisfied, from what had come out of their meeting, that the content on the table was sufficient enough to warrant a full blown game plan. This in turn, would be faxed through to Whitehall, for the P.M's blessing.

After the briefing, Eastern approached Levinson with the intention of salvaging some details, surrounding Rogan's sudden, thus far, unexplained death. "Heart failure old boy, according to the paramedics at the scene, it was quick, so he wouldn't have suffered. Yes, that's what the autopsy will show."

"I see, so, where was he found?"

"Slumped behind the wheel of his car, in the agency's underground car park, terrible business old boy, he was only fifty eight you know."

"As you say, his age is irrelevant, the old 'Grim Reaper' doesn't take any prisoners, does he? By the way, who found him?" Strange to say, that Levinson at this point, appeared to be outwardly uncomfortable, at Eastern's systematic grilling.

"Uhm, lets see now, yes, a cleaner. Apparently, Rogon's body was slumped forward onto the steering wheel, causing the horn to continually sound off."

"So the engine was still idling then?"

"Well, yes, I presume so, of course, it must have been, otherwise the horn wouldn't have sounded off. Well, I must be off now. Milton will be in touch, regarding any official statement connected to operation 'Cuckoos Nest'." Sometime later, relaxing in the comfort of his flat back in Hove, he had cause for concern, as he related his earlier conversation with Levinson to, Joan.

"I'm sorry, Joan. Call me over zealous if you like, but I've got this foreboding feeling, that something is amiss."

"Do you want to share it, darling?"

"Rogon's death, it's all too bloody clinical, and convenient for my liking, but then again maybe you're right, I can't bring him back, can I?"

"You're not God, if that's what you mean, but I am struggling with the concept surrounding his death. I know you too well, Mike. Once you get your teeth into something, you won't let go."

"It's Levinson who alerted me to have hidden doubts, when I was questioning him; it was almost as if he was reading off an auto cue, when he answered me back. That'll be the next thing, Rogon's funeral."

"That won't be for some time yet, darling. In the meantime, you've got our Mister Brezznov to deal with. You need to put all your energies into that."

"You're right of course, Joan. I've promised, Rogon that much if you remember?"

Eastern was feeling restless; a full week had elapsed, since his arrival back in Hove. When contact was finally achieved, the agency's timing was as predictable as a chocolate fire grate. "Who the hell can that be at this hour?" Eastern growled.

"You'd better answer it, Mike, it might be Levinson, or whatever his name is."

"I think you mean, Milton but yeah, you're right, it could be important." Checking his watch, he lunged at the phone. "Eastern, speaking. You do realize its six a.m. who is this?" A pregnant pause ensued, followed by the melodramatic tones, from an excitable, Milton.

"I apologize for the inconvenience Mister Eastern. I have been authorized to tell you, that operation 'Cuckoos Nest' has of now been officially approved. A 'code red' will also be enforced, as from eight a.m. today. Thereafter, a car will be at your disposal an hour later, message over." He then hung up.

"I don't suppose for a minute you heard that, Joan. It was a message via, Levinson. I'd better get up, get my self ready and packed, can't believe its happening at last."

"Happening?"

"Yeah, sorry, operation 'Cuckoos Nest', its all systems go. Just after ten thirty am that morning, he arrived back at Spooks HQ, situated somewhere in London. On hand to greet him was, Levinson himself.

"Good to have you back dear boy, we have a big nut to crack, wouldn't you say?"

Eastern muttered something like, 'come back, Rogon all is forgiven,' under his breath, and followed him into the briefing room. As he had anticipated, Anthony de Ville and CI Rogers were present.

"If you'd all like to be seated gentlemen, then we can proceed with...." Stopping short, he acknowledged, Milton's presence, as he silently entered the room, "ah, there you are at last. Coffee's all round I think, Milton we have a long day in front of us.

Once seated and fully relaxed, Levinson went on to clarify the

P.M's decision to sanction operation 'Cuckoos Nest'. "If I can reiterate on the confirmation, I suggest that Mr de Ville start the ball rolling." The latter explained, that he would put a full blanket coverage, advertising campaign into place, the subject being, the 'Kimberley Legend'. For authenticity sake, a room at his auction house, would be made available. For the sale itself, should either himself, or a representative of his, decide to participate in the proceedings. "Quite clearly," he emphasized, " any interest Brezznov shows, in his desire to obtain said stone, would be via phone bidding."

"How confident are you, de Ville that he will be in a position to outbid other prospective buyers?" Enquired, Levinson.

"Under the circumstances, at best, I'd have to say eighty per cent certain, bearing in mind his fanatical diamond perversion, and the finance he's accrued, that could be a conservative estimate. Going on from that, I have taken steps, to instil professional bidders, in situ, on line, phone, and even in the auction room itself."

"Are we talking a coup of some kind here, old chap?" Enquired, Levinson.

"I realize its a pun, but it all depends on ones values, If you see where I'm coming from? Primarily, the third-party bidders, are instructed, to ensure that, Brezznov will come out on top. From my standpoint, and an educated guess to fall back on, he will, at the end of the day, find himself the owner of the 'Kimberley Legend',"

"Hmm, I'm impressed, Mr de Ville. You've obviously got every aspect covered.

Lets hope that our enigmatic victim, rises to the bait. In ignorance, I presume you will place a substantial financial figure on the 'Kimberley', to include a flexible fixed reserve.?"

"Absolutely, the fact that the reserve is, as you say, 'flexible', means that we will have full control on a bidding plain. The price-ceiling, will also act as an incentive to draw, Brezznov in. I would like to add at this stage, if I may, that, as a reputable international renowned auction house, I'm totally unaccustomed to this type of practice, but when needs must, I suppose...."

"........it becomes necessary to 'turn the cheek', I think Is the phrase you're looking for Mr de Ville." Interrupted, Levinson. "I thank you for your time and input, and I will throw your ideas, open to those present, later during the day. With regard to your concerns over reputation sir, should our combined 'cheek-in-jowl' plan, interfere with future trading, you would be completely exonerated, and I have the P.M's written word on that."

Eastern, made a bad attempt, to smother a chuckle, at Levinson's interpretation of the proposed 'scam'. "Stitching, Brezznov, up like a fucking kipper, would be more like it." He told himself inwardly. Levinson then brought him down to earth.

"CI Roger's, unfortunately sir, you have a big cross to bear, in a word, overall security of operation 'Cuckoos Nest'. I strongly suspect, the word 'nightmare', has figured highly throughout the last week? saying that, I feel sure, that when you have laid out your case, it will prove to be incontrovertible."

"Patronising bastard." He mused, " where the hell are you, Rogon? I'm missing you already." Roger's raised one eyebrow at an acute angle, signalling Levinson's, definition of 'the bollocks' as, Eastern would have put it, before opening up.

"Security, small word, one hell of a responsibility. As we all know, in a case like this, It means that I have had to empower the use of rigid forces, far beyond what I would class as terminally normal. The security alone, alienated to the 'Kimberley Legend', far outreaches any set guide-lines. As such, its contrary to say, I'm forced to keep the home of the 'Kimberley' to myself, merely as a precaution you understand."

Eastern was slowly getting pissed off, with the rhetorical verbal crap on display.

Without any hesitation, he went for the proverbial jugular. "Coffee, anybody?

I know that I could use one." His timing, proved to be faultless. Levinson acknowledged his timing, and called for a short recess. Minutes later, his request matured, "thanks, Milton. "He laughed, "poor old, Rogon and those MI6 morons, don't know what they're missing, the catering staff must have been threatened with deportation." For reasons of his own, Milton gave a quizzical smile, and placed Eastern's coffee in front of him, and added.

"Possibly, Mr Eastern possibly." He then exited the room. Momentarily, Eastern was left to frown, Milton's parting remark, had somehow managed to crawl underneath his skin, and in effect, leave his addled thoughts to have a field day.

"Strange, that's not the, Milton I know, I got the impression that he was trying to tell me something, he shouldn't have. The best................."

"...............when you're ready, Mr Eastern I'd like to crack on dear boy." The over bearing tones issuing from, Levinson brought him back to reality. "As we are all aware, the success of operation 'Cuckoos Nest', hinges on Brezznov's approach toward the 'scam', be it by phone or a third-party mediator. What I can tell you, is that our man in the field, Fuller. Has at last, made contact."

"Presumably, for all the right reasons, one would hope." Echoed Eastern.

"Fortuitous comes to mind, Mr Eastern. It appears that, Brezznov has taken Fuller into his confidence, alluding to our proposed 'scam'."

"Now that is what you call a breakthrough, tell me, is Fuller in a position to expose Brezznov's intentions if any?"

"Nothing that appears to be conclusive I'm afraid."

"Same old, same as, typical Brezznov. Knowing him like I do, he won't even know himself, until five minutes before it all kicks off." Eastern without any forethought, had unwittingly dug a hole for himself, by declaring his keen conflict of ambivalence, twinned with, Brezznov.

"Suffice to say, that's why you're here, Mr Eastern." Levinson concluded.

"Your maverick persona, in the past, has served the agency well. Rogon always spoke highly of you. I for one, suspect that you will be involved right to the death."

Patronising bleeder." Eastern muttered under his breath, "although, thanks for the credit, Rogon. I won't let you down."

Levinson then declared 'any questions' time to those present. Eastern for one, had a problem with the coverage, entailing telephone and Internet bidders.

"I can put your mind at rest, on that account, Mr Eastern." de

Ville ventured, "things have moved on somewhat, since we last met. After taking advice from CI Rogers, I have decided to classify the sale of the 'Kimberley' as being a 'Reserve', and 'Catalogue' auction combined. ."

"Can you enlarge on that? I'm not familiar with the procedure."

"Basically, working in conjunction with a 'Catalogue auction', means that the 'Kimberley' will remain in a Government vault, thus simplifying the security measures, entailed in transportation."

"Amen too that." Rogers concurred, "the thought of having to deliver a 'rock' of that value across London, would have been my biggest nightmare."

"So, you need to help me here, the bidders themselves."

"Yes?"

"How do they get to see the 'Kimberley?"

"Through the normal advertising coverage, or under lock-and-key in a designated location, I've set in place, which in fact comes into force tomorrow morning. It's paramount, that we have complete transparency, in every aspect of the 'scam'. We cannot afford to scare Brezznov, off, the minute he smells a rat......."

"......he'll be on his toes, end of." Eastern cut in. Is there anything else that you think I should be aware of?"

"Monitoring Internet and land bidders will prove a headache. Brezznov as we now, will be bidding under a pseudonym, rather like a 'Private' auction whereby bidders identities are not disclosed. We can only hope that, Fuller will be acting for Brezznov, in which case, we will be forewarned of the alias that he'll be using."

"And at the same time you can track any transaction back to its origin. I like that, so, assuming that Brezznov has now procured the 'Kimberley Legend', he needs to start talking money. Will that become a problem for him?"

"No, not in terms of financial holdings, generally, an immediate deposit will have to be made, with the balance securing his bid, settled within an allotted time scale."

Eastern still wanted more, and pressed, de Ville for more information.

"Payment! how do we stand on that one, can it be tracked back?"

"That, I'm afraid, is rather a grey area, Mr Easter. One can only assume, that Brezznov will have the use of an offshore account, when closing any deal."

"Surely there's a way round that, legal 'scam' or not?" de Ville indicated that he was having a 'bad-hair-day'.

I'm afraid not, I'll refer you to the world of Banking privacy, if I may. Its a principle born within the 1943 Swiss Banking Act. Brezznov or his associate's, I suspect, will have the use of a 'Corporate Debit Card', which if required, can be used at any ATM, and does not entail a large security deposit. Any transactions by way of Banks, Merchants and so forth, are not traceable to the client."

"Shit! surely it can't get any worse, can It?" Shrugging his shoulders, de Ville delivered the only coupe-de-grace available."

"Although I strongly share your sentiments, Mr Eastern I can categorically state, and I quote, 'the only information revealed by the transaction, belongs to the Corporation in its entirety', therefore I'm sorry."

"Eastern slumped back in his chair, looking fully dejected, words didn't come easily. "Brezznov might have won the financial world, but he hasn't won the bleedin' war, he's still in the country, and that, as far as I'm concerned, gives us the edge."

Some thirty minutes later, the meeting was dissolved sine die.

CHAPTER 21
DAY OF RECKONING PART 3

Eastern, was beginning to have reservations, extending over and above, the current Brezznov affair. Three days had now elapsed since his inimical meeting at Spooks HQ. In which time, he had reason to suspect, that his level of uncanny perception, had at times been threatened. "I swear too God, Joan I feel like I'm being constantly shadowed. I could well understand it, if Rogon was still alive, although that regime even died a death, prior to my last mission." Joan didn't appear to share his conviction.

"Whilst I share your concern, Mike. I seriously don't think that, Levinson would be culpable of such an act. What could he possibly hope to gain from it?"

"Guess you're right, Joan. Sorry If I come across as being tetchy, a damned phone call right now, wouldn't go amiss though."

ESP is a wonderful attribute, especially when you're wanting. "I'll get it, Joan. I have a feeling that's, Levinson. Hello...speaking, I understand, thanks Milton."

"Well, that's cheered you up, Mike. You look like the cat-who-got-the-cream."

"I'm back in business, Joan. Anthony de Ville, has forwarded a firm date, for the 'Kimberley Legend' auction to proceed."

"Are we talking sooner, or later, Mike?"

"Forty eight hours minimum, that's as much as I can tell you, Joan. Official Secrets Act, you know how it is, "tell you what, lets celebrate tonight, we can book 'Jamies' again if you like, it owes us, especially after that last ordeal concerning, Rogon." An hour later, they were sharing a corner table together, engrossed in a menu apiece. Some time later, their meal became history, as they savoured another bottle of their favourite wine.

It was Joan who initially picked up on it, interrupting Eastern as she did, when in conversation. She went on to recall a previous conversation, that they had shared, earlier on that day. The topic being, over Eastern's hang-up, concerning a possible shadow, source unknown. Leaning across to him, she divulged her feelings. "Mike I don't want to hear you say 'I told you so', but there's a remote chance that your theory holds water." Amongst other things, She emphasized the fact, that one other diner in particular, for whatever reason, seemed to have taken an uneasy interest in his presence. "Call me stupid, but I'd be surprised if you had any back left, Mike.

The man in question, hasn't taken his eyes off you all night."

"Maybe the guy fancies me, Joan." Joked Eastern, and left it at that.

The following two days flew by, as pre-arranged, an agency car was on hand to whisk Eastern, off too Spooks HQ.

Three hours later following a quick briefing, Eastern was dropped off at the designated auction room, set aside for the sale of the 'Kimberley Legend'. Primarily his role during the proceedings, would constitute acting as an officious observer. In no time at all, the room was beginning to look like a millionaires cattle market. With time on his hands Eastern, took to consulting the catalogue. Minutes later, he wished he hadn't. "Fuck sake!" He muttered, wincing as he did so. "I wouldn't earn enough money in a lifetime, to buy one of these little babies, even the catalogue itself is worth framing."

Breaking off, he glanced at his watch. He noted that the auction, would be kicking   off in five minutes time. Full of trepidation, he instinctively trawled through a sea of faces, on the off chance of finding Brezznov or indeed, Fuller. It was always going to be a long shot, but at the same time a necessary one. His thoughts came to an abrupt close, as the auctioneer focused in on the would be bidders. Finally, following weeks of intense planning, the 'scam' came into fruition.

"Ladies and Gentleman please, If I may draw your attention to lot number five in the catalogue, the State owned 'Kimberley Legend', who will start the bidding." Eastern felt a sudden blood rush, in sympathy with the obscene amounts of money, produced by a spontaneous bidding war, "one point two million pounds with me in the room thus far, I have to tell you that the reserve price has not yet come into play." And so it went on. Phone, internet and would be buyers alike, all intent on one purpose, vying for, Brezznov's 'baby'.

The bidding, had now achieved the undisclosed reserve, and now stood at one point three million. "Do I hear one point five? Ah, a fresh bidder." With no further outside interest, the future of the 'Kimberley' lay in two peoples hands. "Where the hell are you, Brezznov?" Eastern found himself almost shouting. "You know you want it, its there for the asking, fucking do the right thing, its got your name on it."

"Two million with me in the room, do I hear three?"

Eastern's gut tightened, his mind, body and soul, were momentarily lost in translation. His subconscious had now started to play games with him. A distorted vision of Brezznov exposed itself, to mock his futility. 'don't want the diamond, don't want the diamond.' Over and over again, it ranted in a soliloquy mode, each word destined into pummelling his brain. His head was now at bursting point, due to his blood count rising, subsequently, he found himself forced to sit in a ringside seat, to witness a curtain of utter despair, slowly descending into a meaningless abyss.

"With no more bids, I am going to sell.............ah, a fresh bidder on the internet." Almost at once, a hidden reality impetus, cajoled his being back to normality.

"Brezznov! It has to be, Brezznov. I knew that...................."

"...............with outside interest, I am selling at one point six million, and sold!" Crash! The hammer came down, while at the same, the curtain of despair lurking in his brain, lifted in unison.

He hadn't realized it, but beads of sweat were prominent on his forehead, the intensity of the 'scam' had taken its toll on his body.

"I need to get some air, and quick. " He persuaded himself. The rest of the morning proved to be a predictable anti-climax. In contrast, the de-briefing at Spooks HQ following the auction, revitalized Eastern's conception, that Brezznov himself. Had indeed, instigated his short lived moment of glory. Levinson for his part, wasn't found wanting, in the acceptance of the outcome arising from the auction.

"Without fear from contradiction, I think it's fair to say, that our man Brezznov, by his own standards, has unwittingly put himself in the frame. It was touch and go at one point, and I thank acting bidders, agents Bennett, and Groves, for their last minute stand to incite Brezznov. The fact that the ten per cent deposit, for the 'Kimberley Legend' was paid with the use of a Corporate debit card, via an offshore account, tells us all we need to know. As things stand, brezznov, has twenty days in which to complete his bid, prior to collection. On a legal stand, CI Rogers has informed me, that a plan of action, will be put into place to counteract any move that, Brezznov makes."

"What's the position regarding formal charges, as things stand?"

"I wish I could be more positive, Mr Eastern. Unfortunately, old chap, conspiracy to steal is not surrepstitious enough at this moment in time, for us to put him away, for an extended period of time. No, we need to ensure that we catch him 'bang-to-rights'..."

".........and by that, with the 'Kimberley Legend' in his possession," Interrupted, Eastern.

"Exactly, dear boy. Our intention, is to ultimately throw the key away where Brezznov is concerned." It had all been said, their meeting came to a memorable close, leaving Eastern to focus on Brezznov's next move. The next three weeks would become a war of nerves by testing his patience consistent with a 24/7, 'on call' regime. 'bring it on asshole', would figure highly where Eastern, was concerned.

CHAPTER 22
DAY OF RECKONING PART 4

Unbeknownst to Brezznov, due to his erratic mode of planning, he'd inadvertently handed Eastern a favour. By a quirk of fate, he just happened to have been at Spooks HQ, mulling over the auction with Levinson, when the call came through. "Excuse me, Mike. I'd better get that. I'll take it in the 'ops' room, Milton. A couple of minutes later, a jubilant Levinson returned from making his call. "You'll be pleased to know that we're back in business. That was Jonathon Grimes on the phone."

"Grimes?"

"Oh, sorry dear boy, you wouldn't have met him. He's in charge of security down at 'Nympton House'. It's a specialist holding base for State investments."

"Bullion, diamonds and the such like, I presume?"

"Yes, and in this case, home to the 'Kimberley Legend' for the last twelve months. But to get back to the important part. It would appear that our Mr Brezznov has made an application to collect his divining glory, for want of a word."

"Under what pseudonym? I presume he is using one?"

"He's calling himself Frederic Orlando, and yes, before you ask, he's settled the balance for the 'Kimberley' via his offshore account."

"Its just occurred to me."

"Go on."

"What if we're wrong, and he is indeed kosher?"

"Rest assured, Mike. I don't have any qualms in that department, old chap. Out of all the bidders, he was the only one with access to offshore banking. Security picked on it when he paid his deposit. Any bona fide dealer wouldn't have reason to bank outside of the UK."

"Fuller! Its just occurred to me. Has he been in touch recently?" Levinson frowned before replying.

"No, no he hasn't, worryingly enough, although I strongly suspect that he's got his reasons," and added, "I'm certain that, like yourself, old boy, he intends being in on the kill." Little did Levinson know at the time, as to how much truth was attached to his statement. Before their short meeting came to a close, Levinson handed Eastern a sealed dossier, the contents of which contained highly secretive and sensitive information. "It's paramount Mr Eastern that you take on board the relevance of the documents inside. Once your satisfied that you're familiar with the contents, you will need to destroy them per se. I can't emphasise how radically important this knowledge will become, given time. At this stage, I'm not prepared to divulge any information regarding Brezznov's movements, once he has taken possession of the 'Kimberley'. What I can say...."

Levinson then went on to explain that Eastern would receive a phone call, with no designated time label attached, sometime within the next seven or eight hours. Its purpose being to form a radii of action 'area of operation', in conjunction with the Met, to apprehend Brezznov, as painlessly as possible. With that in mind, Eastern would need to remain in situ at HQ, pending the relevant call. Levinson then departed, leaving Eastern to his own designs.

With 'alleged time' on his hands, Eastern decided to contact Joan. He informed her, without digressing, that the following twenty-four hours would be crucial into finally bringing about Brezznov's downfall. Therefore, he would not be returning back to Hove, for a limited period of time..

Cometh the hour, cometh the man. Eastern didn't need asking

twice. The moment he placed his hand on the receiver, he felt a sudden adrenalin rush surge through his body. 'This is what I've been waiting for', he told himself. Rapt as he was, his inner mind still remained terminally housed in one direction. With all points leading to Brezznov. "Speaking...of course....yes, in thirty minutes...goodbye." His hand was shaking as he replaced he receiver, not that he'd have been aware. He drew in on his breath, choosing to regulate his irregular breathing. A single convulsive shake of his body, and then it was over. 'As from now', he insisted, Mike Eastern is back in business.

In no time at all, his two immediate colleagues, were making themselves known, and conducting an induction plan. 'I'm the arresting officer supreme, Chief Superintendent Dyson, ably assisted by DS Grant. He went on to state that, Eastern's role, would be one associated with government representation, and lastly, that firearms would be limited to specialist police marksman only. Their intended destination, when they had finally managed to get away, seemed to take longer than Eastern had foreseen. Some time later, their unmarked car came to rest, adjacent to a large suburban house. Dyson peered through the car window. Seemingly satisfied, he spoke. "Well, gentleman, as always, we have a job to do, so let's do it with the minimum amount of fuss. Hopefully there won't be any bloodshed. Okay lets go."

"Christ. You're one cool customer, my friend," Eastern remarked. I'm with you. Let's do it."

"Now remember, as I said before, once we gain entry, I'll do the talking. If I suspect that it's all going to kick-off, I'll give you the nod. Please God it won't come to that." DS Grant took his emotions out on a large brass knocker. Moments later, the door opened. Confronting them was none other than a flabbergasted-looking, Brezznov.

"What the................."

"Good morning, sir. Mr Orlando, or should I say Brezznov? May we come in?" Waving their ID cards in his face, the pair made a move to gain entry, as pre-planned. Eastern at this stage had made himself scarce, to avoid a multiple altercation.

"This is fucking harassment. I don't have to stand for this shit!"

demanded an irate Brezznov. Due to their pushy persona, Dyson and Grant were now well-embodied inside the house. Akin to a clockwork charade, Dyson stated his case.

"Victor Brezznov, I have a warrant for your arrest, for conspiracy to murder, fraud and grand larceny. Read him his rights, Sergeant." Brezznov was now beside himself with rage.

"That's total bollocks. I haven't left the house for weeks. I've got witnesses to prove......" He stopped in short flight, as Eastern suddenly made himself known.

"You...you bastard, Eastern. You've set me up. You're dead! Dy'e hear me?"

"You did that yourself asshole." By now, he was almost screaming with utter loss.

"I'm far too clever for that. I'll fucking buy my way out this, you see if I don't."

"Actually, Victor, in one sense we didn't find you. We didn't have to. The 'Kimberley' did it for us." Dyson smiled for England, as Eastern continued to lay into Brezznov.

"Maybe you're not listening. Your diamond told us exactly where to find you."

"You're lying, that's crazy talk."

"Not this time, Victor. Your egoistical ambition to own the 'Kimberley' has backfired on you. In fact, it's brought about your downfall. What you didn't know, is that the diamond had been previously bugged. It led us right to you. Plain and simple."

"Impossible! There's no poxy way it could have. Besides, the deal, when I bought it, was legal, and I have all the necessary paperwork to prove it." This, time, it became Eastern's turn to laugh, as he screwed the verbal dagger home.

"You'll have a lifetime on your hands to do that, Victor. As for ownership, I'll dwell on that one in a minute. Right now, you've got a fucking great big bug problem to deal with. Have you checked the 'Kimberley' itself?"

"You're talking in riddles. A diamond is a diamond, you asshole."

"And that's where we differ, my friend. This particular one happens to be special. Let me explain. Transparency is a much-maligned word, Victor. Have you got any thoughts on that?"

"Yeah, you and yer smart words, you're talking bollocks." In the background, looking on, Dyson and Grant exchanged what could be mistaken for a well-rehearsed smile.

"Are you going tell him, Mike. Or shall I?" interrupted Dyson.

"So it fucking talks now does it? You fucking puppet, tell me what?"

"For the record, Brezznov," explained, Dyson, "the 'Kimberley has been coated with a transparent liquid, incorporating thousands of microscopic sensors. The 'Kimberley' was tracked from the second it left 'Nympton House'. Forensic science, fortunately, has moved on somewhat, since you've been accustomed to daylight. You can work the rest out for yourself."

"My diamond. It has to be mine. It was an open deal, I can show you a full comprehensive file on the paper work."

"I was relying on that, Victor," Eastern cut in, "you don't know it, but that file now reverts into being Queen's evidence for the prosecution." Brezznov was losing it fast. His demeanour began sinking faster than the Titanic. He was almost pleading for a form of acknowledgment.

"No! what do I need to know you bastard?" Eastern's face epitomised the word 'satisfaction', as he deliberately took his time, intrinsically explaining the cold hard facts entailing the sale and background data, alluding to the 'Kimberley Legend'.

"Victor, the diamond you allegedly bought, was recovered from the proceeds of a 'safety deposit box' heist that went wrong, some twelve months ago. Since then, it has been stored for transit in a State holding bay, while awaiting probate documents, due to the fact that nobody has come forward to claim ownership of it. So, until that has been confirmed, the diamond is classified as being stolen property. Suffice to say, in your inflamed ego trip, that's exactly what you have bought stolen property and as you so rightly point out, Victor, you, have all the necessary papers to prove it. Bad mistake. You've messed up big time by shooting yourself in the foot. It's not looking good. Need I go on?"

"I always thought you were a smart bastard, Eastern. I had you figured right from day one. This ain't over yet I promise you."

"Yeah, well thanks for reminding me, Victor. I can well recall you stating on occasion 'you're out of your league, Eastern'. You'll now have time to reflect on that, because I'm the man who brought you down. I instigated this 'scam' and I'm here to see it through. Shortly, you will be just another State statistic. I can't speak for the likes of Steadman and Stowlowski, or, in fact, the others I don't know about, although one thing I did manage to pick up on, was your extreme allergy towards porridge. I can see you becoming a long-term 'hunger striker', Victor. long may it reign, you asshole!"

Averting his attention away from Brezznov, Eastern, glanced across at DS Grant. The smug look he enthused spoke volumes. "How the mighty fall. Put the 'bracelets' on him, Grant," he asserted. "Just get this pile of shit out of my sight before he contaminates the room."

Unbeknownst to his aggressors, Brezznov had other ideas, which didn't include the likes of Eastern. Without hesitation, he whipped out a pistol he'd secluded in his smoking-jacket pocket. "Hold it right there, I'm not going anywhere," he ranted, "It isn't over yet, now fucking back off, before I put your brains on three walls!"

"Give it up, Victor. You're going nowhere, except into custody. Killing us would be futile. You'd be 'mullered' before you stepped through the door. There's more marksmen out there than you have ideas, and right now you don't bleedin' have any."

"I always figured it would come down to this, Eastern," he fired back, "I may be going down, but I'm taking you with me. That way, we can share a cell together in hell." Eastern froze. From out the corner of his eye, the vision of a figure began to emerge from behind Brezznov. Oblivious to what had transpired, Brezznov intentionally manoeuvred the pistol toward Eastern, "It all ends here, asshole. Keep my bunk-bed warm." Cocking the firearm, a mask of addled hate and insanity masked his face. Taking aim, he slowly tightened his finger-grip on the trigger.

In a split second, Eastern suffered a moment of deja vu, as his sub-conscious revealed a similar situation he now found himself in. That particular day he got lucky. This time around, 'Lightening' owed him nothing. To all intents and purposes, he'd now become a dead man walking.

His gut instinctively tightened. In response, his throat hardened. 'Can't breathe....choking...head bursting'...nauseated...body tensed in expectation from whom knows, what? From out of his pre-empted misery, a loud explosion invaded his space, and then it was all over. His eyes fluttered open, rivulets of blood began to form unique patterns, as they cascaded down his face. Squinting through blood-soaked eyes, Eastern watched as Brezznov's body toppled forward. The mask of perdition had now gone, and that included half of his face. This in turn could now be found dispersed over Eastern and his two colleagues.

Through semi-glazed eyes, Eastern's 'vision' had now suddenly materialized. As it drew near, he realized that his alleged vision had now morphed into a flesh and blood third-party, prominent in his hand, a '38 Colt 'Cobra' hand gun. A sustained silence followed, in which time Eastern had managed to retain a form of sanity. He gazed down at Brezznov's lifeless outstretched body in front of him. Hardened as he was, the gaping hole at the back of Brezznov's head was a sickening scene, and caused Eastern, to momentarily choke. He turned to face Dyson and Grant, both struggling to find their composure. Forcing himself back round again, he swiftly averted his attention toward the figure now facing him.

Words didn't come easily. Slowly, recognition crushed any doubts as to the benevolent figure's identity. "Fuller! It is Fuller, isn't it. Where the bleedin' hell did you come from?" Gasped, Eastern.

Grim faced, Fuller took his time before answering. "That, in itself, is a long story, Mister Eastern. My preference, right now, is to clear up this bloody mess, "He replied coolly. Nodding in a brisk business-like manner, Eastern shook his hand.

"You're welcome to that, and what a poxy mess. Any closer, and you would have taken his head clear off. I'll thank you later. In the meantime I'll get on to Levinson, and put him in the picture."

In no time at all, the house and the crime scene, as a whole, became infested with security from every branch. In terms of his immediate future, Eastern had no qualms, it was, as he had previously stated to Rogon, ' time to bow out. I'm all done here.'

The de brief, back at HQ later on that day, produced an air of optimism. All thanks to Brezznov's less fortunate and un-rehearsed demise. Levinson wasn't short in showing his gratitude. "Results, gentlemen, that's what we as a team aspires to. The PM will be proud of you all." Eastern glanced skyward, to hide his mirth.

"We." He told himself, "where the fuck was you Levinson, when it was all coming on top? Come back, Rogon, this idiot is a poxy glory hunter." An hour later, he signed a mission-release document, cleansing himself from any liabilities arising from the Brezznov case. And so it was written. Mike Eastern, late of Spooks, re-entered the real world as we know it.

"Joan? Yeah, I'm free at last. I'm on my way back to Hove right now." His mobile was on overtime.

"That's wonderful news darling, I can't wait to see you. No more 'Cuckoos Nest' to worry about. I'm so pleased for you."

"God, I'm relieved. I feel this is the first day of my life, Joan."

"Yes, I'm only just beginning to understand. In a manner of speaking, you could say that 'you're the Spook who flew over the 'Cuckoos Nest', couldn't you?"

EPILOGUE
THE FUNERAL

Seven weeks had elapsed, since Eastern had broken his ties with Spooks, in which time, the word 'contentment', had taken on a whole new meaning. From the adrenalin rush of a roller coaster scenario, to living a cat-on-a-hot-tin-roof existence, had long faded into obscurity, leaving a keen sense of 24/7 normality, to embrace his life. What, you might ask yourself, could possibly induce him, into turning the clock of circumstance back?

Whatever thoughts you might volunteer to tender, in defence of such a situation occurring, remember! We are talking Mike Eastern here, so think on. As a minor suggestion, quote, 'God made the world in seven days, and executed the law and the rules within'. In sheer contrast, Eastern, on a good day, would have no problem in breaking every rule in the book! So you see the problem I'm having to deal with here.

In the end, it took the ferocity of a simple envelope that when opened requested his presence to attend a funeral. Not any funeral, I hasten to add. This one, just happened to be his late 'plastic' partner in crime prevention the unforgettable Rogon.

I think I'll let Mike Eastern do all the talking from hereon.

"Uhm, the day of the funeral, you ask. Yeah, I'm not going to forget that in a hurry. Thinking back, the minute I woke that morning, I felt an impending sense of foreboding, that cremating Rogon was only a rehearsal for what was deemed to follow. I'd just finished breakfast that particular day, when Joan happened to mention that it was raining stair-rods outside. Glancing out of the window wasn't a good idea. God, how I hated the rain and even more, bleedin' funerals. Joan, bless her heart, did her best to cheer me up."

"One things for sure," she said, "Rogon's not going to get wet, where he's going."

Cremations bother me, but I could see the point she was making. Highgate cemetery, situated in North London, can be a daunting place for some people. Not that Rogon would have had a say in it. The fact that he was a by-product of the 'manor' made sense. Highgate would be his final resting place. Oh, before I forget. Did I mention that Joan didn't accompany me to the funeral? She made an eleventh hour decision not to go. On reflection, I sincerely think that, at the time, she new something I didn't.

By the time I arrived at the cemetery, the rain had ceased. Funny, I remember laughing to myself and saying, bloody Rogon. You always did get your own way. After paying the cab off, I made my way across to the Service Chapel. You'll be in good company here, Rogon. I said, there's a lot of famous people buried here, for instance. Karl Marx, and, if you're looking for the 'craic', Jeremy Beadle. On second thoughts, he wouldn't have been your cup of tea. Anyway, you're on the west side of the cemetery. People always say it differs from the east side. Spooky. A bit like you and me, really. Know what I mean?

I really didn't know what to expect, as far as representation was concerned. Apart from myself, there were only three or four officials from the agency, present, Levinson included. Bloody sad when you think about it. His family, for want of a word, consisted of Milton, and whoever he came into contact with at the agency. I don't mind telling you, I felt bleedin' gutted. There was a man who'd given his life to the State. And for what? Following the service, I decided to make a quick exit. As far as I was concerned, I'd done the business . There was no way I wanted to get involved with officialdom. Knowing my poxy luck, I got ambushed by a hungry reporter, desperate for a column-filler.

I mean, how sad is that! What a way to make a bleedin' living. Did you know the deceased at all? he enquired. I've reason to believe he was an unsung hero. Now you know me. I took more crap and bloody grief from Rogon than most people would, in a thirty-year relationship. And he's unsung? I must be a fucking working angel. I told myself. So, to get back to the reporter. Know him, you ask, you want to know if I knew the guy? I was a bit heated at the time. I knew him. You were saying? I cut the guy short. For some reason, I suddenly felt that I was in a verbal wilderness. I needed to take stock of the situation. Nobody had ever questioned my affiliation toward Rogon. I told him I was sorry, I was somewhere else. Seriously, do you know what? No! I really didn't know him at all, I said. Now fuck off. Trouble was, deep down, I knew I was right. Plastic and flesh and blood isn't the best recipe.

A word, Mr Eastern. Levinson, fortunately, had pre-emptied a possible altercation. 'A favour, if you would, old chap? That! Really got too me. For the last two months, I've had to put up with 'old chap', 'dear boy', and now this pompous bastard decides to come back into my life again, begging me for a poxy favour. I mean, don't these people get it? As I said before, Rogon was now excommunicado, all I want to do now is to go back home and get on with my life. Full stop. 'Mr Eastern, please, It won't take a minute of your time.' He was bloody insistent, I give him that, So I thought to myself, oh what the hell, it can't be that important surely?

What's on your mind, Levinson? I asked him. I've got a cab arriving shortly. There's somebody I'd like you to meet, before you go, he said. Now I am pissed off, as you can well imagine. The last thing I needed, was a bleedin' trip down memory lane, with an ex Mickey Spillane look-a-like. Pointing with his finger, Levinson then drew my attention toward a figure standing close to the cemetery entrance. A colleague of mine would like a word with you. Does this colleague have a name? I fired back. That's for me to know, and you to find out, Mr Eastern. Bloody mind games I thought. No change there then.

With that, I left Levinson and strolled across toward the figure who, I noticed, was standing with his back to me. I can be bleedin' cynical at times, but then you know that anyway. Its just that I had this weird feeling that something, or other, didn't feel right. For instance, how many people do I know, fully dressed in black garb and matching Bowler? I asked myself. I stretched out and tapped the figure on the shoulder. Excuse me, I said, I believe you want a word? What happened next will remain tattooed on my brain until I'm dead.

Slowly, the stranger turned around. Confronting me, and wearing a 'Silicone Valley' smile, was none other than Rogon! For a full fifteen seconds or more, I just stood there, mouth agape, blinking, looking like a bloody Zombie. So help me, I fucking froze, I tried to speak, I felt numb. It was like somebody had wedged a ruddy great house brick inside my mouth. It can't be. You're fucking dead, was the best I could come up with at the time. I mean, how stupid is that? I thought. So I continued. We cremated you twenty minutes ago. Then he opened up.

Hello, Mike. Yes, indeed it is I, Rogon. And no, fortunately you didn't cremate me, although I expect there were times when it had crossed your mind. It's good to see you again. Its been far too long. But the service, the cremation, even your reported death. What the hell is going on? He then looked me in the eye, as if he'd never gone away.

A sham, Mike, a total and utter sham from start to finish. The whole thing was so bloody surreal; it felt like we were both having a chat over a cup of tea. I'm still in a daze, nothing is working for me, I asked him the most obvious question that comes to mind. Right, so you're here. Who, then, was the poor bastard in the coffin? 'I never made the arrangements, Mike. He was quick to add, I left that to the backroom boys. Next you're going to tell me, is, that this bloody charade is legal, I suppose. Again, I can't comment on that, Mike. Let's just say that Whitehall will go to extraordinary lengths to appease the PM.

I remembered laughing at the time, and thinking, fucking Brezznov wouldn't agree with you, Rogon. But I still had a problem with Rogon's alleged death. I couldn't figure out what he was gaining out of it, on a personal level. So I confronted him. Putting Brezznov to one side for a minute, it still doesn't explain why you went to all this trouble. There has to be a bigger reason.

He nodded, like only Rogon nods. Basically, Mike. I, we, the agency, did it all for you! Well, I told him straight. Don't patronize me, Rogon. But he continued. You see, my friend, weeks ago, when you told me that the Brezznov mission would be your last. I wasn't prepared to let that happen. For me, this charade, as you put it, has been my way of saying I don't want to lose you, Mike. I might have been out of the frontline, owing to my alleged death, but I have never allowed myself to be that far away from you, if you know what I mean?

I can relate to that, Rogon, I added. It all makes sense to me now. You've been my shadow for weeks. The restaurant, for instance, even Joan picked up on that, amongst other occasions. Does that mean that you're in then, Mike.'? Strangely enough, I didn't have a problem answering him. Rogon, I said, for somebody who's gone to all that trouble, just to prove a point, and then yeah, I'm in.

Funnily enough, I went on, I don't really feel as If I've been away. I swear to God, he had a twinkle in his eye at the time. There and then, we both shook hands. I waited around and watched him leave. He hadn't got very far when he turned round. I always said you'd make a good Spook, Mike, he shouted, and then, just as quickly, he silently disappeared. Like a perpetual shadow, he melted away, lost to the world, in a backcloth created from a thousand and one gravestones.

For a minute or so, I chose to remain there, grabbing at what form of sanity was available. Believe it or not, I didn't give a shit at the time at what could have been on offer. As far as I was concerned, my mind was already made up. See you around, Rogon, I shouted back at him, not that he would have heard anyway. I considered that he must have been as rapt in his own mystique world, as I had become with reality. I can also recall thinking to myself, that the expression 'life-after-death' was, to my mind, totally believable. Knowing that Rogon himself had aspired to do the oracle. Smiling generously to myself, I turned on my heel and walked away.

The end.... maybe!

Acknowledgements

I would like to thank my wife Sheila, for her tolerance
and support throughout. Also to Margaret Austen for her
proofing and editing services, and not forgetting
Julie Shillingham for her in depth appraisal of the book
prior to printing. I'd also like to thank James Watson for his
superior computer back-up assistance.
And last but not least, my thanks to Gibson Publishing
for services rendered.

Also available by Gary Tulley

Once Upon A Spook

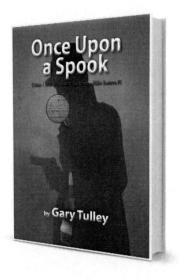

Gary Tulley